IN SEARCH OF THE
LIGHT

*The
Adventures
of a
Parapsychologist*

SUSAN BLACKMORE Ph.D.

 Prometheus Books

59 John Glenn Drive
Amherst, NewYork 14228-2197

To my parents

Published 1996 by Prometheus Books

00 99 98 97 96   5 4 3 2 1

Library of Congress Cataloging-in-Publication Data

Blackmore, Susan J., 1951–
    In search of the light : the adventures of a parapsychologist / Susan
Blackmore.
        p.   cm.
    Rev. ed. of: The adventures of a parapsychologist. ©1986.
    Includes bibliographical references and index.
    ISBN 1–57392–061–4 (paper : alk. paper)
    1. Parapsychology. 2. Blackmore, Susan J., 1951–   . 3. Parapsy-
chologists. I. Blackmore, Susan J., 1951–   Adventures of a parapsychologist. II. Title.
BF1031.B57   1996
133.8′092—dc20
[B]   96–16260
                                                                     CIP

Printed in the United States of America on acid-free paper

This book is a personal story and so it is made by all the people who influenced me. I would therefore like to thank everyone who appears here, as well as the many who do not, but who nevertheless contributed to my work. I have frequently put words into people's mouths and in each case I would like to thank them for giving me the permission to do so. I would also like to thank Tom for his endless help, support, and encouragement, though he says I shouldn't: "For richer or poorer and all that stuff," he says.

Finally, I know that one reason I enjoyed parapsychology so much was because of all the friendly, open, and encouraging parapsychologists whom I met. I thank you all for keeping me entranced by this impossible subject.

Susan Blackmore
August 1986

When I first wrote *The Adventures of a Parapsychologist* my intention was clear. I reckoned there must be many other young people searching for something science did not give them, and turning to the paranormal and the New Age. I had learned the hard way what happens when you put psychic phenomena to the test and I wanted to share my experience with those other hopeful people.

Ten years on I am delighted to have been asked to update the book for a new and revised edition. Although I have to admit to being embarrassed by some of my own tale, I am struck by how well it still serves my original purpose. It is a simple personal story of how an ardent believer in all things weird and wonderful put her own beliefs on the line and ended up having to change them.

Susan Blackmore
Bristol, England
January 1996

One

The Fish is Hooked

I always wish I could remember. I wish I could remember just how I felt about parapsychology all those years ago when I first began. I wish I could remember what it felt like to believe passionately in the possibility of the paranormal and to be fired with enthusiasm for tracking it down.

And I wish I understood memory better. Perhaps if I did I could bring back past experiences and halt the inevitable slipping away of self into the past. Perhaps I could tell an accurate story of my adventures as a parapsychologist.

In any case, the desire to understand memory and consciousness is as much a part of this story as the desire to understand the paranormal. It is a story of many false paths taken and many pointless questions asked. It is the story of how I embarked on ten years of research into the paranormal and where that adventure took me.

At the age of eighteen I lay on a Devon beach, keeping a beady eye out for a certain young man and his sailing dinghy and reading Rosalind Heywood's *The Sixth Sense* (Heywood 1959). In spite of the distractions, something of her enthusiasm took hold of me. She hinted at the interconnectedness of all human beings, at the mysterious nature of consciousness, and at the way science ignored what might turn out to be man's greatest potential.

She introduced me to the different forms of extrasensory perception (ESP). There is (1) telepathy, the transmission of information from one person to another without using the senses; (2) clairvoyance, the direct perception of objects or events without sensory means, and (3) precognition, seeing into the future. She touched on psychokinesis (PK), the effect of mind on matter, and introduced the notion of psi, the hypothetical process underlying all these capacities. Through her book I first heard of the Society for Psychical Research and the experiments conducted since the 1880s on mediumship, traveling clairvoyance, and survival of bodily death. It is Rosalind Heywood I have to

7

thank (or not) for my initiation. I was hooked, though I did not realize it straight away.

Parapsychology has everything a hook needs. It is mysterious and alluring. It has just enough "scientific" evidence to provide bait, while at the same time it is rejected by most orthodox scientists, the inspiration for a crusading spirit to shout "I'll show them." And that is, I suppose, what I wanted to do!

It was during my last year at school that I turned down my hard-won place at medical school, after a traumatic realization that I really did not want to be a doctor. Instead, without very much understanding of what was involved, I decided to study psychology. In the autumn of 1970, I went to St. Hilda's College, Oxford, to read PPP, or physiology, psychology, and philosophy.

University was a shock. On my first day there, before I had even begun to get my bearings, my tutor gave me a piece of paper on which was written my first essay title, "The Role of Sodium Ions in the Nerve Action Potential," and a list of references. I had a week in which to write it. I didn't know what a reference was or how to use a journal library. I had a vague idea of what sodium ions were but not a clue about the "nerve action potential." My first essay was a disaster. But the next week's essay, "The Role of Potassium Ions in the Nerve Action Potential," was a little better.

In the midst of all this there was "Fresher's Fair" at which all the societies tried to grab new members. There I madly joined all kinds of things from a choir to the Psychology Society, and among all these I put my name down for the Oxford University Society for Psychical Research.

In the excitement of my first weeks I soon forgot all about the OUSPR, until one morning, while I was still loafing about in my room, there was a knock at the door.

"Come in," I called, imagining it might be one of the girls from the neighboring rooms.

In came a tall young man with dark eyes, long curly brown hair, and tight corduroy jeans. I quickly straightened my dressing gown and invited him in.

"You put your name down for the Psychical Research Society," he began.

"Oh, so I did," I said, somewhat nervously. I had forgotten all about it since then. "Are you a member?"

"Actually," he laughed, "I think I am the only remaining member there is! I was trying to find someone to start it up again with me."

I looked at him doubtfully. I wouldn't have a clue how to run a society, and I had no idea what it would entail. But I did like him, and he was a "second-year"—much revered—so I said I would.

People often ask me how I first got interested in parapsychology, and I usually tell them that it was Kevin, rather than Rosalind Heywood, who was to blame. With him I started up the society again. We invited witches and Druids to speak to us and we even joined a coven. We had lecturers from the Society for Psychical Research (SPR) in London who told us about experimental work, and we soon began experiments of our own. We attracted about a hundred members, and each week three of us—Kevin, our friend Vicki, and I—would cycle round the fifty or so colleges pinning up notices about our meetings. It was hard work but exciting.

Later on in the year Kevin's lack of enthusiasm for his school-work finally got him expelled, and I was left in charge of the society. My tutors disapproved. They made it clear that parapsychology was a waste of time, that it had nothing in common with "real" psychology, and that they hoped it was just a "passing phase" which would not encroach too much on my proper work. I hate that more than anything—being told that something I care about is just a "passing phase." I daresay it happens to all children as they go through the same phases as their parents once did, and their parents try to tell them what is happening. But from the inside it is quite different. I thought parapsychology was important.

I also challenged my tutors' view of what "proper" work was. Gradually creeping up on me came the notion that their idea was very limited. At the heart of psychology must be the desire to understand human experience and behavior, and yet they were apparently dismissing as unworthy of consideration whole chunks of it—perhaps even the most important bits:

Several questions, or protoquestions, began to niggle at me.

• What does it mean for "me" to recall something which "I" once experienced in the past?

• What is happening when you seem to be in contact with something "larger" than yourself?

- Why is it that some experiences feel "more real" than others?
- How can a physical and physiological brain give rise to consciousness?

* * *

These were not well-formed or sensible questions, but they were not yet well-formed thoughts. It was just the beginning of trying to understand some important facets of human nature. And in those three precious years at Oxford two processes worked side by side to mold those questions into better shape.

On the one hand there was my "proper" work, which tried to reduce the questions into answerable shape. There were practical classes dissecting rats and frogs and injecting foul chemicals into living brains. There were essays to write on the physiological basis of memory and the psychology of perception and learning. There were projects with rats pressing levers in boxes and fish swimming about in tanks and visits to the mental hospital for tutorials on schizophrenia.

Mostly I loved it. Contemporary work on neurotransmitters was exciting, and John Eccles, world-famous neurophysiologist, had hinted in his book at the relationship of "mind" to the synapses (though my tutor implied that this was mere senile dementia). I could see the weakness in current theories of memory, and I loved the challenge of trying to improve on them. Above all, I was learning how to ask questions more clearly and how to design experiments to answer them. It gave me at least the beginnings of rigorous thinking. But it made me rebel against reducing all the interesting questions too much.

The reverse process was at work in many of my other experiences. Three of them were of lasting impact: my introduction to psychoactive drugs, a part of university life in the late hippy era of the early 1970s; an out-of-body experience I had in my first term at Oxford; and a trip to India at the end of my first year.

All these served to stretch out the questions I wanted to ask way beyond anything I could see the means of answering. But they were exciting questions; and, in the face of my experiences, I was not going to abandon them just because I could not see any way of answering them.

I suppose all people experience dissonance to some extent when they ask far-reaching questions they cannot answer. Many people come

to premature and ultimately unworkable answers and just stop thinking. Others go on wondering but never have the means or motivation to
track down the answers. Some accept the answers given by religions or
tradition rather than have no answer at all. In science one can do none
of these, but the same dissonance fuels the scientist's motivation. At
one extreme are the really exciting questions, which often cannot be
clearly formulated or which prove to be unanswerable, and at the other
are the most easily answered ones, which are limited and even boring.
In between are the questions that provide scientific progress. I suppose
the best scientists manage to keep sight of their deepest questions and
let those guide their more mundane experimental work.

Whether I ever succeeded in doing that this story may tell, but in
the beginning I certainly failed. I conceived a theory which was "premature and unworkable," and I hatched a desire to show all the
psychologists that they had been missing out on the most important
clue to understanding mind and memory—the paranormal.

Two

The First Mistake

Why did I come to think the paranormal was so important? I can only say that, like so many others (and just as illogically), it happened through personal experience.

During that first term at Oxford, the activities of our Psychical Research Society expanded in all directions. We even took to having ouija board sessions in my room in college. Four or five of us laid out letters in a circle around a table, placed a glass in the middle, and positioned our little fingers on its upturned base. We then called out (in true spiritualist fashion and in great seriousness), "Is there anybody there?" Within a few moments the glass usually began to move and spell out comprehensible words and phrases. We always appointed one person as the "scribe" for the evening so that we could keep a record of every pearl of wisdom obtained from the glass, as well as all the jibberish. We always treated the glass with respect, as though there were "someone" inside it; that "someone" often responded by giving his or her name and details of his or her life and death.

I had first done this at boarding school, where it was (quite rightly I believe) forbidden. One night several of us sat—with a lookout for the teacher—cramped around a tiny table between the dormitory beds. We "contacted" "Simon" who claimed to be the spirit of a teenage boy who had died in a plane crash at the age of eighteen. He had been a Beatles fan (as were we all), but he hadn't heard their latest record, which we obligingly rendered for him in ghastly girlish song!

"Simon" told us his name, address, and the date of his death. Then some days later, while I was away, one of the girls involved looked up his phone number in the telephone book and plucked up courage to ring.

"Can I speak to Simon please?" she asked.

"Oh," came the reply, "didn't you know? Simon was killed last year in a plane crash."

Whereupon my friends ran terrified and giggling from the phone.

Or so the story goes. I long believed this story, and it had a great impact on me. After all, I can well recall the singing and the excitement of getting a name and address. It was only later that I laid more importance on the fact that I was *not* there at the time of the phone call, and that, in any case, memory, including my own, is highly fallible. And we had kept no record of any of the events. Now I was determined to record everything carefully.

Calling up "spirits" through the ouija board proved equally popular with new Oxford students. So we set up these regular séances in college, where there were no teachers to catch us. The content was rather different. Quotes from Rilke about *Sturm und Drang* and rantings in Middle English replaced the Beatlemania, but the general mix was familiar. On many occasions we were given such checkable information as dates and places of burial. We eagerly went out on expeditions to romantic Oxford graveyards, bravely carrying our thermometers, infrared cameras, tape recorders, and notebooks, hoping we might even find a visible spirit in the process. We never did, but somehow we never seemed overly disappointed, even when we didn't find the right name on the gravestone or catch a spirit's image on film.

It was after one of these séances that something extraordinary happened. I was tired—extremely tired. Over the previous three or four weeks my initiation into Oxford life meant 9:00 A.M. mornings but later and later nights, eating Marmite toast cooked on someone's gas fire, and drinking first-class college port in dark panelled rooms until all hours of the morning. This particular evening I had been sitting for many hypnotic hours pushing a glass around a table (or being pushed by it—it is hard to tell after even a few minutes). At about 11:00 P.M., I went to a friend's room for coffee, where the three of us, Vicki, Kevin, and myself, sat smoking, drinking coffee, and listening to rather loud, heavy, rock music.

I sat cross-legged on the hard floor and lapsed into my tired imagination—flowing with the music and inhabiting beautiful, winding, leaf-lined tunnels. As I became more and more lost in my inner wanderings Kevin suddenly asked, "Where are you, Sue?" Well, where *was* I? It was one of the hardest questions I have ever had to answer. My "imaginary" world was so real that I was there. As I struggled for a better answer I suddenly saw below me, myself sitting cross-legged on the floor. And so began nearly three hours of the most exciting, challenging, and vivid adventures I have ever had (Blackmore 1982a).

It seemed to me that "I" was up at the ceiling and looking down on the room below, where my own body was sitting. I seemed to be able to see from above everything that happened, to hear perfectly normally, but to be free to travel about as I wished. I somehow knew that that body down there was "mine," and yet it seemed quite unimportant, and I was happy to forget about it for awhile. Nothing before had ever seemed so real or so intense. It was nothing like just imagining I was floating, and it was nothing like a dream either. In any case I was wide awake. My body was still sitting there, upright on the floor, and talking rationally about all that was happening.

I had no ready explanation, although I toyed with many possible ones. But one thing was certain: The experience was important to me—and the psychology and physiology I was learning in my "proper" studies had nothing to say about it.   ,

In contrast, the occultists and spiritualists I kept meeting did have something to say about it. They told me I had experienced *Samadhi* or that I had had an out-of-body experience or a mystical experience. They told me it was astral projection and that my astral body had temporarily separated from my physical body so as to travel in the astral planes among the finer vibrations, beyond the merely physical. They told me that I was psychic and that I had a great future ahead of me as a healer or a clairvoyant.

I was fairly sanguine about all this eagerness, but because these people appreciated my experience I was drawn to their teachings. Right from the start I found them intellectually unsatisfactory, but at least they had *something* to say about what had happened to me. All through that year we had Theosophists to speak to us and occultists to demonstrate their "powers," and I seemed to be surrounded by these alternative ideas.

* * *

I suppose that is partly why I conceived a great desire to go to India, where I imagined I could learn far more of these ideas. In the long, three-month vacation at the end of my first year I did just that. During the summer term I searched newspapers and notice boards for groups going overland and eventually found one with an ex-army truck driving to the Hindu Kush in Afghanistan and on to Kashmir for a pilgrimage.

I joined the three-month trek in July 1971. We drove slowly through Europe, camping as we went; to Turkey, where we stayed in a bug-infested youth hostel in Istanbul; to Iran, where we were chased and taunted; to Afghanistan, where we were robbed of some clothes and food by bandits and locked up in a police station for a night! As we progressed farther east, everything gradually changed, and we all changed with it—something that could never happen by flying there. By the time we reached Delhi we were almost prepared for the poverty, begging, and disease. We were adept at cooking local rice and vegetables and used to a vegetarian diet. We were thinner and browner and more or less ready for our pilgrimage.

We walked with thousands of Hindu pilgrims from Pahlgam in the Himalayas of Kashmir to the Cave of Armanath. It is a fairly arduous three-day climb along narrow rocky paths, across wide plains, and over several desolate passes with stunted trees and breathtaking views to the final destination: a gaping glacial cave where the icy lingam resides. This holy piece of phallic ice grows and shrinks with the phases of the moon and is at its peak at the August full moon. Anyone who touches it then becomes immortal; and we joined the thousands of devout Hindus who sought immortality.

Walking in high altitudes is exhilarating. Walking alongside cripples, seeing legless beggars dragging themselves on their arms while rich women are carried in Sedan chairs, is distressing. But walking with holy men and sharing their food is inspiring. By the time I had bathed in the glacial river and waited before the lingam in the icy cave, I was prepared for transformation.

As I rushed out again into the clear mountain sunshine to sit with a circle of orange-robed holy men, smoking Bhang from a great pipe, I honestly felt immortal.

On the walk down the mountains I gave away my shoes and walked with bare feet. I vowed often to myself never to forget what I had experienced—knowing, I suppose, that a greater part of me would forget and that remembering would not be easy. For memory was the only connection I had with that eighteen-year-old schoolgirl, dressed in a purple uniform and taunted for being good at physics, who had decided not to become a doctor less than two years before, and now that didn't seem much of a connection.

When I came back to physiology and psychology, it was with a lot of experiences I could not ignore and a lot of questions I could not answer. I had experienced all kinds of states in which the quality of consciousness seemed to be quite different. But what is consciousness? What changes in altered states of consciousness? Why should drugs, or walking, or altitude, or just different ways of thinking change oneself so much? I didn't even know whether these were sensible questions, let alone get close to answering them.

Then I wanted to know about memory. How is it that people can remember things? This is not a crazy question, and psychology does not have an adequate answer. It is question that fascinated me on every level, from asking how I could remember the actions of a little girl of years before, to asking how one can so easily forget life's lessons once learned, to how information can be stored in living tissue.

Generally speaking, psychologists assume that information gained through experience is stored by means of some change in neural structure and that this stored information makes possible a reconstruction of at least aspects of the original experience. The precise mechanism involved in storage is very much an open question, but few doubt that it will one day be found.

Philosophers have far more diverse views. For example, Ludwig Wittgenstein wrote, "I saw this man years ago: now I have seen him again, I recognize him, I remember his name. And why does there have to be a cause of this remembering in my nervous system? Why must something or other, whatever it may be, be stored up there *in any form?"* (Wittgenstein 1967, p. 106).

More recently, H. A. Bursen (1978) and S. E. Braude (1979a) have argued against the "myth of the internal mechanism," rejecting altogether the notion of there being a memory trace.

* * *

As a student I was not much aware of these arguments, nor of all the complexities of research on memory. I knew only that there was no clear answer to how memory is stored, but that obviously memory works! I also knew—or thought I knew—that people could communicate with each other by telepathy and that no one is isolated from anyone else. It seemed to me (and how hopeful one can be in ignorance) that the problems of memory could be solved by acknowledging this unwelcome fact.

Theosophists and other occult groups have the notion of the Akashic Record, in which everything that ever happens is written. By magical or spiritual means some people can read the Akashic Record, and then everything is visible to them. There are also varying ideas of "other worlds." For example, according to Theosophy, which is loosely based on certain Eastern religious teachings, there are seven planes of existence (Blavatsky n.d.). Beyond the normal physical world are the etheric and astral worlds, and beyond them the higher and more rarified spiritual and mental planes. These teachings, in which I became increasingly immersed, colored my thinking and lay behind my "memory theory of ESP" (or should I call it the "ESP theory of memory"?).

Perhaps, I argued, memory is not stored in individual brains at all. Perhaps the role of the brain is one of recall but not of storage; it transforms and processes the information but does not hold it in store. I proposed that in committing something to memory we, as it were, throw it out into a kind of ether. It is stored in some way outside of the individual in some store that is accessible to anyone, not only to the person who put it there. I imagined it might just be a fact of nature that information persists. It is for retrieving the information that we need brains.

If this were so, then the hunt for the physiological basis of memory (then in so much trouble) could be seen as doomed to failure. And this idea was awfully appealing to a student having to grapple with all its intricacies. But more important, recalling something from memory would be essentially the same as telepathy. In the one case, I would be retrieving something that I had stored myself in the communal "out there" store. In the other, I could be recalling something that you had stored there. Both would use the same process. Memory could be seen as a special case of the more general process of ESP.

An interesting question then becomes why I should be able to retrieve my own information more easily than I can retrieve yours. My answer was that it was because my own thoughts now are more similar to my own thoughts in the past than they are to any of yours. So a general principle of "like attracts like" (one of the central occult tenets) could be seen to underlie the whole process of memory. To take it to extremes, gravity could even be the ultimate example of "like attracts like."

It was exciting. Could I change the face of psychology with this revolutionary insight?

I have to put it this way—for this is how I thought. I wasn't totally arrogant, but I was certainly naively hopeful. And that naivete had its benefits. The genuine pleasure I derived from working on this "theory" gave impetus to my work. I might laugh at it now, but if I hadn't thought then that it was both original and workable, I would never have worked so hard. I worked at psychology. After all, if I was going to take my theory anywhere I had to have a good grasp of the psychology of memory and learning, and I needed to learn all I could of physiology, philosophy, physics, and anything else that seemed relevant. But most important was that this idea seemed to bridge the gap between my fascination with the paranormal and occult, and my interest in "real" psychology—or so I thought.

I have to point out, in case you have not noticed it, that I was already making an interesting and fatal mistake. I was interpreting the "realness" and vividness of my own experiences as meaning that they were "paranormal" or "occult." It is an easily made and common mistake, and it took me many years to see it for what it was.

But at that time, as a second- and third-year undergraduate student, I did not realize it. My paranormal theory was, for me, a way of resolving the dissonance between my experience and my knowledge of psychology, a way of bridging the gap between the questions that fascinated me and the ones I could actually answer. Now I could face up to the "unanswerable" questions. I thought I had an answer.

Three

How Do You Become a Parapsychologist?

What should I do with my answer—my theory of ESP and memory? I knew that what I really wanted was the chance to put it to work, to design and carry out experiments to test it, but it was not easy to find such an opportunity. As the end of my degree course approached, I had to decide what to do next, and I panicked. It was much like deciding not to be a doctor all over again.

I applied to a teacher-training college, but when I was accepted I realized that I did not want to be a teacher. I applied to other universities for postgraduate study. I did not get the place I thought I wanted—to study the physiological basis of memory at Exeter University. Instead I was offered a place at Sussex to do research on pigeons. But I didn't want to work on pigeons. When I contemplated actually going there, I felt my life closing in around me and my hopes failing. After all, I wanted to be a parapsychologist.

So how does one get to be a parapsychologist? The answer "With difficulty" is true but not very helpful. It is not even easy to say what counts as "being a parapsychologist." There are no postgraduate courses in parapsychology of any kind in England. There is no "official" way to become a parapsychologist. Yet other people had apparently managed it. And if they could, I could.

Miraculously my physiology tutor noticed a newspaper advertisement which announced the Perrott-Warrick Studentship in Psychical Research, and how she laughed at my excitement when she showed it to me! This sounded too good to be true. It was administered by Cambridge University (although no space was provided there for students) and offered about 2,000 pounds per annum to study any aspect of psychical research. I immediately set about applying.

But I faced problems. My memory theory was poorly worked out, and I could not then see any clear way of testing it. Indeed, I began to doubt whether it was so wonderful after all. So I proposed to study paranormal effects on plants. I remember my interview well. I went before a large board of elderly and impressive Cambridge dons, in a spacious paneled room, and I waffled. I convinced both myself and them that I really didn't know what I was talking about. All my inspiration and excitement could not produce worthwhile experiments or testable ideas. I was clearly not a good bet on which to spend the 2,000 pounds. Also I had not arranged a place to do the actual research. Only later did I discover that I should have found a university willing to take me on as a Ph.D. candidate before I applied for the Perrott-Warrick Studentship. Needless to say, I did not get it.

I decided to "go away." I'd go to India again or go and live in a commune or something. But fortunately I never did. Through pure chance I met Professor Terence Lee from Surrey University and was offered a place in a master of science program in environmental psychology. When I got to Surrey I discovered quite unexpectedly a Ph.D. student there studying parapsychology. His name was Ernesto Spinelli, and he was working on ESP in young children. At last I could see that it was possible to become a parapsychologist. All I had to do was find a way to get a Ph.D. place to study some project in parapsychology.

The Ph.D. system in Britain is not quite like that anywhere else in the world. Typically, the student spends three years on a piece of research, either entirely independently or with minimal help. There are usually no courses to take or lectures to attend. It is simply a question of proving that you can endure three years of designing your own research, carrying it out, and writing it up as a thesis at the end. It is possible to do research on almost any topic, but first you have to find someone willing to act as your supervisor. Second and far harder, you have to find the money. If you go for research areas which are highly topical and have obvious relevance to contemporary theoretical or practical problems, the chances of a government grant are good. If you go for something a bit more obscure the chances are less. If you go for parapsychology they are close to zero. Nevertheless, I was determined to try.

By 1975 I had finished my M.Sc. and got a part-time job teaching psychology to architects in London. At first it suited me well because I had enough money to live on and enough time to start on my great ambition—to become a parapsychologist. I joined the American Society for Psychical Research as well as the British SPR and took subscriptions to the four main parapsychology journals. I set up a card-index system for references and set to work reading.

But it was extraordinarily hard. On days when I wasn't working I began to get up later and later, and without tutors breathing down my neck and assigning essays, I found the reading increasingly difficult. For the first time I began to doubt that my ambition was strong enough. However, I began writing to many universities about the possibility of doing a Ph.D. in parapsychology.

Oxford and Cambridge are obviously among the nicest places to be. Their replies to my inquiry were straightforward at least. From Oxford: "I enclose a list of supervisors. From this I think you will see that parapsychology is not a subject which any member of this department could supervise." And from Cambridge: "I would not advise you to consider this Department if your interests are in parapsychology . . . I would advise you to pursue your application elsewhere."

A lot more hopeful was Edinburgh, where Dr. John Beloff, a lecturer in psychology, had long been pursuing research in parapsychology. He had one or two Ph.D. students, and so I wrote to him. He sent me back a wonderful piece of advice, and I have often wondered whether I should not have taken more notice of it! It was neatly typed and duplicated:

A Note of Warning to Candidates Contemplating Postgraduate Work in Parapsychology at the University of Edinburgh

Dr. John Beloff is willing to act as supervisor to any postgraduate student wishing to undertake a thesis on some topic in experimental parapsychology provided that he considers it to be feasible. . . . It would only be fair, however, to point out that to embark on such a thesis would, in present circumstances, be to take a considerable gamble with one's career. First, because the outcome of any research in this field is still so uncertain that, at the end of three years, the candidate may find himself with insufficient data to support a Ph.D. thesis. Secondly, the prospects of a full-time career in parapsychology, in this country at least, are virtually nil.

I read that warning and ignored it. I did not want a career; I wanted to study parapsychology.

On a university ski trip to Scotland in the spring, I decided to visit Dr. Beloff. I found my way along streets of tall houses to a dreary old building. From the gloomy hall, dark wooden stairs led up to winding stone corridors, and there at last was a door marked "Parapsychology

Laboratory." Just seeing that door was a thrill. I knocked cautiously.

"Come in." A rather distinguished-looking man with graying hair got up from his desk and held out his hand to me.

"Dr. Beloff?" I inquired. "It is so kind of you to invite me to come and visit."

"Not at all," he said. "It is a pleasure to meet people who are interested in our perplexing subject. I believe you want to study for a Ph.D. in parapsychology." I nodded. "Do tell me something about the work you want to do."

Nervously I tried to tell him, as coherently as I could, about my memory theory and my ideas for testing it, about Ernesto's work, and about the prospects at Surrey. In no time I found myself arguing against his view that paranormal phenomena might be evidence for the separability of mind and matter. I realized how much I missed being able to talk about parapsychology and how little opportunity I had at Surrey.

"Would you like to see some of the sights of Edinburgh?" asked Dr. Beloff, and soon we were out in the cold spring sunshine, walking up Princes Street, still talking about parapsychology.

I found John Beloff charming, in a quiet and restrained way. I was extremely nervous and probably spoke far too much and too fast, but there was so much to take in. When we returned from our walk, he introduced me to his doctoral students, and I heard all about their experiments.

At that time, as for many years, the researchers at Edinburgh were generally failing to find any ESP, apparently no matter what they did. But this didn't seem to suppress their determination to carry on or to dent their belief in the phenomena (Beloff 1973). It was laughingly referred to as a "trans-Atlantic effect." In the United States, researchers find ESP, but in Edinburgh it's too cold! Naturally I shared their conviction that it was worth going on searching. It was fascinating to ponder why ESP should appear elsewhere but not in the well-controlled environment of the Edinburgh Parapsychology Laboratory.

Was it really just the geography? Or could it have something to do with the experimental atmosphere in Edinburgh? Was the rather stuffy and formal department inconducive to such an elusive phenomenon, or could there be something wrong with the methods they were using? I was familiar with the idea that the experimenter's belief is crucial—

that if you don't have sufficient belief and motivation, you may block any potential ESP (White 1977), but these people seemed to have deeply held beliefs and powerful motivations. I pondered the question with great interest. Oddly, I don't think I even considered the possibility that ESP does not exist.

This visit was for me the beginning of meeting "real parapsychologists" and hearing about real live parapsychology experiments. The other "real" parapsychologist I met was Alan Gauld. A lecturer in psychology at the University of Nottingham, he had done considerable research on hauntings and poltergeists and written a classic work, *The Founders of Psychical Research* (1968). It is an enormous scholarly book which, much later on, I used in preparing my lectures, but then I felt inadequate because I had not yet read it. But Alan Gauld was certainly not one to test me on whether I had read his books! He invited me to visit and told me about his work and his students' projects while we walked around the pleasant grounds of the university.

I was thrilled that he gave so much of his time to discuss the things that mattered the most to me. But, like John Beloff, he could not provide any funds for a Ph.D. student.

In the end Terence Lee provided the solution. I could carry on with my part-time teaching in London and work part-time on a Ph.D. at Surrey. He would be my supervisor. My friends at Surrey thought I was mad, but in October 1975 I began work for my degree in parapsychology at the University of Surrey.

Four

Starting to Test My Theory

Finally, all my reading in parapsychology was leading somewhere. Now my file-card system had a concrete purpose, and I could write essays for someone else instead of just for myself. I read everything I could find, from occult magazines to parapsychology journals and "real" psychology books on memory.

It was hard work to be teaching half the week in London and studying in Guildford, but in many ways the two were a nice counterbalance. When I got tired of reading and began to feel that lone studying was selfish and pointless, I could look to my "useful" teaching instead. When the teaching became a chore and the architecture students a bore, I could remind myself that I was "pushing back the frontiers of knowledge" with my brilliant parapsychology.

I was also rushing backward and forward to Oxford. The previous year I had lived with John, a philosophy student and musician, in London. John had encouraged me to find a Ph.D. place, and with him I spent endless hours discussing the philosophical problems of the paranormal. He was back now in Oxford, and I spent much of my time there. Indeed, we were planning to get married the following September, so as the year went on it was increasingly dominated by parents' plans and difficult decisions—and even by arguments and traumas: Where would the wedding be? Whom should we invite? What time of day should it be?

But the year was also increasingly exciting as far as parapsychology was concerned. I began to get to know Ernesto Spinelli better. When I was first introduced to him, at a meeting of postgraduate tutors, I felt in awe of him. He was tall and dark (and reputedly an Italian aristocrat), with a huge head of frizzy brown hair. He spoke with a soft American drawl which, for some unaccountable reason, always intimidates me. So it was nice to discover that he wasn't so terrifying after all, to have lunch with him in the student bars, and to learn more about his Ph.D. work and his ESP experiments with children.

Then one cold winter afternoon he telephoned me to say that he was supposed to be lecturing at a weekend course on communication but was too ill to go and would I do the lecture for him? I said that I would, although I was very nervous. John and I went for the weekend to a lovely country house, and I lectured on paranormal communication— my first parapsychology lecture. There were lots of questions, from people who wondered whether telepathy could be electromagnetic, to those concerned about whether we survive death, and many who just wanted to tell me about their experiences. And in those far-off days I had not become sated with endless renditions of psychic tales.

It was a year of meeting more and more parapsychologists. In May I went to my first parapsychology conference, at Cambridge University. It was both a pleasure and a shock. There were some excellent papers but some really pathetic ones. Perhaps most disorienting was to hear a famous physics professor and Nobel laureate talking about transcendental meditation. He claimed to present his "scientific explanation" of T.M., but to me it seemed to explain nothing. Although I very much enjoyed talking to him and found him helpful and interesting, he left me very bewildered.

Much better, I thought, were Ernesto's paper on his research and one by Carl Sargent, then holder of the Perrott-Warrick Studentship. I was very impressed by Carl. He seemed to take a very strong, almost behaviorist line, described meticulously designed experiments, and displayed a commitment to psi backed by wide-ranging knowledge of the literature.

Some months later, on a summer visit to friends in Cambridge, I spent a whole day with Carl. He was about my age and very striking in appearance, dressed all in white with his half-open gleaming shirt exposing a shock of reddish curls. He had wild hair and penetrating eyes. I was torn by feeling so much in common with him but also so many differences. I had little interest in his talk of psychoanalysis and the personalities of pop stars. He smoked heavily and nervously and liked to work entirely at night. But he delighted me (and put me to shame) with his knowledge of parapsychology. He claimed to have read the entire body of parapsychology journals since the 1930s, and when we touched on any topic he poured forth exact references, names, and dates. He had an impressive filing system, all cross-referenced by subject, and was unreservedly generous in helping me with every question I asked. In no way could I ever be, or would I want to be, like him, but he became an example of hard work and dedication.

As the summer wore on, the wedding got nearer and nearer and the traumas worse and worse. I dug myself into them and battled as hard as I could. Then one evening, when I was trying to forget it all, in the bath, my sister came in to brush her teeth.

"Susan?" she asked, through a mouthful of toothpaste, "What would you do if you didn't marry John?"

"If I didn't?" I repeatedly inanely. It was a question I had never asked myself before. I had been going to marry him for so long. "I suppose I'd buy myself a house, and perhaps I'd live in Guildford, and, well, I don't know really."

But it was one of those questions that, once asked, cannot be unasked, and I couldn't stop thinking about it. One bright and fevered day I suddenly realized, with one of those awful flashes of insight that often come just in the nick of time, that I could not marry for philosophical argument alone. In spite of four years together, and only a few weeks before our wedding, I backed out.

*   *   *

It was not a decision I have regretted, but it was one that took some getting over. I had to get away, and I thought up all sorts of ideas for spending the summer hitching to Africa or going to the USSR or back to India. But John Beloff formally and authoritatively advised me that I would be making a grave mistake. The Annual Convention of the Parapsychological Association was to be held in 1976 in Utrecht, one of its rare occasions in Europe, and I could not miss that if I were serious about the subject.

Serious I certainly was! So I went to Scandinavia with a busload of young people and then left them all in Amsterdam a few days before the conference. Hitchhiking to Utrecht, I found a campsite, put up my tiny tent, extricated my only (crushed and dishevelled) skirt from my rucksack, and made my way to the conference.

I suppose I had expected to be overwhelmed with wonderful evidence for the paranormal, but things weren't quite as I had imagined.

The first night there was a magic show with some fairly impressive card tricks, cold readings, and "telepathic" drawings. But what was so amazing was not the tricks but the reaction of the audience. As we all filed down the broad stairs afterward, I overheard amazed voices crying, "Why, that guy must be psychic!" "How could he have done that without telepathy?" and so on.

Was this how parapsychologists reacted to simple stage magic? If so, it didn't say a lot for their ability to detect fraud or deception. But I comforted myself with the thought that the people near me were probably not experimental parapsychologists and could in fact have been just visitors to the conference. It was years later that a parapsychologist went so far as to express in print his opinion that parapsychologists are poor detectors of fraud (Cox 1977).

Another surprise was to find that Sir John Eccles was to be the after dinner speaker (Eccles 1977). Eccles had written about the effect of minds on synapses. Could I pluck up enough courage to speak to him?

One day, as I began to learn the important conference skill of missing the boring papers, I found that he was among the group of fellow-skivers. He was old and gray, quite severe looking but not too ferocious to approach, and I eventually got out my question.

"Sir John, you have talked a lot about mind being something other than brain and not located in the brain—but what about memory? Is memory stored in the brain or is it only in the mind?"

He looked at me with interest and obviously took my question seriously. Then he explained that it had to be in both. Memory was stored in both the mind and the brain.

"I'm sorry, I don't understand," I mumbled. "Do you mean there are two stores?"

He nodded, and I just stood there staring blankly, as the crowds of people wanting to talk to him intervened. That wasn't any kind of answer, was it? That didn't get us anywhere at all. I was so disappointed. Had my tutor been right about him after all?

During the rest of that exciting week, I inwardly thanked John Beloff for having persuaded me to go. I met people whose names had been only references in journal articles to me: Rex Stanford, William Braud, Jerry Solfvin, John Palmer, and Bill Roll. I began to understand some of the difficulties and controversies in the subject—the necessity of convincing the critics and skeptics of the reality and importance of psi, the feeling that parapsychology might be a proto-science in search of a new paradigm and headed for a great future, the determination to be a science and not a pseudoscience (Johnson 1977), and the doubts and difficulties involved in the experimental work.

I came back yet more convinced that I had to put my memory theory to the test, but I was still not sure how to do it.

It is not easy to start one's first experiment. There are all kinds of excuses that get in the way: I must read all these papers first; I must learn more about statistics; if I start too soon I'll do it wrong; I must see my supervisor once more before I really begin. The most insidious of all is the thought that you want your first experiment to be *perfect*.

I sometimes wonder whether I would ever have begun had it not been for a most fortuitous chance.

Ernesto Spinelli and I had been grumbling to each other that there seemed to be no chance to give any lectures on parapsychology at Surrey. Terence Lee had vaguely hinted that he might organize a couple of classes for us, but nothing had happened. Then someone in the General Studies Department suggested to me that I might "offer an option" in parapsychology as part of general studies. I didn't have a clue what this meant but soon found out that all undergraduates at Surrey had to have two hours a week of some subject entirely unconnected with their main subject of study. This might be contemporary theater, man in society, physics for sociologists, or indeed anything in which someone had "offered an option." So I set about designing a course in parapsychology. It was to be twenty weeks long, so I made out a timetable with a series of topics from telepathy and clairvoyance to dowsing, Tarot reading, and astral projection.

The bureaucratic process was set in motion until eventually I was called before a committee of senate. There, shaking with apprehension, I sat in silence at the vast table while other "options" were discussed and courses planned by all these people who seemed to know each other well and do this sort of thing all the time. While they discussed, I was mentally rehearsing all my answers should they question the usefulness of my subject or the organization of my course.

The chairman began, "Parapsychology, eh? Should we all hold hands and turn the lights down? Hee hee hee!" Titters of laughter rippled round the table, and I raised a weak smile.

"Do you think our late vice-chancellor is with us now?" interposed someone else. There were more titters and an even weaker smile from me.

Then a middle-aged lecturer cleared his throat. "Mr. Chairman, I would like to ask who is going to teach this . . . er . . . course . . . and what his or *her* qualifications are."

I was not only surprised but by now infuriated. I burst out, "I thought I had made it perfectly clear that I propose to teach the course myself, and if you are asking for my qualifications then I can tell you very simply. [The tittering was stopping, and I noticed slightly embarrassed stares.] I have a degree in physiology [slight nods of approval] and psychology from Oxford [stronger nods], and an M.Sc. from this university. . . ." But he did not let me go on.

Apparently no one had any other questions. They didn't want to hear about my plans for the course, for practical classes, for essays, projects, or anything. Year 11 Parapsychology Option, as far as I knew the only course of its kind in the country, was launched.

It was to start with the 1976–1977 year. I did not know until the week we started how many students I was to have. Early that week, I went into the General Studies office with trepidation to ask. What if no one wanted to take parapsychology? The secretaries began laughing.

"We've had terrible trouble with your course," they told me. "It's really upsetting the balance. You have over seventy students already!"

* * *

And so it was that I found myself with about 130 students for two hours every Monday afternoon. Apart from the terrifying prospect of lecturing in a large lecture theater, there was the excitement of teaching my favorite subject. But more important still, I couldn't turn down the opportunity of having so many willing subjects to test. I had to begin my ESP experiments straight away.

My first experiments were far from perfect, but at least I did them. I settled down into an effective, if punishing, routine. On Tuesdays and Wednesdays I traveled two hours each way to London to teach the architecture students. On Thursday and Friday I prepared all my lectures, marked essays, and tried to do as much reading on parapsychology as I could. Saturday I tried to keep free, and Sunday I spent frantically preparing my experiments to carry out on Monday.

On those long Sunday evenings my friend Kim and I drew and redrew target pictures, sealed numbered lists in envelopes, tossed dice, stuck pins in random-number tables, and typed out questionnaires and answer sheets—all to be ready for Monday.

Somewhere in between all that I had to run the Surrey University Society for Psychical Research, organize psychology seminars, and go to other meetings and lectures. Yet, somehow I managed to analyze the results of the experiments as I did them, often staying up into the early hours of the morning with heaps of answer sheets and my trusty calculator, because I didn't want to waste the opportunity to test so many subjects. So I kept it up—one experiment a week for twenty weeks. And, as it turned out, for several years.

Of course some of the experiments were designed primarily for the students' benefit, but many were aimed at testing my memory theory of ESP. I still had the very real problem of bringing a rather vague and wide-reaching theory into the realm of the testable. Whether the theory were right or wrong (or useful or not), it was only worth pursuing if I could draw testable predictions from it and design experiments to carry out those tests.

I started by tackling the fairly simple question of whether ESP more closely resembles perception or memory.

Most traditional views of ESP treat it as a weak form of perception, somewhat analogous to a very faint radio signal that can barely be picked up or a very distant voice crying amid a loud noise. This lies behind the folk term *sixth sense* and the notion that certain people are more "sensitive" than others (Heywood 1959; Sinclair 1930). Other theories deny there is any perceptual basis to ESP and argue that it is more like a "meaningful coincidence" or synchronicity. This is Carl Jung's "acausal connecting principle" (Jung 1955). Such theories suggest that information in the sender and receiver just comes to correspond in some noncausal way.

As I read more, I discovered that there were also other memory theories as well as previous surveys of similarities between ESP and memory (Roll 1966). At first this upset me. So I wasn't saying anything novel after all! But it also encouraged me, for I had more to work on, and certainly no one had systematically set about finding out whether ESP was more like memory or perception. This became the main question I wanted to answer. If traditional views were right, ESP was more like perception. If my memory theory was correct, it was like memory.

One of my first experiments used the confusion of drawings to find out. I designed several sets of three drawings. In each set the key picture (a caterpillar, for example) resembled two other pictures; one (a butterfly) was closely associated with it, while the other (a train) looked very similar but was not associated with it. In the actual experiment the target picture (the caterpillar) was sealed in an envelope and hidden from the subjects. All the subjects, my hundred students, sat in their class with a sheet containing many pictures. They had to choose which one they thought was the target; the whole process was repeated many times.

This seemed a good test of the main question. If ESP is like perception then the confusion should be a perceptual confusion— between the similar-looking pictures. In other words, when the cater- pillar was the hidden target the subjects should more often pick the train than the butterfly. But if my memory theory was correct then they should confuse the two pictures which are associated in memory and pick the butterfly more often than the train. My expectation was clear. I carried out the experiment and eagerly analyzed the results.

I was wrong. I was wrong in more ways than one! My very first experiment launched me into the beginnings of a quandery which took me more than ten years to resolve.

There were any number of possible outcomes which would have provided progress. If the students had picked caterpillar most often, with train in second place, I would have had to conclude that perhaps the perceptual theory was better than my memory theory. I would have been disappointed, but I could then have pursued perceptual theories with more confidence.

They might have picked the caterpillar most frequently but not picked the train or the butterfly more often than all the other unrelated pictures. This too would have been disappointing. It would have meant that this method was not able to distinguish between the theories. I would then have had to design better methods.

But what happened was none of these. There were simply no meaningful results at all. Neither train nor butterfly (and their equiva- lents in the other sets of pictures), nor even caterpillar, the actual target, was systematically picked more often than one would expect by chance. In other words, there was no sign of any ESP.

After the effort I had put into this first experiment and the enormous disappointment of its results, I felt moved to write in my diary, "Pretty pathetic! I concluded that parapsychology is all a lot of rubbish and I should do something else!!"

Five

The Doubts Begin

Of course I did not do something else. I was still hooked. Those multifarious other experiences still beckoned. And the feeling that my theory could account for them lured me on.

Our student Society for Psychical Research provided much of the inspiration. Just as at Oxford, we had lectures from psychical researchers, when we could find them, and from occultists of all kinds. We also ran experiments and got together to look for ghosts or hunt down ley lines. We had séances, used the good old ouija board, and sat around in semidarkness peering at each others' auras.

Auras are fascinating. There is no doubt that if you hold out your hand against a dark background and look at the space just beside the skin, you will begin to see a faint glow around it. Under some conditions it is possible to see colored halos and other more complex effects. If the fingers of two hands are pointed at each other and gradually brought together there comes a point at which the two auras seem to reach out and combine into one; and the reaching out effect seems to vary with the relationship between the people. But why?

First of all, the light skin against a dark background provides high contrast and good conditions for after-images. As the eyes move slightly but rapidly about (as they always do), an after-image builds up around the edge of the hand and produces a light blur. Colored after images can also be formed. But what of the other effects? Might they be paranormal? These were the kinds of questions we tried to explore in our evening meetings, and we found no easy answers.

We soon gained a great deal of encouragement in the form of Julian Isaacs. One day Professor Lee told me that a new student was coming to see him about the possibility of doing a Ph.D. in parapsychology.

"I can't spend all day with him," Lee told me. "Will you take him for lunch and show him around a bit?" Of course I said I'd love to. At last I might have someone else to discuss things with.

Julian was not at all what I had expected. Very tall, with an untidy mop of receding fair hair, he talked so fast and with such a profusion of neohippy slang that I could barely understand him. But I fear I misjudged him at that first meeting. We were both the sort to get aggressive in our nervousness and to show off with nothing but clever-sounding arguments. We sat outside, eating lunch at a student snackbar, and we made an odd combination. Then as I got to know Julian better, his nervousness turned into an endless source of enthusiasm and energy, and he inspired our student society to all sorts of new endeavors.

The first involved a new method for producing paranormal physical phenomena, like the movement of objects or spontaneous productions of sounds. In the old days of psychical research, especially in the heyday of spiritualism around the turn of the century, tables reportedly tipped up or even lifted right into the air, people were levitated, voices appeared from nowhere, and a mysterious substance called ectoplasm was exuded from the bodies of mediums and fashioned into the forms of spirits (Gauld 1968; Kurtz 1985).

In more recent years the number of physical mediums and the production of ectoplasm has declined dramatically—some say because of improved techniques of detecting fraud. However, in Canada, a group run by George Owen had recently been successful with a radically new technique (Owen and Sparrow 1976). They decided to invent their own "spirit." They called him Phillip, invented a fictitious past for him, and called on this imaginary entity to communicate by moving a table or rapping out answers to their questions. Apparently he cooperated and did many of things that spirits have traditionally been supposed to do, like moving a table about, creating raps and bangs, and answering questions through a code. The group even recorded the raps on tape and made films of tables in the air.

The idea was that, by relinquishing their own responsibility and pretending a "spirit" was doing it, the group allowed their own paranormal powers to operate. It is an attractive idea: that we all have paranormal powers but our fear prevents them from being manifested.

Taking this lead, we set up our own "sitter group" in Guildford. We began by having an artificial ouija board session in which we invented our person (or spirit) and asked him to communicate through the letters. We called him Oliver and spent many enjoyable hours making up his history, family, friends, and life in London's East End.

Gradually we could hand matters over to him, and we received sensible answers to our questions. In later weeks we sat around a small table and patiently waited for him to lift it or rap with its legs or do anything at all.

We cajolled him, shouted at him, pleaded with him, and tried to entertain him. We talked about him, asked him questions, and sang to him. We even had a special birthday party for Oliver; choosing the appropriate Cockney foods and beer, and singing his favorite songs for him. In return the table creaked and groaned; it even swayed a little, and once or twice we thought we heard faint raps—but then once or twice we all gave helpful shoves or pushes too! It seemed very uninspiring for the hours and hours we spent "with" Oliver.

We knew we had to be patient. The Phillip group had continued for years. But either our patience ran out too soon, or there was something wrong with the method. After more than two months of regular meetings we decided to call it a day. Fun we had had, boredom we had also had, but paranormal phenomena we had not.

Much more encouraging were my explorations into the Tarot. Back in Oxford, one of Kevin's many gifts had been teaching me to read the cards. He taught me well. He made me practice as much as I could, and he told me to write down every reading that I did and keep a complete record, never to read the cards for money, and finally not to consult any books but let the cards themselves be my teacher. In this way, though I don't think I had any special "gift" for it, I became a fairly good Tarot reader.

The method I used was to sit quietly with the "querent" at a table and ask him (or her) to shuffle the cards. I told him to think about his own life or any special question he had and to shuffle until he felt happy with the cards. He was then to cut the cards three times with the left hand and pass the pack to me. I took ten cards, one by one, from the top of the pack and laid them out face down in the pattern of the "Celtic Cross." One by one I turned the cards over, and, according to their position in the cross and whether they were upright or reversed, I interpreted the person's life. I used to go into a sort of reverie myself, and out of the pattern of pictures would come a complete story: a person's childhood, struggles and happiness, love affairs and ambitions, hopes and fears.

By the time of my first Ph.D. experiments I was working a lot with the Tarot. At the Surrey "Fresher's Fair" we offered a free Tarot reading to everyone who joined our SPR. This proved to be a powerful draw, and there were many takers and many new members. After that I began a Tarot training group, and once a week a small group of us met in the Union. I gave a brief talk on a few of the cards, and then we all practiced doing readings for each other. All of us learned to read the cards quite well. Again and again people told me I was right. They asked me how on earth I knew so much about them and how the cards worked. I didn't know how the cards worked; I only knew that it was yet another mystery.

Of course, I had a few ideas. Could it be just good guesswork and practice at getting to know people? That seemed unconvincing as an explanation, especially since there were odd facts such as the same card tending to appear again and again for the same person. My special card was the Queen of Wands, while other people repeatedly found the Moon, the Ten of Swords, or the Lovers in their readings. This couldn't just be chance, could it? My knowledge of the oddities of chance was reasonably good but not my knowledge of the way chance plays tricks on people's perceptions. There were many other relevant psychological processes that I had not yet come across (Alcock 1981; Marks and Kammann 1980). Confronted with the mysterious workings of the Tarot, and with no better explanation to offer, I found myself always leaning toward a paranormal explanation.

As far as paranormal explanations were concerned, I seemed to be making some progress. I believed the Tarot might work in two possible ways. The simplest was that the whole process was due to telepathy. The Tarot reader simply picked up information from the general memory store "out there." The information was relevant to the person who had shuffled the cards because the reader was thinking about him or her and about sharing ideas. It was similarity of ideas which made telepathy operate, according to my "memory theory of ESP." The problem with this formulation was that it made the cards redundant. They would have to operate just as a kind of hook for ideas, or a picture around which to weave the telepathic input—much as a crystal ball may do. But also it didn't explain why particular cards kept on coming up for certain people. So this notion wasn't entirely satisfactory.

However, the ESP theory also had to account for clairvoyance, and this meant that objects and events had to produce ideas or "memories" that could be picked up in the same way. If this were so, then perhaps the cards had associated with them a great mass of ideas, perhaps all the ideas ever thought by the people who had come into contact with them. If there was some process that guided ideas together, then it would bring the right cards to the surface at the right time. Superficially this seemed to account for the operation of the cards as well as for the way the special cards kept coming up. It also fit with such occult teachings as the importance of keeping the same pack always with you, keeping it carefully wrapped in special material, and never letting other people touch and contaminate it. Indeed the more I thought about it, the more details my theory seemed to account for. At the time I mistakenly took this for an advantage.

My ideas waxed lyrical on other topics too. The whole business of imaginary spirits was perfect for my theory. If a group of people all thought up an imaginary person and kept on thinking about it, they would give it a reality as far as the world of memory was concerned. If their ideas were strong and clear enough, then surely other people would be able to pick them up too. That "spirit" should be accessible to other mediums and psychics, once it was sufficiently thought out. And if psychokinesis works at all, then it should work just as well for this kind of spirit as for a "real" spirit.

It was fun thinking this way. It was terribly exciting to be trying out new ideas, experiencing new things, grappling with occult notions and trying to make sense of them all. And there is nothing wrong with having fun in science. Indeed it is often the fun of thinking up new hypotheses that carries one through the arduous job of testing them and doing long and difficult experiments. But looming ever larger and larger were several grave problems.

First of all, my supervisor and other psychologists with whom I discussed my ideas clearly thought I was going too far. They thought it was pointless to waste time on such obviously occult ideas. ESP was bad enough, but Tarot cards were quite beyond the pale. And as for imaginary spirits moving tables—well! It was made quite clear that I could do experiments on ESP, but not on these other "weirdos."

This problem would not have been insuperable. It meant only that I had to keep my more extreme interests to myself, or reserve them for the SPR meetings, and keep them out of my thesis. I didn't have to stop thinking about them.

Far more important was whether the theory could be made to work. I faced a lot of opposition from people who claimed that it was unscientific or pseudoscientific or that it did not fit with current psychological theory. This forced me to think in some depth about the difference between science and pseudoscience.

* * *

The problem of the demarkation between true science and pseudoscience has been central to the philosophy of science, and I had to learn more about this. I also had to recognize that what was "scientific" or not was not only the theory itself but what one did with it. Science abounds with crazy theories. Most of them turn out to be useless and are thrown out or forgotten. A few turn out to be brilliant and world-shattering and transform whole areas of science. But it is hard to tell in the beginning which is which. If a theory is going to be of any use at all it has to pass at least three tests. Roughly speaking, it has to account well for existing data. It has to be internally consistent—make sense. And it has to be able to predict new findings (whether in new or old data). If I was going to make my theory work and convince my superiors that it was worthwhile after all, I had to tackle all three areas.

The first was the easiest and the most fun, but then it always is. Fringe areas of science abound with theories that "explain everything." Indeed I had begun by making the very obvious (and very common) mistake of thinking that the more a theory explains, the better it is. In fact it is very easy to think up theories that explain everything, like that things move because angels push and pull them and that there is a different kind of angel for every different kind of motion. However, such a theory is totally unselective about the things it explains, and it fails utterly on the second and third tests. It provokes further questions like "What pushes and pulls the angels?" and it cannot predict any new findings. Was my theory just as bad as this? I didn't think it was, but clearly it was time to struggle seriously with the second two problems.

Niggling doubts had begun to set in.

Six

The Theory Starts to Fail

For all my commitment to my theory I had to admit that it had its problems. There were three principles upon which the whole idea depended. And the more I thought about them, the more impossible they seemed.

The basic idea was that thoughts or ideas (or something) were stored independently of brains in some common store. They could then be reached by anyone who thought or imagined sufficiently similar ideas. The three essential principles seemed to be: (1) the division into units of "ideas" or "thoughts"; (2) the notion of similarity; (3) the principle of varying strength or potency of ideas.

Each of these was problematic. The whole theory worked on the notion that it makes sense to talk about ideas independently of the system that is thinking them and that they can somehow be divided up into units. After all, if I am going to get hold of an idea of yours by telepathy, then there has to be some sense in which that "idea" existed as a unit "out there" in the communal store. The more I thought about it (and philosophers have been thinking about it for hundreds of years), the less sense dividing thoughts up into units seemed to make.

Of course I was not alone in trying to do it. A few previous paranormal theorists had done precisely the same thing. H. H. Price, an Oxford philosopher and the very aged president of our Oxford SPR when I was running it, had propounded a theory of the "psychic ether" (Price 1939). This "ether" contained individual "ideas" that could become associated with buildings or people, so giving rise to hauntings and ghosts. But Price never satisfactorily resolved the problem of what counted as an "idea."

Then Whateley Carington, one of the best-known psychical researchers in the 1930s and 1940s, had put forward a theory that involved "psychons" (Carington 1945). However, he too had neglected to explain just what constitutes a "psychon." Was my idea of an elephant a single psychon? Or are there separate psychons for each of its ears and trunk and tail? And even worse, was a different psychon activated each time I thought of an elephant since one can never think exactly the same thought twice?

Neither of these theories resolved the problems; nor did mine. More important, I could see no way to make the theory work without having to assume some kind of units of ideas. I tried to formulate it using only a continuum of ideas instead of separate units, but this only threw me harder up against the second problem.

The second problem was that of similarity. What did it mean for two ideas to be more or less similar to each other? Is my idea of an elephant more like your idea of an elephant or my idea of a giraffe? Is that question answerable in principle? Of course there are many dimensions along which one could decide similarity. But if this theory was to work for everyone, then nature would have to have intrinsic dimensions of similarity. Everything seemed to point against this. There are infinite ways in which things can be similar or dissimilar. It makes sense that humans (and other animals) should use some categories and not others in trying to understand their world, but it is something quite different to imply that nature has preferred dimensions of similarity. And, if it did, what are they, and how on earth would we find out?

I seemed to be arguing myself into a hole!

Finally there was the question of strength. If I fleetingly think of a large gray animal, this surely should not have the same effect as if I clearly and carefully imagine the beautiful, solid, and detailed roamer on the African plains. But what is the difference between these two? Are there bigger "ideas" in the store, the same ones represented more times, or some tagged with a label saying "good clear idea," or what? The more I thought about it the less sense it all seemed to make.

You might be wondering whether these arguments apply to all thinking and whether by generalizing them we could show that thinking is itself impossible. But in fact none of these are problematic when applied to one person's thinking. Within one organism or one brain or information-processing system, it does make sense to talk about units (such as bits of stored information in a computer), and similarity can be internally defined in any ways that suit that system. Finally, strength can be determined in terms of repetition, multiple storage, or any number of other mechanisms. All the problems arise when a comparison is made with a different organism or person or system, in other words, when you are trying to incorporate telepathy. (I should add that the problems are even worse if you want to incorporate clairvoyance too.) So gradually the problem of explaining ESP began to seem harder and harder.

I struggled with these ideas. And I was very lonely. I tried to explain to my supervisor, Terence Lee, but he wasn't particularly interested, and he was far too busy to learn much about the subject. I think he felt that my theory might be a harmless diversion, but the real work was experimental. What he cared about was that I should get on with some good experiments. In many ways I agreed, but I did so want my theory to make sense.

I then tried to talk to Shivesh Thakur, professor of philosophy at Surrey, who was supposed to have an interest in psychical research. He was happy to discuss it but could provide no insight into my problems. I tried to talk to Ernie Spinelli, but he seemed quite uninterested in the sort of theoretical problems that plagued me.

Until a few months before, I had had John with whom I could easily have talked all this through and with whom I longed to talk now. There were advantages to being on my own though. I realized with pleasant surprise that I was actually free to do whatever I liked. So, with my parents' help, I decided to buy a house in Guildford. Like so many English towns, Guildford has a standard kind of house at the bottom of the housing market. There are rows and rows of terraced houses, built at the end of the last century, with two or three rooms "down" and two or three "up." I found a typical house with a long narrow garden, only a mile from the university, and with rather pretty intricate brickwork and beds of roses in front. My mother found a cooker and a fridge, and a table and a bed, in the second-hand section of the local paper, and in junk shops I bought chairs at 50 pence each and saucepans full of ancient cutlery. Then I turned the main living-room into a study. It was there that I sat, with only my faithful cat, Lucifer (otherwise known as Lucy), for company and thought about the problems of ESP.

In some ways I was lonely. I had always lived in college or in shared student houses of one kind or another, and I wasn't used to living on my own. But in other ways I flourished. There was so much time to sit and think. And think I did. When I wasn't scoring answer sheets or preparing lectures, I wondered why I couldn't really remember what it had been like being at Oxford, or how the existence of ESP was to be reconciled with psychology. I cooked meals on my own and ate them in silence. I didn't have a television, and I rarely went out. In spite of an extravert appearance, I have always found myself choosing to stay at home rather than go out. I rarely went to parties or evenings in the pub; and, although I always thought I ought to go to the cinema or theater, somehow I never could be bothered. Instead I immersed myself in ESP and memory. How could I make sense of ESP?

I tried to work out just what needed explaining. As far as I could see, there were all the forms of psi: telepathy and clairvoyance, precognition and psychokinesis. Then there were ghosts and apparitions and hauntings of various kinds. And finally there were all those experiences, like out-of-body experiences or near-death experiences, in which people seem to travel in other worlds. It was these last, with which I'd had some experience myself, that most impelled me. I couldn't abandon looking for explanations when I had such a clear recollection of my strange experiences.

It seems odd to me now that I didn't notice what I was doing. I was just making the assumption that all these things are related and that they are all paranormal. Having made that assumption, I began by trying to explain ESP.

However, it was clear by then that my theory was in serious trouble. I would have to put all my energies into my experiments and hope that they would show me the way. It was thus that I worked on a long series of experiments. With my routine of one experiment a week I could afford to make mistakes and to learn from them. In this way, I gradually got better and better at experimental design.

All the experiments involved statistics. Most ESP experiments do: The subjects have to guess which word or picture or symbol is the "target" from among a number of other words, symbols, or pictures. There is always a certain probability that they will get the right one by chance. In every case the "chance hypothesis" is used for comparison. Only if the subjects score significantly better (or worse) than chance can you conclude that "psi-hitting" (or "psi-missing") might have occurred.

But even then you cannot conclude that it was definitely ESP that caused the deviation from chance. It could have been a fault in the design of the experiment, or a lack of good controls, or sensory leakage with the subjects able to see the targets or even to cheat. Only if the experiments are really well-designed can you conclude that the deviation was probably due to some paranormal effect.

One thing I learned, at my initial expense, was how to avoid the dangerous "stacking effect." In one of my early experiments I enclosed a list of target pictures in an envelope and kept it on my desk at the front of the class. All of the students had to guess the order of the pictures inside. This they did most successfully. "At last," I thought, with a mixture of disbelief, excitement, and pleasure, "at last I have found some ESP. Here we go—"

But, in the midst of excited speculation on why this experiment worked when the others hadn't, it gradually dawned on me that there was a problem here. What if the first target I had used just happened to be the most popular? I had about a hundred people all guessing at the same list of targets, and any effect of preferences would be exaggerated by the number of people guessing at the same thing. I pondered this for a while and couldn't work out whether it mattered or not.

I think it was Carl Sargent who finally enlightened me. He seemed to know everything about designing ESP experiments and, as usual, was the one to point out my methodological flaws. He made me feel extremely ignorant, but he helped me a great deal. He explained that this was the "stacking effect" (Greville 1944). There are ways to calculate it and so allow for it, but the only safe solution is to use individual target sets for each subject. Then any effects of preference don't "stack up," and normal statistics will apply.

Many previous experiments have suffered from this problem, especially those on television or radio in which large numbers of viewers have all tried to guess at the same hidden target. I was slightly comforted to know that I wasn't alone in making this mistake. But I had to get my experiments right, even though it meant much more work. You cannot just have one target set but must make one for each subject. So my Sunday evenings became even more work. I didn't mind the hard work; it was exciting to be doing real experiments at last. But as I ironed out the initial flaws and designed experiments that were more and more carefully controlled, any slightly promising effects seemed to disappear. I had obviously been wrong in attributing a few early successes to psi. They were almost certainly due to a "stacking effect." I looked forward to being able to do better experiments and to test my theory in even better ways, but I have to admit that I began to get a little despondent.

*   *   *

It was obviously time to take a break from all this frustration. During the Easter holidays of 1977 I went on two skiing holidays, first to the Alps with my family and then to Scotland to race for my university ski team. It was there, on the freezing and rainy (yes both at once!) slopes of Cairngorm, that I first set eyes on Tom Trościanko.

My ski boots were so old that they were made of leather. I couldn't race in those, and so I reluctantly decided that I would have to rent some. It was not entirely a success, and I struggled in vain to do them up tight while standing on a steep slope in the driving snow.

"Will somebody help me with these boots?" I feebly asked the other racers around me. Some chivalrous young man immediately dropped down into the snow and helped me, but standing by, laughing, was another member of his team. He was clearly delighted at my predicament. If the captain of the Surrey team couldn't even do up her boots, then that was one team they were sure to beat. He, I learned later, was captain of rival City University—rivals for bottom place that is.

One night, after a hard day of racing, we had an evening of Broom Ball, a sort of free-for-all ice hockey played with brooms, a beach ball, and no rules whatsoever except that there are two goals. People hit each other with brooms, stole the ball and threw it away, knocked each other over—and very few of us even knew how to skate. After this dangerous melee was over, we all sat around in the bar, and there, chatting with the rest of his team, I noticed the man who had been laughing at me. Without his ski gear and layer of ice, I could see his curly fair hair and soft moustache. His face was rather boyish, and the corners of his mouth seemed always to be turned up. I couldn't resist it. As I walked past, I winked at him.

The result wasn't quite what I had intended. He got up in the middle of his conversation and walked straight up to me. I growled at him, pretending to attack him like a wild beast, and in no time we were clutching one another.

I hung on to him tight, not sure whether I was glad or terrified. I had no idea what to do next, so I challenged him to think of something. "Race you to the middle of the ice," he said. I tore myself away and ran as fast as I could out of the bar. He was after me. I could hear him clattering around the tables and slamming through the door. We went down the stairs, along the rows of seats by the ice-rink, and he was gaining! In a final attempt to escape I rushed out onto the ice and slid, in a long tumbling heap, across half the rink. "What on earrth do you think ye're doing?" cried a deep and angry Scottish voice. "This ice has to be rrready for the morrning, and ye've rrruined the surface. Come here," the voice bellowed.

The two of us stood sheepishly by, looking guiltily at those obvious marks across the smoothness of the ice. Together we apologized, were forgiven, and went quietly back to the bar. There I learned that his name was Tom. He was in London to do a Ph.D. on the psychology of color vision.

"Do you have a girlfriend?" I asked, trying to sound disinterested and casual.

Tom smiled an odd smile at me, "Yes I do," he said, as my heart sank and I tried not to feel disappointed. "Her name is Pat. She's an artist, and we live in Ealing. I've known her a long time."

I could tell little from his tone of voice, but I imagined them together, relaxed in their own flat, surrounded by trendy paintings and artistic decor, happy and permanent. I should obviously not get involved. I told myself I would just enjoy the rest of the week there and then get back to work on my own.

Seven

Psi is Always Around the Next Corner

The following week was the First International Conference of the Society for Psychical Research, held at The City University in London. It didn't escape my notice that that was Tom's university. Indeed, as we'd said goodbye, amid the chaos of stacking skis and students into the right minibuses, Tom had said he might come and look me up there.

It wouldn't be true to say that I hardly thought of him during the next few days! But certainly I had to work very hard. I was about to present my first conference paper. Many years later I would give such papers without anxiety, but for that first one I was terrified. I started then a practice which I always continued: I learned what I intended to say more or less by heart so that I could speak entirely without notes. I practiced to myself, pacing up and down the corridors of City University, discreetly peeping into doors just in case Tom was hiding there, and pretending I was concentrating solely on my paper. Also that day I did my first live radio broadcast. It was only for the local London radio station, but I felt important talking about our conference and the special subject of parapsychology.

The paper went well and provoked a lot of comments and questions, but it must have made extremely dull listening. I didn't dare mention my own theory (with all its problems), and I had precious few experimental results to present. So I discussed various kinds of possible memory-ESP theories, a very dry and abstract presentation. What I remember now is the audience. My parents had come to support my efforts, and as I waved self-consciously I noticed a familiar face behind them. There was Tom! My previously well-controlled nerves produced a pounding heart and shaking hands, and I struggled through three theories of ESP and memory with my mind elsewhere! Now Tom was hearing about my work. Now he was stepping into my normal life with all its problems. Or was he? As we went off to have dinner together I reminded myself that he was living with someone else.

In all the excitement I forgot about my worries over the experiments. But not for long. As soon as the conference was over I had to get back to them. I had sorted out my initial troubles, had learned how to design a reasonably good ESP experiment, and now I ought to be able to get down to the testing in earnest.

My experiments all had the same aim—to see whether ESP was more like memory or perception. There were three main kinds of experiment:

1. Studies of the errors and confusions made in ESP (Blackmore 1981a).

2. Studies of correlations between ESP and memory (Blackmore 1980a).

3. Studies of the effect of varying target material on ESP (Blackmore 1981b).

The first type I have already described. We know from psychology experiments the sorts of errors and confusions people make in both memory and perception. For example, if you are shown words very briefly and then asked what you saw, you are likely to make mistakes based on how the words look. You might confuse *house* with *horse* or *cough* with *bough*. If the words were spoken you would never confuse *cough* with *bough,* but might confuse *now* with *bough.* On the other hand, if you were asked to remember words, you would make quite different mistakes. You would be more likely (at least in certain kinds of memory task) to confuse words according to their meaning. You might remember *pony* instead of *horse* or *branch* instead of *bough.*

The study of errors has proved a very powerful technique in psychology, and I thought it could be so in parapsychology too. However, I was in for a disappointment. I spent countless hours drawing pictures or hunting through special lists for the right words. But I never got an answer to my question. I did not find one sort of error more than others. Indeed I only found errors. The responses my subjects gave were totally unrelated to the targets. How could I ask what kinds of errors predominate in ESP, if there were only errors and no ESP?

My second approach concerned correlations. If ESP is like remembering, then people who are good at ESP should also be good at remembering. I spent many more days and nights designing experiments to test memory ability. My long-suffering students now had to learn lists of words and recall them in various ways, ticking off targets they had seen before or trying to recall as many as they could in a brief time. When I got zero correlations I thought I ought to combine the ESP and memory tests into one and bent my energies to that tricky task. After half a dozen of these kinds of experiment I had to admit that I had got nothing other than more failed ESP tests and correlations with memory that varied nicely around the zero level. Not very encouraging.

The final method was to use different kinds of target materials. For example, it is known that it is easier to remember words if they are easy to imagine, while the easiest to perceive are usually those most frequent in the language. For example *elephant* is easily imageable and therefore easy to recall, while *existence* is not. *Hauser* is rare in English and is therefore hard to perceive if, for example, it is blurred or shown only for a short time, but *house* is common and easily perceived.

I therefore used words of different imageability and frequency, carefully controlling for word length and other variables. It meant more late Sunday nights preparing well-balanced lists of words suitable for tests, typing them out, and duplicating them. And the results? Just the same, I am sorry to say. I could never find out whether imageability or frequency had any effect on ESP, because I never found evidence of any ESP. My results were steadfastly close to chance.

One is always looking for scores that are significantly different from chance, that is, by convention, those which give a probability of less than 1 in 20 that they were due to chance alone (or a p-value of .05). Of course, by chance alone, results are sometimes spuriously "significant." On the average, if you do twenty experiments, one is likely to come out "significant" just by chance. At one point I calculated that I had performed thirty-four independent significance tests and just two were significant—remarkably close to chance expectation.

I was getting no ESP.

"Why not? Why not?" I interrogated myself as I worked alone in my new study. "It isn't fair. Other people can find ESP—or so they say, or so their journal articles say [see, e.g., Wolman 1977]. Why can't I?

"Have I done something wrong? Is there something fundamentally wrong with me? Do I have the wrong subjects or use the wrong methods? And what on earth can I do now?"

I still very much wanted to know whether ESP was like memory, and I very much wanted to understand all those odd experiences I had had: the out-of-body experience, the experiences in meditation, the ouija board, the Tarot, and the auras. But how?

* * *

Fortunately, I soon had someone to talk to, someone to share the frustrations and disappointments with, someone who took a heathily down-to-earth interest in my obsession with parapsychology. One morning when I arrived at the university, the secretary called me over. "A young man has been ringing you. He's rung twice already and says he'll ring again. He didn't give his name."

I wondered if it could be Tom, but why should he ring the university? I had given him my home phone number, and he hadn't called there. But it *was* Tom, and he said he'd come to dinner at my house that evening. It was that evening, as I watched carefully to see whether Lucy the cat took to him or not and whether he was good at washing up and picking the right vegetables from the garden, that I learned he had already left his flat in Ealing.

He went to live in a small gloomy room in a dreary part of Clapham, in South London, with a Polish landlady who spoke little English. It was in her untidy kitchen that Tom first cooked a meal for me. There were candles and flowers and everything beautifully laid out on the table. He made delicious salads with Polish delicacies and crunchy red kidney beans. It was only years later that we realized how long those beans should have been boiled! But upset stomachs did nothing to detract from the romance of the occasion.

It was there, looking up from the narrow lumpy bed at the mottled and cracking ceiling, that we planned our future and cried about our apparently insurmountable problem. We had another grim autumn coming up. I had my two jobs, and Tom had his thesis to write. We only knew one thing—we wanted to do them together and we wanted to be married first, even though we'd known each other only a few weeks.

I had had enough arguments about weddings with my parents. I knew they liked Tom and was sure they'd be delighted if we were married. But no such luck. With my interests at heart they tried to persuade us that it was much too soon to be sure and that I was only "on the rebound" from John, and wouldn't it be better to wait until the spring?

"So the birds will all be chirping, I suppose," put in Tom rudely.

But we didn't want to wait, and in the end my parents organized our wedding with enthusiasm. This time there were no traumas or arguments about what time the wedding should be, whether to sit down or stand up for the meal, or what color the flowers should be.

That September, five months and eleven days after we first met on a cold wet mountain, Tom and I were married. We had a wonderful party and then slipped off to the train to spend our honeymoon night on a British Rail bunk heading north. We had a delightful, exciting, and scary fortnight in a tiny two-man storm tent on the wind-swept northern isles of Shetland. It was dark from 7:00 P.M. till 7:00 A.M., and the only evening entertainment was to stay in the tent and play Scrabble by torchlight or to brave the weather and go out to The Booth, where local fishermen stood in their wet-weather gear to buy a few pints. By day we cooked on our pebble fireplace or watched the seals on the beach by our tent or walked on the bouncy heathery moorland.

* * *

It was a shock to return to Guildford. Another year, another lot of students, and all the problems of my experiments to face. But I now had Tom sharing my house, writing his own thesis, and helping me struggle with my problem.

My problem was simple. I couldn't find any ESP.

"But what does it mean to say I can't find any ESP?" I pestered him.

"What do you mean, what does it mean?" he brought me down to earth with a smile. "It probably means there isn't any, and you might as well stop looking for it."

"But it isn't that simple." I went on. "What about all those other people who *have* got results?"

"Well, what about them?" he countered. "Maybe they're wrong and you are right. Maybe they haven't done their experiments as carefully as you have or something. That's possible."

"Yes I know it's possible, but I may never be able to find out whether it is so. And what about the negative definition of psi?"

This was something I had begun to worry about in earnest and discussed at great length with Tom. ESP is traditionally defined negatively. The *Journal of Parapsychology* describes it as, "ESP (Extrasensory Perception): Experience of, or response to, a target object, state, event, or influence without sensory contact." It is that last phrase that is so important: *without sensory contact*. It means that you can never be sure whether you have found ESP or not. Finding it depends on finding something which cannot be explained by sensory contact, and that means having to be ever more and more sure that sensory contact is ruled out—hence all the many precautions I had taken in my experiments.

This negative definition is problematic enough if you find extra-chance scores, but it becomes even more so if you find nothing. If you keep on searching and don't find psi, there never comes a point at which you can say that it doesn't exist, only that your experiment didn't find it. Some people have even argued that negative results can tell you nothing about psi. According to this view, any amount of negative results can contribute nothing to the controversy over the existence of psi, and unless I could find out something positive about psi, all my work would be quite useless, and I might as well not have bothered.

I went to my supervisor with this problem.

"Do you think my results are worth anything?" I asked him anxiously. "I mean if I can't find something as elusive as psi, and negatively defined too, what can I conclude now?" He shook his head, led me over to a more comfortable chair, and sat down next to me. "I really want to know what you think," I begged. "What am I to do now?"

"Well, if you really want to know what I think," he finally conceded, "as far as your thesis is concerned it doesn't matter whether your results are negative or positive. The only thing that matters is whether you have planned your experiments well, designed them properly, and written them up clearly. So you needn't worry about that.

"And as for what to do next—well, I always told you what I thought. You should be doing experiments like Ernesto's. If he can get such outstanding results with young children, I don't see why you shouldn't. Your memory experiments just aren't working. Go out and do some work with young children. Then you'll find some ESP."

I took his point. He was sensible and down to earth. And I had to find some psi. But I wasn't happy. I really didn't want to do any experiments with children, though I wasn't quite sure why.

That night I had a very long, very hot bath and struggled with my many confusions. I lay in my newly acquired bathtub, looking through a crack in the faded pink checked curtains, which I had inherited with the house, to the outlines of bare trees outside. I thought again and again about the negative definition of psi. Perhaps I ought to redefine psi, but I had tried to tackle that one countless times before and had never made any headway. Yes, it would be nice to redefine it, but how? I had no answers there.

Perhaps the whole subject was impossible! Was I wrong even to be trying? Was the whole scientific enterprise inappropriate for understanding these things?

Perhaps I should just forget all about scientific research, I thought, leaning toward escapism again. But I rejected that route smartly. Science is extraordinarily flexible and can surely be bent and expanded to incorporate the paranormal if need be. Science is not the rigid set of rules and tedious procedures some people make it out to be. It is a very general approach to asking questions. What lies at its heart is the process of trying to understand the world by asking questions, by thinking up possible explanations (or theories or hypotheses), and putting them to the test. It really doesn't matter too much what sort of theories or what sort of tests, just so long as one listens to the answers they provide. What characterizes pseudoscience is its refusal to listen to the evidence.

I did not like my evidence, and I did not really want to listen to it. I wanted there to be ESP, and I wanted my theory to be right. But nature was telling me I was wrong. Very reluctantly I decided it was no good clinging to a useless theory. I would have to shelve it for the time being. Perhaps I would even have to abandon it altogether.

With feelings akin to parting from a dear friend, mixed with a certain amount of enjoyable relief, I sat up and ran myself some more hot water.

I may have been abandoning my theory, but I was not going to take an utterly pessimistic view. My negative results certainly told me something: that is, that my predictions were wrong. However, that finding wasn't very informative. The really useful results in science— whether positive or negative— are those that surprise people. They are those that contradict existing theories or that provide unexpected support for new ones. All my results did was to confirm what everybody already thought. Perhaps it was this, rather than the negative definition of psi, that was the real problem. If everyone else had shared my expectations, and I had found them to be wrong, then that would have told us a great deal, but of course they didn't. People who did not believe in psi (and I was surrounded by them at Surrey) were not at all surprised by my lack of results. Indeed, I was often told that the results simply proved that I had done my experiments properly and got my controls right.

On the other hand, people who did believe in psi did not seem surprised either. My results did nothing to dent their belief. They simply put my failure down to the fickleness of psi or to my own lack of belief in it. I stared into the pretty soap bubbles. It was so easy to imagine I could burst them by thinking about it! Did I or didn't I believe in psi? It really wasn't as simple as that, was it?

I recalled a recent conversation with Julian as we were walking across the campus one gloomy English afternoon.

"Julian, why do *you* think I can't get any psi?"

"Why do *I* think you can't? I don't think you can't. I just think you have a mental block about it. You are so hung up about having to understand it and make theories about it that you can't believe in it. If you could just believe it was going to work, it would. It's a psi-mediated experimenter effect."

I knew all about psi-mediated experimenter effects. The idea is that the experimenter, purposely or not, uses his own psi ability either to encourage or block the psi of his subjects or even to act as the subject himself, with the "real" subjects being quite superfluous. If this were so, it made sense that the experimenter's beliefs could be important. Believers, or sheep, might score higher than disbelievers, or goats, and this sheep-goat effect might apply to experimenters as well as subjects (Palmer 1971, 1972; White 1977). It also seemed to fit with the notion that the presence of skeptics can disrupt otherwise successful experiments.

"But, Julian, I know I am pretty skeptical now, but honestly I *did* believe in psi when I started, and even my earliest experiments didn't work!"

"Oh really, Sue," he said, "do you expect me to believe that? Do you really think that you believed in psi, and then a few failures changed your mind? I think you were always a skeptic."

"But I wasn't. I mean, I did expect my first experiment to work. I mean——well, I suppose there is nothing I can say to convince you. In fact it's rather interesting, isn't it. I cannot even be sure myself. I suppose I could read my diary, and that would give me a clue, but it isn't easy to be sure about your own past beliefs, is it?"

"I don't know," Julian waved his long arms dismissively. "The important thing is now. You don't believe in it now, so you don't get results now."

"All right," I said, "then what can I do about it now? I can't just decide one day to believe and then do an experiment and it will work, can I? You can't just change your beliefs that way."

"Well, you'll just have to find something you do believe in then, won't you?" he said simply. He made it sound so easy.

I remembered this conversation painfully. I couldn't *make* myself believe. I kept my eyes steadfastly on the curtain's pink stripes and tried to think what this meant for my research.

And suddenly I was mentally thanking Julian. I realized that I needn't wallow in these abstract speculations forever. There *were* things I believed in. I jumped out of the now tepid bath water with renewed determination. Professor Lee wasn't going to like it, but too bad! I made myself a promise. I would do those experiments with children, but not right away. In the meantime I had something else I wanted to do. ESP might be around the very next corner.

Eight

Explorations into the Tarot

I believed in the Tarot. Since those early days, I had gone on using the cards, both for myself and for others. In fact by now I'd been reading them for nearly eight years. And time and time again the cards had impressed me. Something interesting was obviously going on. I wasn't quite sure what, but there was something. The failure of all my other experiments may have cast doubt over my own theory, including the way it accounted for the workings of the Tarot, but nevertheless the Tarot obviously worked, and I might be able to find out how. I might even find a better theory of the paranormal, or I might find that psi manifested itself in the cards while being shy of laboratory experiments.

But the main thing was that I believed the cards worked. So if there were a psi-based experimenter effect, I could relax and look forward to some interesting results. I began to think about how to test the Tarot.

However, I was becoming overwhelmed by the number of things I had to do. My experiments had failed, my theory was proving useless, and my only present hope was for an experiment I could not even tell my professor about. I had to worry about whether ESP really existed or not, whether this question even made sense, and where I could go from here. I had also promised to do some experiments with children, and these would be time-consuming and difficult. And on top of all this, I was still teaching environmental psychology to architecture students. The endless traveling to and from London was a strain. I just didn't seem to have the time and energy to tackle everything at once any more. Could I find a way to give up the classes in London and concentrate entirely on parapsychology?

Professor Lee was clear in his opinion: I would be mad to give up my only foothold in *real* psychology and a *real* job, and I would never get money from a government research council unless I changed to *real* research. I thought he was probably right there. But I was fed up with working constantly—weekends and evenings and always under pressure. Tom said that if we had to live without my income, we would manage and that I shouldn't work myself into exhaustion. Right, but then it was back to that old problem of how to fund research that most people think is a waste of time.

Quite by chance I saw an announcement that the Science Research Council was offering a new kind of grant for parttime Ph.D. students who wanted to do a year fulltime. It sounded perfect. It was for students with a "proven ability" to work for a Ph.D. on any scientific subject. I thought that, in spite of my results, I had probably proved my ability to do Ph.D. research and hoped that my supervisor would recommend me. The SRC might well rule out parapsychology as not being scientific, but there was no harm in trying.

I put in my application to have one year's grant to study ESP and memory. If I got it I would do those long-promised experiments with children. But I knew I wouldn't hear the result for some months, and there were only ten grants being offered in the whole country, so I tried not to hope too hard.

In the meantime I was already hard at work, designing an experiment to test the operation of the Tarot cards. I had two things in mind: First, I wanted the test to be realistic. It had to incorporate and test a *real* Tarot reading, and it wasn't to destroy the very thing it was trying to find by turning it into a sterile laboratory test. Second, it needed to control totally for "normal" influence. Only if the controls were good enough could we conclude that the Tarot worked paranormally. (Back to that negative definition again.)

There were many things to control for. In a normal Tarot reading the "querent," who has come for the readings, sits right in front of the reader and responds to the things the reader says. Obviously the reader can tell immediately the sex, age, and general appearance of the querent and can get a good idea of what kind of person it is. Then she can use all the feedback given. By unconsciously watching the subtle responses to suggestions and any vague comments, the reader can guide her reading toward the right answers. This isn't to say that these processes necessarily play a large role in Tarot readings, only that if you want to find the paranormal element, you have to rule them out. This would mean that the reader and querent had to be separated from each other.

On the other hand, that was beginning to destroy the whole feel of doing a Tarot reading. What about the intimate sitting round the table, the ritual shuffling and cutting of the deck, and the slow and thoughtful laying out of the cards? All these had to remain or I felt it wouldn't be a fair test.

Then how was I to assess the outcome to decide whether it was successful or not? Obviously I had to develop some method for statistically evaluating how successful the readings were. There were methods available for doing this. For example, one can get ratings from subjects on how good they think readings are. You can use other people to judge how accurate they are, and you can use the ratings in calculations based on what would be expected by chance. If the scores come out better than chance would predict, and the controls are all good enough—hey presto—you might have psi.

I put all this together and concocted a simple experiment to test whether the Tarot cards work normally or paranormally.

In one of my parapsychology classes I explained to my students that I wanted to do a Tarot experiment and that I needed ten volunteers to be subjects for two sessions and one to be an assistant experimenter. The assistant had to be someone with experience doing Tarot readings, perhaps someone who had been to my Tarot classes or someone who had been reading the cards for a long time. He or she would also have quite a lot of work to do in this experiment.

At 5:00 P.M. we all met in the student union in a quiet room off the bar. There were far too many volunteers, and I had a hard job picking ten. A student named Linda, from my Tarot group, turned out to be an excellent assistant. There were two sessions. Each of the ten subjects had two readings, an "ordinary" reading and a "test" or controlled reading. On that first occasion I did half the ordinary readings, sitting face to face with the students. After the reading was over they had to rate it on a scale from 1 (totally incorrect) to 7 (totally correct). Since there was one card representing the future, most of them felt they couldn't give a score of 7. Most of them put 6! So far, so good.

The test readings had to be done without me present. So one by one Linda took the students into the quiet room and carried out the first part of the reading. She got them to relax and think about themselves, shuffle the cards, cut them three times with the left hand, and give the pack to her. Once they had gone she wrote down the order of the top ten cards. She gave each card order a letter (A to J) and wrote out a list of the students' names with their corresponding letters. This list she sealed up in an envelope and put in a safe place. Finally she made out a list of ten card orders with their letters (but no names, of course) to give to me.

Meanwhile the students who had done their bit were plying me with drinks, and we were all doing more readings and discussing how the Tarot might work. We were looking forward to the second session at which we would find out how well the cards had performed.

In the meantime I found myself a quiet, uninterrupted evening and set myself to do the ten readings. I sat quietly in my study at home with my old worn and beloved pack of cards. They were the same cards Linda used—the only time I have lent them to anyone else.

I took the first list of ten cards, imagined I had someone sitting there with me, and laid out the cards. I went through in my mind, just as I would in an ordinary reading, what all the cards meant. Then I wrote it down as clearly as I could and went on to the next. Later on I typed up the ten readings and gave each of them a number (1-10). I made a list of which number related to which letter and kept that sealed in an envelope.

The next week at five o'clock we all met again in the union. Linda was there with her list in its envelope, and every one of the ten subjects was there, including one who had struggled there with the flu. I gave each of the ten a list of the ten readings with their numbers. They had to read them all and give them ratings (just as they had for the ordinary readings) and then pick which they thought was theirs. When they had done that, they had to put all the other readings in order from the one which fit them the most to the one that fit them the least.

When it was all done, Linda and I put together our lists of names, letters, and numbers and worked out which reading was meant for each person. Then we could find out how far down the rating list everyone had put their own reading. According to chance they should average a score of 5.5, but if the cards were working paranormally the subjects should have put their own reading higher up the list. I had brought along with me the tables needed to apply a statistical test to their scores (Solfvin et al. 1978). We would know straightaway whether the result was significant or not.

Together we compared the lists and drew up the scores. With some trepidation and real excitement, I looked it up in the tables. I hardly dared to look—but yes, it was significant!

The ten subjects had, on average, put their own reading in fourth position, which was significantly higher up on the list than chance would dictate. I shouted and laughed and everyone clapped.

It · as my first genuinely successful result, the first I had obtained in an experiment that I thought was well-controlled. We had many drinks to celebrate and sat around in the union for hours discussing what this meant and where we could take it from there.

Of course the test readings were not rated as highly as the ordinary ones. It seemed that the "normal" factors probably provided a large effect, but there seemed to be some paranormal effect as well. Now I had to address myself to the question of where it came from. Was it that the cards were moved about into the appropriate positions, or was I just using psi when I made out the readings, with the cards playing no role? Feeling better than I had for weeks, I cycled home to the supper Tom had cooked.

Gradually I began to tell people about this experiment. I didn't think it was suitable for presenting at a conference or even a seminar at Surrey, but I told my parapsychological friends about it.

* * *

First, I told Serena Roney Dougal about it. I had first met Serena a couple of years before when she had rung me up one day, quite out of the blue, to ask whether she could meet me to discuss parapsychology. I was always pleased to meet anyone interested in parapsychology and arranged to meet her at the architecture school. As I sat there waiting for her I wondered what sort of person she would be and if I should have invited her to our scruffy coffee room. But in a moment Serena was there, quite out of breath and bedraggled by the howling wind outside, with a chaotic toddler in tow. She had long straggly fair hair, blue jeans, and a multicolored coat, and she quite threw me with her mischievous smile, which seemed to alternate with a deeply worried look.

We talked for a long time, with little Colva running and falling about among the tables, and although we were totally different in many ways, we got on very well. Whether I was able to help in any way I have no idea, but, soon after, Serena went on to do research for her own Ph.D. in parapsychology.

Since then I often met her at parapsychological meetings and visited her in the half-demolished street in South London where she lived. She seemed to have experienced almost every conceivable psychic phenomenon and to know all the magicians and occultists around. She was a marvellous antidote to the dull disbelief of a normal psychology department.

When she heard about my Tarot experiment she was delighted. "There you are, Sue. I told you so," she said. "It is just because you believed in it. You'll never get anywhere with those boring tedious memory experiments. All those poor students getting bored in classes and having to fill in endless forms. Psi doesn't come to order and just won't let itself be experimented on like that. But if you treat it right you can find it. Oh, I am glad."

Her enthusiasm was infectious and it all seemed right. Perhaps psi was just that kind of odd thing—almost as though it had a will of its own. It didn't want to be caught in the laboratory.

"Well, what do you think this means, Serena?" I was excited too. "Do you think I could turn this into a repeatable experiment or would that be spoiling it too?"

"Oh, typical!" she responded. "You always want a repeatable experiment! Can't you be content with one successful result?"

"No, I can't!" I knew she was partly teasing. "I'm not going to try and force it, but I'd like to know why this should work and not my other experiments. I'd like to do more experiments to find out."

"Well, it could be all sorts of things. They were all friends of yours, you were having a good time, you are very much 'into' Tarot, and you expected it to work. And also it was your very own experiment—not for your thesis or anything. I think that's important too."

None of those things was especially easy to investigate, but they were not impossible either. "Right," I said. "I'll have to get on and find out just what is happening here. Oh, Serena, you have no idea how wonderful it is to have even one little experiment that works. It really makes all those months and months of failures seem like nothing!"

"Well, don't go and spoil it all," she admonished. "The Tarot doesn't like to be messed about either!"

Things were quite different when I described my success to Carl Sargent. I made regular visits to Cambridge to see my many friends there and often met Carl as well. I even gave a lecture on my Tarot experiments to the Cambridge University Society for Psychical Research. Most of the audience seemed genuinely interested, but Carl was not impressed. He stood up to inform me that I had a serious flaw in my design.

I gulped; I was sure he must be mistaken. I had been very pleased with my experimental design. That's why I had been prepared to give a lecture to the Cambridge Society about it.

He explained carefully and precisely. I had used Solfvin, et al.'s statistical test (1978), but this assumes independence of the ratings. Since my subjects all knew each other, their ratings wouldn't be independent. So I couldn't use the test.

I breathed freely again. "But that can't possibly produce any spurious results," I said. "The subjects did all know each other. Indeed most of them were very good friends and were in my parapsychology course and in my groups together. But they had no idea which reading was meant for whom. So it couldn't possibly produce spurious results, could it?"

But Carl persisted. It was not, he argued, a question of whether they could have known about each other's readings—only that their ratings wouldn't be independent.

"But I don't see that," I persisted grimly. "Why should knowing each other make any difference?"

Carl did his best, but I was not convinced, and the audience obviously wasn't that interested. I gladly dropped the discussion and turned to the other raised hands: the questions about different cards, and layouts, about the relationship of Tarot to the Kabbalah or to ritual magic.

It was only when I went away and thought about it that I began to see the force of Carl's argument. It was not that the subjects could possibly know which reading was meant for whom; it was a question of the assumptions of the statistical test. Imagine that among the group there was a very gregarious, loud-spoken, and jolly student whom everyone knew well, and imagine that (quite by chance) there was a reading which fitted him precisely. In this case all or most of the others would think this reading must be his and therefore could not be theirs. They would all be doing the same thing, and in this sense their ratings would not be independent. This kind of nonindependence could come about in all sorts of ways. To be valid, the statistical test I had used had to have independent ratings. So I couldn't use it. All the other tests I could think of assumed independence too. Suddenly I realized, yet again, that Carl really did know a thing or two about experimental design and that I would have to try the experiment again with people who did not know each other.

I decided to do it all exactly the same way but to advertise in the student paper for volunteers to come to the union one evening at 6:00 P.M.

Everything started extremely well. Exactly eleven people showed up, and one of them wanted to be the assistant, so we didn't have to disappoint anyone. This exactitude of the number of people was just the kind of thing I'd come to expect of the Tarot—or was it just coincidence? We all sat around having a drink and a chat about the Tarot, and I explained what we were going to do.

Again we did the two kinds of readings, and the new assistant carried out her tasks efficiently. Exactly a week later we met for the denouement! We matched up the names, letters, and numbers. We compared the lists and drew up the scores. I got out my statistical tables and——

Nothing! It was bloody chance again. I could have cried. I felt awful and sorry for all those kind people who had come to take part with such enthusiasm. I didn't know what to say to them. I don't remember what I did say. I only know that I tried to keep cheerful during our drinks in the bar and to impress on them that it was valuable research, even if the results weren't quite as I'd hoped. Then I went home to Tom, thoroughly dispirited.

"How did it go?" he asked cheerfully.

"Don't ask," I replied. "It didn't work." He looked sympathetic but not unduly surprised. Tom had been learning to read the cards too and was even a subject in one of these experiments, but he didn't share my great expectations.

I didn't bore him with all my miseries. I went to bed early and opened my diary; it always helped to pour it out in writing. I gazed at the white sheets and white blank page—June 7th, Wednesday—and recalled the bouncing step with which I had set off to the university that pleasant morning clutching my Tarot readings and papers.

"Well," I began writing lethargically, "my experiment didn't work. Of course I am disappointed. . . . but now I have to think hard again. I have been assuming that group ESP experiments don't work, but Tarot does—do I now move over to including Tarot in my expanding black areas? Surely not—do I then seek to account for these results in some way and then to find out in further tests whether this holds? Or do I change my approach completely? And if so how?"

By the time I had finished my written speculations I felt much better. I went back to two possibilities and would have to face one or the other of them. Either there was no ESP and the original positive results were due to the flaw Carl had pointed out. Or, alternatively, there was ESP, and the second experiment didn't work for some other reason.

Serena was quick to point out possible reasons. "I told you, Sue," she said, "you shouldn't keep looking for repeatable experiments. You never feel the same the second time round, so you don't have the same enthusiasm, and that may prevent it from working."

"But that's not true," I protested. "I mean you're right that you can never feel the same, but I was terribly enthusiastic. It looked as though I was at last onto something."

"Yes, but you were expecting too much this time. It mattered too much to you. Psi appears most easily when you aren't depending on it or trying too hard."

"Oh, Serena, I know all that stuff about psi being better when you're not trying, but I really think I wasn't trying more or less this time or last time."

"Well, I'll tell you another important difference," she went on. "All those subjects in the first test were friends of yours, weren't they? And they were all interested in the Tarot and cared about it working? And you all had a good time larking about and having fun, didn't you?"

"Yes."

"Well, the second lot were just anybody. They wouldn't have the same motivation and interest. So that could be why it didn't work, couldn't it?"

"I suppose it could, but even that's pretty hard to test. If you have to have people who don't know each other, then you can't all be friends and have a good time doing it."

"No, well, you can't expect to be able to get the right atmosphere for the Tarot *and* squash it into a lab experiment. You see, it's telling you something!"

But that was the whole point. I was still far from sure what it was telling me. The simplest, and in some ways the only correct, conclusion was that the first experiment was flawed and had to be rejected and that the second one didn't work. Ergo, no ESP—yet again.

But then again there were a lot of parapsychologists eager to make something of that first success. And I supposed some of Serena's arguments could be right. On a trip to the United States a friend suggested I should use parapsychologists as subjects. They would care about the Tarot and the results. She offered to be an experimenter and suggested that we could do it all by post. We had a deal.

We did everything the same way, but the material all went by mail. The subjects were all enthusiastic parapsychologists. Probably they all knew each other, but they did not know who else was in the experiment, so that didn't really matter.

There is little point in describing this experiment in any more detail. It all went well, except for the results; they were just about at chance level. These "special" subjects were unable to pick out their own reading from among all the others (Blackmore 1983).

I was glad I had not told Professor Lee about these experiments when I began. It might be cowardly, but I was glad he wouldn't be able to laugh and say, "Told you so!"

So now I really had no excuse but to have a go at those long-promised experiments with children. And there was one definite ray of light on the horizon. That long-awaited letter from the Science Research Council had finally come. I had got the grant. In October I was to start a whole year working solely on parapsychology.

Nine

Young Children as Psychic Subjects

It was wonderful to have a grant at last, to be a fulltime student again, but it also meant that I no longer had any excuse for putting off those experiments with children. And why had I kept putting them off? To tell the truth I was a bit scared. It was one thing to carry out experiments with the students who were about the same age as I was, who rapidly became my friends, and who were there every Monday afternoon. It was quite another to contemplate finding nursery schools and getting permission from teachers.

As Ernesto Spinelli was so ready to point out, I had had no training in developmental psychology and no experience of experimental work with children. The children themselves were not the problem. I had a younger brother and sister and lots of much younger cousins. During university holidays I had run an art group in a friend's house doing painting, drawing, theater, and all kinds of crafts with children of about three-years-old and up. It wasn't the children I was worried about; it was the process of getting the experiments organized.

I went to Ernesto. "Professor Lee thinks I ought to do some experiments with young children," I began. "I'm sorry to sound stupid, but can you tell me how you set about it?"

Ernesto patiently explained. His basic method was quite simple. It involved two subjects, a "sender" and a "receiver," and a series of outline drawings to be used as targets. The aim was to transmit the right drawing from one to the other. It was essentially the same task as in most of my ESP experiments. But of course a lot of work goes into making it suitable for young children.

To do this Ernesto had had a pair of colored boxes, called the "Guessing Machine," constructed. One was the sender's box and the other the receiver's. The sender and receiver were children from age three up, and adults as well, but he usually paired two children of the same age group.

Ernesto and two assistants began by getting to know the children and playing games with them. When it came to carrying out the ESP tests they demonstrated the "Guessing Game" with the aid of two puppets. The puppets wore little thinking caps and the two children could wear caps too, to help them think of the right picture. The sender sat on a little chair in front of his guessing machine and looked at the five pictures on its front. Beneath each picture was a button to press. The sender had to choose which picture to "send" and then press the appropriate button.

On the other side of a screen, or in a different room altogether, the receiver sat in front of a similar box with a thinking cap and puppet to help; the child guessed which picture the sender was looking at and pressed that button. The pictures were lined up in a different order on the two boxes so that mere position effects would not interfere with the results. If the same picture was chosen by both children, then a chime sounded as a reward for a correct guess. All the button presses were automatically recorded for later analysis of the results.

Ernesto's results had already been most impressive. Others before him had had success with young children (see Blackmore 1984a), but his results were outstanding—and apparently lawful. He found that when he used children of under eight years of age, they were able to guess the right picture far in excess of what chance would predict. Indeed the youngest groups were scoring something like 20 percent above chance expectation, which is exceptional in ESP experiments. Usually the differences from chance are of a few percent at best. Here were really obvious successes. With the older children the effect became less and less, and above age eight it settled down to about chance. Adults scored only at chance too. Ernesto seemed to have found that Golden Fleece of parapsychology, a repeatable experiment. All you had to do was use children under eight years of age.

He was even beginning to find other fascinating effects. For example, the scores were best if the two children were of the same age rather than different ages. Indeed they were better still if they were paired for IQ rather than chronological age. And in addition the effect was apparently suppressed if they had to do a complicated task at the same time, but it was not affected by soft music.

All this seemed to fit nicely with Ernesto's theory of paranormal cognition. He suggested that ESP (or paranormal cognition) originated from the same process that made normal cognition, or thinking, possible. Both involved the connection of two separate "meanings" to form a new "meaning"; the difference was that as children reached the age of eight they became better able to make more internalized and self-centered mental connections and lost the ability to make external (or paranormal) ones. In other words, growing intelligence suppresses ESP (Spinelli 1983).

His experiments and conclusions reflect a common belief that babies and "primitive" peoples are more psychic than we educated westerners; that somehow it is "natural" to be psychic and that we lose it by concentrating so much on the intellectual rather than intuitive side of our nature. If Ernesto was right, he was turning this folk belief into "real science," though I did have some doubts about his theory, especially what exactly was meant by a "meaning."

Somehow, I never got to see the experiments in action, at least not with the young children. However, when Ernesto submitted a draft of his Ph.D. thesis, I was able to learn more about the details of the experiments. Professor Lee gave me the thesis to read, and I took it straight home and read it right through from beginning to end one long afternoon, making reams of notes as I went. My supervisor had asked me for my comments, so he obviously thought they were worth having. I suppose I was flattered—so often my downfall—so I took the task seriously. I wanted to say something intelligent about it.

Promptly at 12:00 noon the following Wednesday I knocked, a little anxiously, on Professor Lee's door.

"Well," he began, "what did you think of Ernesto's thesis?"

"Isn't Ernesto here?" I asked. I didn't really want to talk about it without him. It would be much better if we could all discuss it together. But apparently he wasn't to come. I felt very much on the line, but I held out my list of comments and began to explain. "I don't know whether I have missed something, but I just don't understand why he used that experimental design for most of the studies. Can you explain why he allowed the sender to choose the target picture?"

"Certainly. I advised him to."

"You what?" I blinked at my professor. "You thought he should do it that way? But that's ridiculous. It invalidates the entire procedure, doesn't it?"

"Come now, Susan, don't exaggerate. If Ernesto had chosen the target picture at random, the first child would not have been really involved in the experiment. You can't ask a child to concentrate on a picture and expect him to be able to do it for long, as an adult might. But if the child has to make a choice, his *will* is involved, and perhaps that helps in ESP. That's why I suggested Ernesto do it that way, and I am sure it is better."

"But . . . but . . . but there is no point in doing the experiments at all unless you can be sure that any significant results are due to ESP, and if you do it this way they could be due to the two children having the same preferences—not ESP at all!"

Professor Lee didn't look convinced, so I went on, "Look, imagine two children confronted by a set of five pictures. What will determine which one they choose? It could be which one stands out most, or which they like most, or which reminds them of the story they heard that morning. Two children who know each other and are of the same age are quite likely to choose the same picture."

"Oh, I see," said Lee, "I see what you're getting at, but of course Ernesto controlled for all of that. You haven't read the thesis carefully enough. As you can see, he set up test trials in which he gave children all the pictures and asked them to pick out ones they specially liked and disliked. Any extreme ones were removed from the set. All the ones he used in the final experiments were about equally popular. So you see preferences cannot account for the results."

"But they can," I exclaimed, trying to think of a way to explain myself clearly. "It is quite different to test the pictures in the abstract than to test them in the context of five choices on the box at that moment. Preferences might only show up in the right context. Imagine these two children again. They have both just come from the same class and have had the same story read to them, about an elephant. Now if one of the pictures is an elephant, they are both likely to pick it. And Ernesto doesn't know anything about the elephant story and certainly won't write it in his experimental report. He will think they both picked it because of ESP. You just can't use that method. No parapsychologists will accept it as evidence of ESP. The target has to be chosen randomly."

But Professor Lee had yet another argument. "Your supposition might work, but I think you would expect it to have more effect for concrete pictures, wouldn't you?" I nodded. "Well, half of Ernesto's targets were abstract shapes, and those produced just as many hits. So your argument really doesn't stand up. In any case the most important point, you know, is that not all his experiments were done with sender choice. The majority were, but Ernesto also carried out further tests in which the target was randomly selected, and those gave exactly the same results."

In fact, Ernesto had tested one thousand children in his first series. It was only after this mammoth achievement was completed that he decided it was necessary to confirm the results with randomly selected targets. He then began new experiments in which he tested a further two hundred children, without the problem of sender choice. The target picture was selected by using random-number tables.

Ernesto didn't expect these experiments to give as good results because the sender would take on a much more passive role. But he was surprised. The results were just as good as before. It seemed to make no difference whether the sender chose the target, or whether it was randomly selected. It worked just as well either way (Spinelli 1977; 1978).

Had all my arguments been misplaced? Had I been determined to find any argument at all—however unlikely—to dismiss the evidence for psi? As I thought it over, I was still convinced that the "sender-choice" studies could not be considered as good evidence of ESP, but I could see no fault with the later ones. Perhaps this really was evidence for ESP—experimental evidence, convincing evidence.

* * *

Now I began to wonder whether I would be able to get results as good as Ernesto's. I began by reading journal articles about ESP experiments with young children and learned that previous researchers, especially in the United States, had used a wide variety of designs and still claimed to have found ESP. The simplest, and very successful, used colored candies, with the color being the target to be guessed (Drucker et al. 1977). I decided that simplicity was a virtue and that I should start with something like this that did not need "guessing machines" and chimes.

Having decided on that, I could no longer keep putting it off. It was time to find some children. First of all, I rang up the local Council Nursery School, a large, well-run school in old-fashioned buildings near my home. I arrived one warm spring afternoon to meet the headmistress.

"Good afternoon," I began politely when she received me in her office. "It is very kind of you to see me. I don't know how much you know about the experiments I would like to do, but——"

"I believe they have something to do with the paranormal, do they not?" she asked.

"Yes, that's right." I launched into my prepared explanation. "It has been found that very young children do far better at tests of telepathy than adults do, and it is very important for our understanding of the paranormal that we——"

"Yes, I see that," she broke in, "but you know this is a Christian school, and I am a practicing Christian?"

"Er—um—yes," I ventured uncertainly.

"We have no objection to your testing the children and perhaps doing some experiments, but when it comes to the paranormal I am sure our parents would agree that we do not want to put our children at risk in this way. I do hope you understand."

I did understand one thing. There was absolutely no point in arguing that my experiments would not put them at risk of damnation or the devil, or—well, what did she think they were at risk of? Also I could not assure her that it would do them no harm at all. Just conceivably, working with the paranormal, especially with young children, might be harmful. I was not going to force myself on her if she had genuine fears.

I had far more success with the playgroups. In England, most towns and villages have a playgroup which is run by independent organizations with the help of parents. They take children from three years of age until they go to school at four or five, and they are just what they sound like—a time for organized play with other children. I visited several local playgroups and found them ideal for what I wanted. There was no bureaucracy, and I was invited to come in and get to know the children.

So instead of spending my mornings working alone at my desk or going to the library, I went off to the playgroups and played with three- and four-year-olds, painting and building and running and jumping. And gradually working out how to do the experiments.

I took along my favorite toy owls, a large soft one called Oggy

Boggy and her baby owl called Baby Bog. These were to act like Ernesto's puppets and help the children to guess. I made "thinking caps" out of silver foil and ribbons. I found old sheets to build screens across the room, and I went to the sweet shop to buy lots and lots of M&Ms for the targets.

Of course I would need an assistant, so I advertised in the student papers; in the meantime Tom helped me get started. We turned up one morning bright and early and constructed a tent out of the sheets. Inside we put a tiny table and chair for the receiver to sit at with a row of five different-colored candies laid out on it, and at the far side of the room another table and chair.

With great trepidation I went off to ask whether any of the children would like to play a guessing game.

"Yes! yes!" "Me! me!" they all clamored, and I realized straightaway that if I wasn't careful we'd have a lot of tots waiting outside! So I let in Robin and Sarah and encouraged the others to return to their play.

Tom sat with Sarah and, using his random-number tables, selected a colored candy. He then shouted "Ready!" and I asked Robin which color Sarah was looking at.

"Red!" he yelled, grabbing the sweet quickly and eating it before I had a chance to stop him.

We sorted out our beginning hitches. Tom built a switch for the sender to press. This turned on a light to tell the receiver when it was time to guess and provided unexpected fun for the children. We gradually learned how to run the tests quickly and efficiently so that the children didn't get bored. We finally settled on a simple procedure. Each pair of children did ten trials. The sender was given an M&M to look at, pressed the switch, and then the receiver guessed. The experimenter announced the result and wrote it down, and if the guess was right we all had a candy. Yes, the children insisted that we eat M&Ms too. I have never felt the same about those little chocolate-centered sweeties again!

At first I was too concerned with getting the procedure right and making it fun for the children to worry much about the results. But, it gradually began to dawn on me that they were not going well. In fact, by the time I had finished the first series of experiments, it was quite clear what the results were going to be—just chance.

I had a brief period of being despondent, but I was already working on the next phase of the experiments.

Professor Lee had made it perfectly plain that he thought my memory experiments were a waste of time. But what if I could incorporate some of my ideas into an experiment with children? I have always loved drawing and painting, and I relished the opportunity to design some pictures to use as targets.

My idea was simple, although the implementation of it was quite troublesome. I wanted to have sets of three pictures. Each set had to have a central picture which was associated with two others; one should be of the same thing but look very different. The other should be quite different but look like the same thing. It was rather like my earlier experiment with caterpillars, trains, and butterflies, but this time the pictures had to be convincing to the children and fun to look at. I painted many and tried them out with many children until I was satisfied. In the end I had ten simple sets of three. For example, in one set there was a cat standing up. This looked very similar to another picture of a tiger but looked quite different from a cat lying down. And I checked with groups of children to make sure that they always called them by their right names: "tiger" and "cat."

These were my targets in the next series of experiments. The children knew nothing of the complications. They simply saw pretty colored pictures from which they had to choose. We all had great fun with these experiments. The children pressed the switches and laughed at the pictures and were entirely convinced they would know what their friends were thinking about. There were always five potential targets and ten trials for each child, so by chance they would get two right in any session. And two right was enough for each child to go away feeling successful. But two is all we got.

By the end of the summer term of 1978, the entire experiment was completed, and the results were analyzed. It was quite clear that the results were just as they had been with adults. There was no tendency to confuse the pictures that looked alike nor to confuse those of the same object, nor (and much more important) to choose the "right" picture at all. There wasn't any evidence of ESP. Young children might be very psychic. They might produce lots of ESP for Ernesto Spinelli. But they would not do so for me.

Why not? Why should Ernesto get such good results and not I?

What was I doing wrong? Would it ever work? Would I ever be able to understand how ESP works, and when and why? I wasn't doing very well so far. I was even beginning to wonder (ever so slowly) whether perhaps I was never going to find any ESP—or even (dare I consider that possibility) that there was no such thing as ESP. I had to get to the bottom of it. Most immediately, I simply had to understand why Ernesto got such good results while I did not.

Ten

Why Can't I Find Psi?

There were only two possibilities. Either Ernesto was really getting ESP, and there was some reason why I did not; or he was not getting ESP, and his results were due to some unnoticed error or other "normal" effect.

I agonized over this dilemma for many months. As I cycled to and from the university, or down to the station, or across London to the Polytechnic, I had argued myself round and round in circles.

"You have to accept it; Ernesto has something you don't. He can elicit psi, and you can't. You must just keep at it. Sooner or later you'll find a way to get psi."

"But for goodness sake, how long do I have to go on? Forever?"

"No—not forever—just until you find it."

"What if I don't ever find it? What if there isn't any psi? Then I'll never find it, so what's the point of going on and on looking forever?"

"Don't be ridiculous. Of course there's psi."

Time and again I would argue myself into accepting that there must be psi. I thought about my own experiences and about all the evidence of everyone else's experiments. I looked around at all the people on the pavement and in their cars. I was sure they all believed in it. But time and again the twin obstacles always set off my doubts.

"Psi doesn't make sense. I can't understand it, and—damn it—I can't find it in my own experiments."

"All right, then. If there isn't any psi, why is Ernesto getting such good results?"

"Well, maybe there is something wrong with his experiments. Maybe there is something wrong with the statistics, or perhaps there are other flaws in the design."

"But you know he has ironed out all those problems you spotted before. His experiments now are very good."

"Well, perhaps then someone is cheating."

"Don't think that!" I admonished myself almost faster than I could think the thought. "Don't let your own lack of understanding and failed experiments force you to think such awful things about anyone!"

It so often came to this in the end. When people cannot believe in psi, they always end up accusing others of cheating. I remembered the famous words of Henry Sidgwick, giving his first presidential address on the founding of the Society for Psychical Research in 1882:

> We must drive the objector into the position of being forced either to admit the phenomena as inexplicable, at least by him, or to accuse the investigators either of lying or cheating or a blindness or forgetfulness incompatible with any intellectual condition except absolute idiocy" (Sidgwick 1882).

Had Ernesto's positive results forced me into this position? If so, I didn't like it. I wanted to get out of it quick. Science is supposed to be about methods and objective criticisms of research, not about worrying over whether little children, students, or investigators might have cheated. Couldn't we just ignore that possibility? Why is it that in parapsychology the question of fraud always seems to come up, while in other fields it is rarely mentioned?

One difference is that in most other subjects fraudulent experiments don't get you very far. You may fiddle with, or even entirely invent, your results. If they are exactly what was expected, then probably you will never get found out, but on the other hand no one will be particularly interested. If they are stunning and unexpected and inexplicable, then everyone else will want to check them out. They will all rush off and try the experiment again, and you will be found out because their replications won't work.

Of course in parapsychology replications hardly ever work. ESP is supposed to be fickle and difficult to find, and no one really expects replications to work. There are plenty of excuses: the conditions weren't right, there were skeptics around, the experimenter didn't believe it would work, and so on. Where replication cannot be used as a control, the problem of fraud is far worse.

Another difference is that ESP is defined negatively (back to that thorny old problem), and therefore you can never be sure when you have found it. The only way to be reasonably certain is to rule out all other more likely possibilities.

The most likely possibilities are sensory leakage, errors in statistics, and other methodological weaknesses. Once those are ruled out, you can always go on to unconscious fraud and even deliberate fraud, either by the subjects or by the experimenters. The history of parapsychological study is littered with examples of all sorts of cheating: from the devious mediums of the heydey of spiritualism (Brandon 1983) to the petty charlatans of the psychic world today (Randi 1982) or the infamous fraudulent experimenters such as Levy and Soal (Rhine 1974; Markwick 1978). The question now becomes, how seriously do you take the possibility of fraud?

I thought back over the well-known critics who had resorted to fraud as an explanation. One of the best-known was G. R. Price, a research chemist who had started a controversy in the prestigious journal *Science* more than twenty years before (Price 1955). He argued that we should always prefer to believe that someone had cheated rather than that psi occurred, even without any evidence. After all, he pointed out, lying and cheating are common human activities, while ESP is incompatible with modern science. He simply assumed that all the evidence for ESP was due to the use of sensory cues, errors, abnormal mental conditions, or—if these more common shortcomings were not enough to explain away the results—fraud.

A somewhat more reasonable line was taken by C. E. M. Hansel, a dryly skeptical psychology professor at Swansea University in Wales. He argued that one at least needed evidence that fraud was possible in a given experiment before preferring that hypothesis. But what is possible? Hansel thought that if a subject could have climbed out of windows, dressed up in disguises, or peeped through trapdoors and thereby achieved good scores, then the experiment was not well designed enough and the results could not be taken as evidence of ESP. In other words, if cheating is even barely possible, there is no ESP (Hansel 1966; 1980).

At the other extreme, some people prefer to assume that fraud is very unlikely, even unthinkable. Such people would require cast-iron evidence of cheating before they would accept such an explanation. I felt trapped somewhere in the middle. I knew that fraud was possible. Subjects, assistants, and experimenters had cheated throughout the history of science (Broad and Wade 1982), but when it came to particular experiments, I just didn't want to have to think about it. Surely it was possible to resolve scientific issues without recourse to the question of fraud, wasn't it?

It depressed me. I had certainly never expected parapsychology to be easy, but I had never anticipated this particular kind of difficulty. I disliked myself for thinking this way, and that was what made me depressed. My solution, as always, was to try harder. I bent myself to the task of thinking this through. I battled with the two main alternatives. Either there was ESP and I should accept it and the consequences, or there were flaws in the many seemingly successful experiments which I had not yet noticed. But I could not come to any firm conclusions.

Throughout all this, as usual, I longed for someone to help me. Ernesto was no longer at Surrey, so I could not talk to him. Professor Lee shared Ernesto's opinion that the evidence for psi was good enough, and I began to doubt my own arguments and my own abilities.

One Monday morning, having prepared my lecture just in time, I dashed over to university and grabbed my mail as I rushed in to chair the lunchtime seminar. I sat down, breathing hard, and saw there was a letter, in a printed airmail envelope, from the *Journal of Parapsychology*. Some months before I had sent off my first journal paper, criticizing previous theories of ESP and memory and arguing that none of them made sense and that they all needed revising.

I couldn't wait until after the seminar. I tried to open the letter quietly and peep surreptitiously at the contents. I glimpsed the first line: "We recommend that this paper not be published in its present form, nor in any form." I read it again . . . and again . . . . No amount of PK was going to change what it said! It went on to say that the paper was badly written and an inadequate review of the literature.

As soon as the seminar was over, I rushed to the phone and rang Tom. He was marvelous and listened and sympathized and said he was sure I would go on to write better things and learn from this one and shouldn't get depressed about it, and so on. Mainly he just listened. At last I put down the phone, wiping away the tears, and braced myself for my lecture.

I marched determinedly over to the lecture theater and put on my jolly lecturing face. I ordered myself not to think about the paper until later and to concentrate for an hour on telling my students about dowsing and how rods and twigs and wires can be used to detect hidden objects, underground water, or even oil. We spent another hour trying it out with rows of cups concealing one full of water and with electrical wires that were secretly switched so as to be live or not. To my intense relief there were about ninety students there that day, so I wasn't a total failure. Students kept coming to my lectures! And we had a great time with the dowsing. Lots of them tried. When one object was hidden among ten cups, they averaged about one in ten located—good chance results, but we had fun.

Afterward, I skulked back to the psychology department, the burden of that letter on me again. Professor Lee was there and free. He took me into his office, put a very large sherry in my hand, and sat back.

"What's up then, Sue? You look awful."

"Thanks," I laughed, "I feel awful. I just got this letter."

I handed it to him. "They don't want my paper. I know that won't surprise you very much. You never thought much of all that memory stuff did you?"

He didn't deny it. "But it's not just that." I went on, fearing that any moment a tear was going to run down my cheek. "My experiments don't work, and Ernesto's do. I can't write decent theoretical papers. I can't find any ESP. What can I do?"

"Well, you could become a waitress or a PE mistress."

"Don't be horrid. You know I want to carry on with parapsychology, but it's a bit depressing, isn't it?"

"Look, Sue, let's face it, there is no easy way to carry on with parapsychology. There is no funding for the subject, and even if you do carry on with it, you probably won't have much of a future ahead of you. There's no guarantee that you'll start getting better results.

"You must face the fact that a *real* career in psychology is out, even with a Ph.D., if you go on with parapsychology. It's a pity, because you'd be good at it. And you have to think hard about it now. There is still time to change the topic of your Ph.D. You could do something with proper memory research if you wanted to, or better still, environmental psychology. That is, if you started on it right away. Haven't you done enough parapsychology yet?"

"No, I haven't," I muttered rather depressedly. "I do want to go on with it."

"But, why? If you were getting results like Ernesto's, I could understand it. Then you might be able to get somewhere with understanding ESP. But you're not!"

"That's the whole point," I expostulated. "If I were getting results like Ernesto's, I wouldn't have all these problems. As it is I just don't understand anything. I don't understand whether there is or isn't any ESP or even whether the question makes any sense! And I can't just walk away from the whole subject because I can't understand it. I want to know the answer."

"Ah, so you want to know the answer to a question which might not even make sense, and you're prepared to risk your career for it."

He was smiling, and I took another large swig of my sherry. I felt better just talking about it. I did know what I wanted to do. Even if the *Journal of Parapsychology* thought I was the pits, I was still going to carry on trying to understand ESP. Career or not, my thesis was going to be on parapsychology.

* * *

But suddenly the prospect of actually writing a thesis was coming nearer and nearer. At about this time Ernesto's thesis was due to be examined. This examination is the culmination of the Ph.D. student's three or more years of research. An external and an internal examiner read the thesis and then meet with the student for a "viva," or oral examination, in which (one is lead to believe) they tear the thesis apart and reduce the student to abject misery before declaring whether he or she has passed. There are no marks or grades or degrees of success. You either get through or you don't. Sometimes you have to do additional work or make changes in the thesis, but in the end you either get the Ph.D. or you don't.

Ernesto was to have John Beloff, from Edinburgh, as his external examiner and Professor Lee as his internal. On the appointed day he disappeared into Professor Lee's room early in the morning and didn't come out. I was anxious all day about it, although I am sure Ernesto didn't realize that. After all, my own similar ordeal could not be more than a couple of years away—and what would I have to show for my work?

That afternoon, when I had to go home, Ernesto still had not emerged. The next day I learned that his examiners were very impressed with the strength of evidence, but because of its controversial nature they felt that some additional experiments were needed under more secure conditions. They proposed that he carry out some additional trials to be observed by outsiders and videotaped in full.

They were obviously concerned about the possibility of fraud—that boogeyman which I had tried to stop myself from even considering. I cannot imagine a Ph.D. thesis on chemistry or biology being queried on the grounds that the experiments were not sufficiently guarded against fraud, but that seemed to be the implication here. That is one of the horrible things about parapsychology. Whether one likes it or not, the question of fraud arises time and time again.'

Of course the examiners were not suggesting, or even implying, that fraud had taken place. They were pointing out that if these stunningly good results were to be published, then people were going to ask whether they *could* have been produced fraudulently. It would therefore be wise for Ernesto to take additional precautions to avoid the criticisms of extreme skeptics.

There is an important difference here between criticizing the experimenter and criticizing the experiment, and I found myself struggling to sort it out. The point at issue is not whether the subjects or the experimenter *did* cheat, but whether the experiments were good enough to give reasonable certainty that they could not have done so. By questioning the experiments, one is not necessarily questioning the integrity of the people involved.

This is a distinction that, for me, took a heavy bashing many years later, but for the moment it served its purpose. I realized that no one was accusing anyone of anything. The examiners were just taking reasonable precautions in the face of exceptional evidence.

The examiners now suggested that there should be a new series of experiments conducted, as before, in a nursery school. Ernesto was not to be present or involved in any way, the session was to be videotaped, and there were to be two eminent psychologists as independent observers who would have the experience necessary to decide whether the experiments were fairly designed and carried out.

I was not in any way involved in the planning of these experiments. After all, they had nothing to do with me. I simply waited with interest to hear how they would get on. Then one day I bumped into Professor Lee, who was rushing along the corridor.

"You can help me, Sue," he called out. "We are supposed to be doing Ernesto's second test experiment this afternoon, but we've only got one observer. You can be the other."

"Okay," I said, and he was gone. I hadn't time to think. I had not heard that the observers were supposed to be eminent psychologists (which I most certainly wasn't). I was only glad that I would at last, after all these years of hearing about them, get to see the experiments in action. That afternoon I set off enthusiastically for the nursery school.

There, in a pleasant and gaily decorated room, the guessing machines were set out. There were the two assistants, each with one child, and all wearing their "thinking caps." We two observers, a London University psychologist and myself, sat to one side against the wall, silently watching.

We observed for some time, and the children did very well. They really seeemed to be getting the right picture more often than chance would predict. I began to get excited; even frightened. Was this really ESP happening right in front of my eyes? Or was there an alternative explanation? I tried to think up some alternatives, and in the break between sessions I asked the assistants many questions about the procedure and the randomization. Somehow I just couldn't calmly accept that this was psi, and I was to go on arguing about the method used in future years (Blackmore 1984; Spinelli 1984). Was it just perversity? A refusal to accept my own failures? A deep fear of psi? Whatever it was, it led me into constant confusion. I just didn't seem able to accept that other people could find psi while I could not.

The next time I saw Professor Lee, he asked me what on earth had been going on in the experiment. At my puzzled expression, he explained that Ernesto was unhappy that I had been allowed to attend the experimental session and that I had asked too many questions and upset everybody.

I was flabbergasted. Had I really upset everybody? Was I always doing stupid things like that? Was I destructive, and was that why I never got results? Was I now so incapable of accepting the existence of psi that I would go to any lengths to escape it, even to the extent of upsetting people? I no longer knew what to think except that I had to take Ernesto's results seriously.

The last of the extra experiments was conducted with two new observers. The sessions had all been taped. The observers were happy with the procedure and the results were fairly good. They were not as good as in the bulk of those in the thesis, but they were still independently significant. The examiners were satisfied, and Ernesto was awarded his Ph.D.

Eleven

Inspiration in St. Louis

On the day of the first class of my third year teaching parapsychology I wrote in my diary, "My first GS class went well. I was a little nervous, but I am much more enthusiastic than last year and less skeptical. I think I'll enjoy it more."

I suppose that if belief were based on just one's own experiments then I should long ago have given up believing in ESP at all. But of course it isn't and can't be like that. No one person's experiments can stand alone, even one's own, and Ernesto's results had obviously made an impression. Also, the events of that summer had done much to obliterate the gloom.

One day during that summer I sat in Professor Thakur's sunny office, leaned back in a comfortable chair, and looked across the Surrey fields toward my house on the distant hill. We'd been discussing Indian philosophy and his childhood and life as a Brahmin.

"I'm off to St. Louis in a couple of weeks, you know," he smiled, "to the Parapsychological Association Convention. How would you like to come with me?" Of course, I could imagine nothing more exciting.

"Oh yeah?" I said. "Are you being funny? I couldn't afford that!" But he persisted. He would pay. We could go together.

Now I was really worried. Was I being paranoid? "I can't go with you," I said, thinking fast. "After all, if I went at all it would have to be the cheapest flights and hitching to the airport. I bet you're not a great hitchhiker!"

"All right, then," he agreed, laughing, "let's see if we can't find some others to put up some money. There are departmental funds for that sort of thing. I'll ring Terence right away if you don't believe me!"

"No, I believe you," I laughed, "but isn't it too late to organize now? I mean I haven't even got a visa—don't you have to have a visa to go to the United States? And what about—well I suppose I *could* do it in time."

And so a few days later I was outside the U.S. Embassy by 7:20 A.M. to get my visa, and then I joined the enormous and well-organized lines of people waiting for standby tickets to the states. Freddie Laker's airline had caused chaos that summer with his ultra-cheap tickets, and as I sat in the cold street it all looked hopeless—until someone from British Caledonian turned up to say that, in order to clear the streets, they had put on an extra flight—to Houston the next day.

On the long and exciting flight I met a Texan called Pedro, who persuaded me not to take the bus all the way from Houston to St. Louis and found me an extremely cheap flight the following day to Dallas and Kansas City. I could get the bus from there, though I'd still arrive a little late for the conference. He even took me to his home for a much-needed dinner before I set off.

Then at Dallas I was told that my flight to Kansas City had been cancelled and I would have to go to St. Louis instead! And so it was that I found myself standing in the heat at St. Louis airport waiting for a promised limousine (though I didn't know what that was) to the university.

"Excuse me," I said, in my best polite English, to a tall and friendly-looking man standing in the line, "Is this the right queue for the university?"

"Why yes," he replied. "You must be English. Are you going to the P.A. too?"

"Yes, yes, I am," I stammered excitedly.

"Well, I'm Charly Tart. Have you come all the way over to see us for the P.A.?"

Wow! Charly Tart, *the* Charly Tart, whose books on altered states of consciousness I had read so avidly and whose views on state-specific sciences I thought so brilliant (Tart 1972; 1975). I hardly knew what to say.

"This is Stan Krippner," he went on, "and this is——" and he proceeded to introduce me to a host of people who had been only ethereal famous names to me until now. And in no time at all we were all scrunched up in a minibus chatting about ESP and PK halfway to the 1978 P.A. Convention.

The next night I went to a party in someone's room, where I sat crossed-legged on the floor deep in discussion with William Braud about magic. I couldn't believe it. William Braud, who wrote those "sensible" papers on the effects of relaxation on ESP, knew a great deal about magic—*real* magic—not conjuring. We talked for hours about submission of the will and freedom to perform magical operations, about the importance of ritual and imagery, until I wondered if I were still in the same world that existed in Surrey.

I remember virtually nothing of the papers. The one idea that seemed to creep through, though, was that a lot of people put faith in the "ganzfeld." There were several papers about this new technique for eliciting psi, including one by Serena (Roney-Dougal 1979).

I knew something about the ganzfeld because I had been a subject in Serena's experiments. Also, Carl Sargent was experimenting with it at Cambridge. It is a method for reducing patterned stimulation and was originally used by psychologists in the 1960s (Avant 1965). The subject lies comfortably in a soundproof room; his or her eyes are covered with halved ping-pong balls (or something else that produces a uniform visual field; white noise (a pleasant hiss) is fed through headphones to the ears. After some time this peculiar condition induces a pleasant state in which images flow more freely and time seems to slow down.

At about the same time, ESP experiments had shown that dreaming seemed to be conducive to psi, but of course experiments on ESP during dreams are difficult to conduct and take a long time (Ullman, et al. 1973) It was originally Charles Honorton's idea that the ganzfeld might provide a much easier way of inducing a similarly psi-conducive state. He reported successful results in the early 1970s (Honorton and Harper 1974), and several other researchers were now reporting their results. It was definitely "the latest thing."

I knew that Carl's experiments were successful too, and now I was hearing about these further successes. My excitement, so close to being extinguished, was aroused again. Perhaps what was needed was to have the subjects in a psi-conducive state. The rationale behind the idea seemed very simple and convincing. Perhaps my memory experiments and the child experiments had failed because of the state of mind of the subjects. Perhaps that one successful Tarot experiment had worked because I got into the right state of mind to do the readings. At least I began to wonder!

I was therefore especially thrilled to meet Chuck Honorton.

Someone at that conference told me a new theory about parapsychologists: the odd thing about them is that they are either very tall or very short. Chuck fell into the latter category. Slightly out of breath, he was round and earnest-looking and more than happy to tell me all about his experiments.

As the second evening of that mind-boggling few days wore on, I found myself testing Chuck Honorton with ESP cards and hitting him with a cushion to make him go faster! Then we began talking about the Tarot, and I learned he had done experiments on the I-Ching. In no time at all we were doing Tarot readings for each other.

I realized then that, though they may talk in public only about experimental controls, statistical tests, and significance levels, most parapsychologists have motivations that run much deeper than just tests for psi. Most of them, and certainly most of the best of them, seemed to be involved in all those things I cared about, altered states of consciousness, stretching the imagination, meditation, magic, and mystical experience—or as Abraham Maslow put it the "farther reaches of human nature" (Maslow 1971). This is what we talked about, late into the night every night. Psi was only a part of a much larger and much more fascinating whole. Or perhaps I should say that psi was the ostensible objective, while quite other, and possibly more interesting, ideas seemed to underlie it all.

* * *

Even the end of the conference was special. I had to find a way back to England and was offered a ride to Durham, North Carolina. Cradle of scientific parapsychology, Durham was where J. B. Rhine had established his parapsychology laboratory in the 1930s and published his early controversial research on ESP (Rhine 1934). There the Foundation for Research on the Nature of Man (otherwise known as FRNM and pronounced *fernum*) now employed several fulltime parapsychologists. Among them was Debra Weiner, in whose battered VW we drove the (to me unbelievably) long way. Debbie put me up in her home, took me to dinner with her friends, showed me round the laboratories where some of those famous experiments had actually taken place, arranged for me to give a talk at a FRNM research meeting, and escorted me down the road to meet the Rhines.

I had never realized that North Carolina is part of the South. I was surprised by the steamy warmth and the wooden houses with huge verandahs and luxurious gardens. As I timidly walked up the path to the Rhines' house I was greeted by the sight of a charming white-haired old lady holding aloft a pair of secateurs.

"Good morning, Susan," she called, "do come and help me. You're a nice English girl, so I'm sure you know a lot about roses," and so it was that I accompanied Louisa Rhine round her rose-filled garden, picking a few choice blooms for the house.

Inside, amid the vases and cut stems, I sat on the edge of my chair but in spite of myself found I was confiding in her all my problems: my inability to find ESP, my series of failed experiments, my determination to continue, and my bafflement at the ways and wherefores of psi.

"You know," she told me gently, "when I was your age I was full of doubts too. Psi is so elusive. It is always slipping away. But in my work on spontaneous cases I found far too much to leave any doubts. And don't worry about being a psi-inhibitory experimenter. I can usually tell a good and a bad experimenter," she said with a conpiratorial wink, "and I can't see any reason why you shouldn't go on to get results in the future. You just persevere."

I felt like an old friend by the time she took me through to a comfortable and tidy living room where the great J. B. Rhine, looking very frail and old, was sitting on a large sofa with his stick beside him.

"You'll have to speak up," she whispered in my ear.

"How do you do," I shouted tentatively. "I am very pleased to meet you," I added, taking the proferred chair and rapidly relaxing as he launched into a monologue of fascinating stories.

In no time he was regaling me with theories on the distinction between the sensory and the nonsensorimotor, which he divided dogmatically from each other with graphic sweeps of his hand across a convenient cushion.

"You are lucky," he told me. "I wish I were your age again. I was enthusiastic—just like you. It is such a wonderful subject. But you know, I wouldn't change with anyone in the world. I've had a life of endless fascination and questioning. I have never stopped to this day. But I couldn't have done it—any of it—without my wife." He peered closely at me, "Do you have a good man?"

I was jerked out of my passivity. "Yes, I do. He's called Tom."

"And does he share your belief in the paranormal?"

"Well," I didn't want to start questioning my own beliefs just now, nor to lie, "yes, he shares my enthusiasm for finding out the truth about psi. He helps with my experiments and criticizes them when I do them badly." I couldn't help smiling.

"Good," said J. B. Rhine, satisfied, "then you'll get on all right."

I diffidently asked whether I might photograph them together. I treasure my pictures as a reminder of two very sincere and kind old people, who died not long afterward.

* * *

And so it was that my own failed experiments came to be set in the context of all that excitement and all that hope. It wasn't as though the people at the P.A. were unrealistic about psi. There were very few who would honestly argue that they had convincing "proof" of ESP, and even fewer who would claim to have a repeatable experiment. Indeed there was much discussion of the problems of unrepeatability and the need for a repeatable experiment to convince the skeptics. However, there was plenty of hope that now, at last, we might have a method that works or a theory with promising leads.

It occurred to me that this has probably always been so. Back in the 1930s Rhine's original card-guessing techniques had seemed convincing, and even repeatable, until others failed to replicate them. Then in the 1940s there was the work of Soal in London with his special subject Basil Shackleton, who seemed always to guess one card ahead (Soal and Bateman 1954). That had once seemed highly convincing evidence, but unrepeatable as well. Then there had been the dream work, initially so exciting, but then becoming unrepeatable (Ullman et al. 1973). And now it was the ganzfeld with its basis in finding a psi-conducive state.

The ultimate failure of all those previous attempts to find repeatable psi did not seem to dull the present hope. I shared that hope and that inspiration. At home my own experiments and their failure had weighed heavily on me. Now, set against all those successes claimed by everyone else, they seemed almost insignificant.

I began then to wonder about something which would later worry me a great deal. How much weight should I apportion to my own results as against anyone else's? It is always tempting to believe your own results rather than someone else's; after all, you know more about them. But science is, and has to be, a collective enterprise. Results must be shared and compared, and no one person can test everything for him or herself. So I had to go on paying some attention to all those other successful experiments.

On the other hand, I couldn't ignore my own experiments completely. Apart from anything else, there would then be no point in doing them at all. Also, I did have the advantage of knowing more about how they were carried out than I did for any other experiments. I was left quite unable to make up my mind how important my own failures were.

This is another of those problems rather peculiar to parapsychology (or at least more pressing there). In most other fields there is rarely a conflict for long. If you disagree with someone else's results you can go on repeating the experiments until everyone comes to a consensus about which of you was right or until some crucial difference in the experiments is discovered. In parapsychology, of course, unrepeatability makes that consensus impossible. You have to agree to differ. I simply put my own failures away in a little mental box marked "my failed experiments" and hoped that they would soon be counteracted, not only by other people's successes but by successes of my own.

The one thing I didn't notice, and only came to reflect on much later, was a curious split in the subject and in myself. All the excitement was really about states of consciousness, and Tarot and magic and ways of being in the world, about human freedom and communication, about love and being close to others. But all the experiments, and all the theorizing, were about psi. The Rhine's lab was the Foundation for Research on the Nature of Man, but it stuck steadfastly to work on psi even though psi seemed to tell us little or nothing about "the nature of man." I was doing just the same. I was fired with enthusiasm for understanding human nature, but I came home determined, yet again, to look for psi.

It is odd how obtuse we can be!

Twelve

Hopes for the Ganzfeld

When I came back to my students, they wanted to know all about the conference and the latest research. They were always asking the awkward questions I was trying to avoid or pushing me into things I didn't even know I wanted to do. In answer to their questions, I began to tell them about the ganzfeld work, and then one bright spark popped up from his seat.

"Why haven't you done any ganzfeld experiments yourself then? You keep going on about psi being elusive, but it sounds as though everyone else can find it!"

They always made it sound so simple, and I had already explained how time-consuming ganzfeld work was. On the other hand, I now had a grant. I would have the time if I got on with it now.

"Well, of course, that's just what I am planning to do," I found myself saying. "Who would like to volunteer to be a subject or to help me with getting it set up?"

A forest of hands went up, and I was committed. It was time to go out and buy some ping-pong balls. Fortunately I was due to give a lecture in Cambridge soon, and Carl Sargent had invited me to be a subject in his ganzfeld experiment. I had already taken part in Serena's experiment earlier that year. She was comparing the effects of subliminal perception and ESP, and I had spent half a dozen sessions lying on a bed at The City University with hissing noises in my ears and the inevitable ping-pong balls over my eyes.

Serena was a gentle and soothing experimenter. In her care I experienced pleasant dreamy half-hours with drifting images of the seaside and sunlit meadows.

Carl was quite a different proposition. Much more forceful, he demonstrated his procedure with a kind of determined conviction that it would work, which was unavoidably catching. (Was this the secret of his success, I wondered?) I arrived at his lab after a restless night in someone's vast and echoing house in Cambridge. We'd all been up late the night before, drinking in the murky wood-panelled college bars after my lecture. The members of the Cambridge SPR had all been outrageous.

"God, Rupert is *such* an awful experimenter!"

"Yeah, you should have seen his controls in that PK test!"

"And what about the experiment with the 'psychic' cat. She was pushed all the way to the target." Beer-glass cats were being pushed to and fro.

"There was a sardine under the correct one."

"No, it was cream. There was a trail across the floor from the starting gate!"

"No, it was Whiskas. You could smell it a mile off." They held their noses and chortled mercilessly, one of them raising his glass to me with a big grin.

I suddenly had a terrible thought. I felt my cheeks flush. Was this whole conversation actually digging at me? Did they think I was an overly fastidious, nosey, and interfering critic who would think up such stupid ideas for criticizing experiments? I was really getting paranoid.

When I left for the psychology labs the next morning, I was excited. Half of me expected—even wanted—to do badly, to show there was no psi in all of this. While the other half was wondering hopefully and nervously, "What if I do succeed? This may be the beginning of finding ESP at last. And what will that mean for my view of the world?" Either way, it was exciting, and I was keyed up for it. Obviously one trial could always be chance, whatever the outcome, but this trial was a special one for me.

Carl was already busy in his impressive lab, a delightfully spacious and comfortable room with easy chairs and a stereo, tables littered with coffee cups and sheets of paper, and a soft mattress in the middle. Off to one side was a control room, invisible behind the one-way mirror, where Carl was to sit while I was "off."

"How's our doubting subject this morning then? All ready for a convincing experience?" someone asked.

"I'm all ready," I responded, pulling a face.

"Cup of coffee first?"

As I drank it, Carl was telling me about his recent sessions and how it was going, why it worked so well, and how important it was. Then it was time to lie down on the mattress.

I had never really fancied the revered Carl Sargent, but there was a certain pleasure in the way he slightly roughly taped on the ping-pong balls, adjusted the headphones, and fiddled with the red light until I was blind and deaf and off in a world of my own; it was rather like the sensual helplessness of being at the hairdresser's or even the dentist.

The noise was loud, like being in the midst of great crashing waves by a dangerous sea. I began to talk about rocks and seaweed, waterfalls and ferns, wet places and chattering streams, knowing that Carl was recording all I said. Then gradually all these died away, and with them my sense of being in that room, that morning, in that experiment. I moved slightly. Yes, I could still feel my arms and legs. I got them really comfortable so that I wouldn't have to feel them again.

"I'm in the garden. I think I'm a snail. I'm crawling under the runner beans. Oooh, it's all slimy and wet. It's lovely, and the grass is enormous. I'm up on the window sill now. I can see down over all the gardens."

I loved my half hour or so of ganzfeld. I visited the seaside, played with beach balls, and felt the sand on my bare feet; I floated in the air and drifted among the trees. It was all pleasurably realistic and unthreatening.

At the end of the session Carl turned up the main lights, pulled off the sellotape, and there was the world again. I had to wake up, sit at a table, and fill in some questionnaires about the experience. Soon Carl was beside me again, with four pictures laid out in front of us, and we went through everything I had said, comparing it with the four pictures and totting up marks for each one. One of those four had been the target and one of his students had spent all that time looking at it. But which one?

There was one picture of some chefs with pots and pans and lots of food, one of a butterfly with shiny wings, one of vintage cars and old bicycles, and one of a beach with people sitting in deck chairs.

By the time we had spent over a half hour going through it all, one of the pictures was beginning to emerge as definitely the best fit. It wasn't totally right, but I had seen so much seaside imagery and had even mentioned deck chairs. It had to be that one. We totted up the scores, and I put the four in order of matching; the beach scene first and the chefs with their food last.

Carl went off to telephone the agent, who soon appeared with the answer. We held our breath. He opened the envelope and held it up to us. It was the chefs!

Carl's face fell. But my reactions were not so simple. Those two halves were at it again: one sorry and disappointed and even angry, the other almost gloating—"there you are; it doesn't work."

We couldn't help looking at the pictures again over coffee, with several of the students joining us. There were things that matched with that picture. I could see how easy it would be to find correspondences after the fact. But Carl was a meticulous experimenter and not swayed by that kind of post hoc "fishing." It was a last-rank miss as far as he was concerned. But there were lots of sessions in one experiment, and he was confident that most of them would be hits even if mine wasn't. And perhaps it was my attitude. I *would* go and get a really good miss!

* * *

That afternoon I took the train back to Guildford, already looking forward to my own ganzfeld experiment and wondering how I should do it. I didn't want to do just a straight replication. It would, of course, be interesting if I got good results, but it would be more interesting still if I could find out something about how and why ganzfeld works—if indeed it does.

I began to have an idea. At the American conference I had heard so much about imagery and inner experience. There were even suggestions that good imagery could aid ESP. So what about the people in my training group? Would they make specially good ganzfeld subjects?

I had started my group earlier that term. Inspired by the conference, I had asked for volunteers for something I had long wanted to do. I realized that in all my experiments I had been leaving out the "experiential" side of things. If psi was dependent on psi-conducive states, then it was time to learn how to achieve those states and what could be done with them. Occult teachings, the lore of astral projection, and magical techniques all emphasized the same three skills: relaxation, concentration, and powerful imagery (Blackmore 1982a).

I had had my own training in all of these. When I was living in London with John, I had been on several courses training biofeedback. The teacher was Max Cade, an extraordinarily unhealthy-looking but empathic and somehow powerful man who used modern biofeedback equipment to especially good effect. We learned to produce alpha-rhythm brain waves at will, to make one hand colder than the other, and to reduce sweating on the palms to almost nothing. But all this was really just trappings. Essentially he taught us Zazen, techniques from traditional Zen Buddhist meditation.

I remember the room well. It was a schoolroom full of desks, with large dingy windows overlooking a sprawling mass of railway lines from which the sounds of trains busily shunting or suddenly screeching came incessantly. The insulation was also less than adequate, and the clatter and chatter of students from other courses periodically burst upon us. Max Cade said he had chosen the most noisy room in the house on purpose. Everyone thinks they can meditate better in the quiet, but we were to learn that we couldn't use distractions as an excuse.

From him I learned to hold the image of a green square steadily in mind. I never quite succeeded with the two rotating spirals going in opposite directions, one changing from red to orange to yellow to green to blue to indigo and to violet, the other starting at violet. I never mastered the art of "just sitting" either.

I also began magical training and belonged to a Kabbalistic group. There we learned to construct rituals, to chant names of power, and to use the implements of magic—or at least the lower and less powerful of those implements. However, the commitment involved in magical training is deep and long and requires great trust in the teacher. In the end I wasn't prepared to undertake it.

Nevertheless, I learned to imagine the inside and outside of a cube at the same time, to hold magical symbols firmly in mind, to construct a duplicate body in imagination, and to shrink and expand in size. Many of these were things I had done spontaneously in my own out-of-body experience all those years before. They were also the imagery skills often used to train people for "astral projection" (Rogo 1983). It was these skills that I wanted to develop further to see whether they were conducive to psi.

When I asked my parapsychology class whether anyone wanted to join a training group, I made it clear that they would have to come every week without fail and that we would be learning imagery, relaxation, and concentration. Eight keen students turned up, and we (and Tom) met every Tuesday in the union.

Our progress was quite rapid. I soon learned that I could produce soothing relaxation monologues as well as anyone else—or at least tolerably well. Many of the others could too, so we took it in turns. We used all kinds of imagery exercises, from imagining peaceful walks in the countryside, to holding images of purple, spotted, seventeen-sided boxes in mind, or becoming an ant crawling on our own nose. We tried several methods for inducing astral projection. Most of us could imagine a duplicate self, remove attention from our senses and our usual bodily feelings, and begin to float.

Somehow, none of us made it any farther out than that. If the aim was astral projection, then we failed. But if the aim was fun and new experiences, we succeeded. The meetings always ended in the bar or got diverted to someone's house for the evening. But, speaking for myself, the best thing was the chance to develop further that kind of mental balance and control that is crucial for meeting the challenges of altered states of consciousness.

So perhaps these skills would help us in the ganzfeld. If imagery was helpful for psi, then all of us should be able to do better after our training than we could have before. I decided to do two things.

First, I would test the ten people from the training group and ten others. Each would do one session with a friend as an agent. I would expect the training-group people to do better—to score higher—than the others. To find out whether imagery was actually an important factor, I would test all the subjects on standard imagery tests before their ganzfeld session.

Second, if there was time and they wanted to do it, I would give some of the students a chance to go on having ganzfeld sessions. They ought to get better with practice and with their increasing imagery skills. I could test their imagery ability repeatedly and compare that with their ganzfeld scores. In fact, there were problems with using repeated imagery tests, and I was worried about how to sort this out. However, the students wouldn't let me keep putting it off.

"When do you want us to come and try the ganzfeld?" they went on at me in class. In no time I found myself committed to testing the first subject the following Wednesday.

I had to buy the ping-pong balls and cotton wool; find suitable sets of target pictures, sort them into groups, and put them in opaque envelopes; prepare and duplicate the questionnaires and transcript forms; find a soundproof room, borrow a white-noise generator and a tape recorder, and scout around for a spare clock and an amplifier, not to mention finding the reclining chair for the subject. Oh, and I forgot I also needed an anglepoise lamp with a red bulb.

Tuesday night found Tom and me struggling with kitchen knives and scissors to cut ping-pong balls in half until at last Tom succeeding in cutting one neatly with a Swiss Army knife. Eventually I was ready for my first subject the next morning.

Two of the students came that day: one to be the subject and the other to be the agent. Mike immediately confronted me with an impossible question.

"Sue, do you really believe this is going to work?" While I tried to compose my thoughts and expression, he went on. "Honestly, you don't look as though you do, and you've never believed any of your previous experiments would, have you?"

"Oh, Mike, I don't know. All I know is that other people have found it works. You are going to go in there and get into a new experience with bright imagery and deep relaxation. Who knows? It might work."

"Yeah, but what about psi-mediated experimenter effects?" He was smirking. I'd make him write his essay on that!

"Let's just forget about that horrible subject, can we? Remember the Tarot experiment? You know I believed that that would work. Anyway, it's far more important that *you* believe in it, and you do, don't you?

They both pulled horrible faces.

"Come on," I said, "time for our first ganzfeld experience."

Chris, the agent, went off to another room to look at the randomly chosen target. Mike was the subject in ganzfeld, and I sat outside his soundproof room, madly scribbling down everything he said. He said enough to make my arm ache. It was different being the experimenter!

When we came to the judging, there seemed to be correspondences everywhere, but eventually Mike put a picture of a lake first because of all his water and seaside imagery. Because he'd mentioned mending cars, he put a picture of a garage with cars second, then some children playing third, and the Eiffel Tower last. I wrote down the final choice and then went off to call Chris back.

He came in beaming.

"You must have got it, Mike," he cried. "I was imagining you in there all that time, under those cars, cursing that engine!"

"Oh, no," we shouted in unison, "it was the cars!"

"I should have known," said Mike. "That image of the cars came out of the blue—like it was not connected with anything that had gone before. I should have seen it was that one. All that water and streams stuff could have just been because of the white noise—sounding like water. I should have ignored that stuff. Of course it was the cars."

And so Chris and Mike went off feeling that they had *nearly* succeeded. And I was already speculating on how easy it is to imagine that you have managed a little ESP, even when the statistics don't show it. Obviously one can say little about one trial, but I suddenly realized how important it is to rely on the statistics and not on vague impressions. Between any half hour's imagery and any picture there are bound to be some correspondences, even some very striking ones. But this is just chance and not ESP. Only the comparison with other pictures and the statistics based on that comparison can show whether there is more than chance operating. Carl knew that, and Chuck Honorton knew that; that's why he had designed the method this way. But I began to see how easily people could be convinced of psi even when it wasn't there.

Well, was it there?

We went on to do the twenty sessions of the imagery experiment. And several of the training-group students had a whole series of sessions. With each one taking most of a morning or afternoon, it was a long job, but they did seem to be getting better.

I was even a subject myself, with my brother Stephen as agent. That was exciting. I had lots of imagery about fishing and fishing rods, about mountains and lakes, about pleasant green scenery. I knew Stephen was keen on fishing and wondered whether that wasn't the reason—until I saw the target—a Swiss mountain lake with a fisherman on a jetty! It made sense. He was my brother and I thought like him, was close to him. If it should work with anyone it should work with Stephen. It rekindled those fires of potential belief and set new speculations flowing. But when we tried it with him as subject and I as agent, it didn't work. And that spectacular hit was lost among all the misses.

The overall results were just as I might have expected by now—chance expectation. Whatever glimmer of excitement, whatever striking coincidences there had been, the statistics were saying "no psi." The apparent improvement with practice was not statistically significant, and the ESP scores did not correlate with the imagery scores. Years before, I might have considered the possibility that statistics were not the way to get at psi, but now I had seen the powerful effects of chance correspondences on people's beliefs. I was beginning to believe that there might be smoke without fire. Or at least that the fire was a normal fire and not a paranormal one. People chose to see psi in those correspondences when they had made the correspondence for themselves.

And so, yet again, I failed to find psi.

Thirteen

Growing Grounds for Skepticism

It was time to do a little thinking and, more urgently, some writing. I was beginning to realize that I had less than a year in which to complete my Ph.D., and what did I have to show for my three years so far? How would it look when written into a thesis?

Writing a Ph.D. thesis is not just like writing several essays. It has to be book-length, with a literature review, details of all the experiments, appendices containing all the data, lists of references, table of contents, and preferably an index. I did not know how long it would take to write, but it was clear I needed to get started.

Typically, Tom had, with complete composure and no fuss, completed his. But he was now desperately looking for a job. Ten years before, he would have had no trouble. The universities were expanding then, and there were plenty of opportunities. Now it was quite different; academic jobs were rare and hard to come by, but Tom was certain he wanted to carry on with his research on color vision. As a last resort, he simply wrote to all the universities where such research was going on to ask if they wanted him.

By now he'd had replies from most of them saying there was nothing doing. But, there was one response that seemed rather too exciting to get overly hopeful about: Richard Gregory at Bristol had suggested that Tom come to visit their Brain and Perception Laboratory.

I had first met Gregory at Oxford when he came to give a lecture to our Psychology Society, but I could remember little other than his dynamism and the wonderful demonstrations of visual illusions he had shown us. I also remembered much of his book *Eye and Brain* (Gregory 1966), a classic which had to be read by all psychology undergraduates. He seemed a fascinating man, and now we had arranged to go to Bristol to see him.

We weren't at all sure what we were going for. Richard had intimated that there was some kind of unspecified job there, and that he actually wanted Tom for it. In spite of the uncertainty, we decided to go and to look at houses on the way. For if there were a job, we would have to move, and we thought we might as well see what the area was like.

We had an extraordinary day. We set off, driving the hundred or so miles from Guildford, and arriving in an area south of Bristol that we had never known existed. The little Somerset town of Midsomer Norton utterly belied its pretty name, with its endless rows of dull grey stone cottages and sprawling new estates. It was an old coal-mining district, the North Somerset Coal Field, which even my school geography had never prepared me for. The countryside was rolling, with almost too-rounded hills, very green and quaintly pretty. But the villages were down-to-earth old mining villages. Slightly taken aback, we began to tackle the Estate Agents.

"We are looking for an old cottage in the country. It must have three bedrooms, a garage, and a big garden. And cost less than twenty-five thousand pounds."

"Ha, ha," said the first man, not unkindly, "You might get a terraced house in Norton or Radstock, but you won't find anything in the villages for that price."

They were all the same. We could have one bedroom and lots of garden, or three bedrooms but no land at all. It seemed rather hopeless. By lunchtime we were in a delightful lakeside village called Chew Magna, where the few shops were all shut for lunch, but the pub beckoned temptingly. We even decided to have an extra pint of the local beer and wait until the estate agent opened again.

"We are looking for," I began my little piece again. And again the man laughed, this time a little scornfully, for Chew Magna *is* rather a superior village! But then he stopped.

"We do," he said slowly, "have particulars of a cottage just being typed up. Would you like to see it? You'd be the first people to look at it."

He went off to the back. "Could this," I found myself wondering, "be the way psi manifests itself—when you really need it? No," said the voice of reason, "it is just extraordinarily good luck."

And so it was. Pear Tree Cottage turned out to be exactly what we wanted. Nearly three hundred years old, it was white with a little porch in front and a great big garden with lawns and flower beds, shrubs and vegetable plots, and even a greenhouse. It needed lots of work, with an almost derelict garage and a public footpath meandering through the front garden (something that could only happen in England). But we loved it. And Tom hadn't even got the job yet, if indeed there was a job! Feeling dangerously hopeful, we went off to Bristol to meet Richard Gregory.

If it *was* an interview, it was the oddest one I have ever heard of. Tom and I found our way to the fourth floor of the Bristol Medical School where, among all the clean and lifeless corridors, enlivened only by the odd medic in a white coat, there was a big orange and pink sign saying "Brain and Perception." Inside was the greatest chaos imaginable, with vast quantities of ancient apparatus lying about amid heaps of books and papers. Professor Gregory was waiting, holding out a huge hand to welcome us with a distracted smile.

"Oh, hello, sorry, I must just finish this letter. I'll be right with you, hang on a tick—make yourselves comfortable in there." He waved in the direction of a small room in the corner. Was I to be there too? I had only come with Tom to see the place. But it seemed I had no choice.

Richard was there "in a tick." He was impressive. He seemed huge, though certainly not fat, with untidy black hair, bushy eyebrows, a fluid and expressive face, and ever-moving hands. His presence seemed to fill the tiny room which, I began to notice, was full of antique typewriters and pieces of telescope. He fired questions at us both. I had barely time to notice the plastic, red-veined model of an eye, or the posters of visual illusions. He talked with contageous enthusiasm about "science" and "life" and parapsychology and color vision, and then all of a sudden he decided it was time for tea at his flat, a wonderful spacious place in a great Georgian crescent with views of the river and Isambard Kingdom Brunel's famous floating docks. Richard seemed tireless as he expounded on the fun to be had from research, while he showed us his collection of antique telescopes. I left Tom poring over them and went upstairs to the little bathroom. There I found an even more fascinating collection: swimming wind-up ducks, boats, fish, whales swallowing other whales, and everything you can imagine to keep a mechanically-minded person happy in the bath!

I began to think that Bristol was the place we wanted to be. There wasn't an actual job, it transpired, but Richard might be able to find some money somewhere for Tom to work there. Several hiccoughs later, and after it nearly all fell through at least once, it was decided he could start in December.

In January 1979, on a freezing and snowy day, we took Lucy the cat and moved into Pear Tree Cottage, the only house we'd even looked at. It was time to stop my experiments, dig over the vegetable plots, and start "writing up."

*   *   *

"Extrasensory perception is potentially of profound importance for psychology and other sciences . . ." I tentatively typed (Blackmore 1980c). Actually, once started, it wasn't so bad, but writing a thesis is a very lonely job. Not only is it a mammoth task—in the end my thesis was more than 100,000 words—but all the time you are writing it, you know that only a handful of people will ever read it. It will just sit in the university library for years to come, gathering dust.

It is not only lonely, but it is difficult to keep motivated day after day, typing page after page that almost no one is going to read. The compensation is the opportunity to deal at length with difficult issues. But, as the snow fell on our new, hardly seen garden, I enjoyed writing about the problems of parapsychology. Indeed the first section of my thesis was about just that.

First, there are the problems of experimental design. In other fields, there are always obvious control conditions. If you want to know the effects of a certain drug, you can compare results *with* the drug against results in a control condition *without* the drug. If you want to study changes in behavior with relaxation or hypnosis, you can use two conditions, with and without the relaxation or hypnosis. In parapsychology, what you cannot do is make a condition without psi. We don't understand how (or even if) psi works. So you cannot have a comparison between "with ESP" and "without ESP" or "with PK" and "without PK." You can, of course, look for the effects of relaxation on psi, but then your measure of psi is likely to be unreliable and the effect small.

All of this forces a heavy reliance on statistics. You always have to compare a claimed psi effect with what would be expected by chance. In other fields the burden laid on statistics is far less heavy. They are an adjunct to finding out how reliable a finding is, how big a difference is, or how strong an effect is. In parapsychology they must be used to find out whether there is anything there at all. If there are any flaws in the use of the statistics, the entire conclusion may be wrong.

Then there is the old problem of negative definitions, which had plagued me for so long. In an ideal experiment on ESP you can show that there is some kind of effect. You can show (by statistics) that it is unlikely to be due to chance. You can show (by adequate controls) that it is unlikely to be due to sensory leakage. And then you have to provide some other hypothesis. And that is all that psi is. Saying an effect is due to psi is saying no more and no less than that it is due neither to sensory contact nor to chance. More than ten years earlier, the psychologist Edwin Boring had dismissed the definition of ESP as "no definition at all." Because of this, he argued, a scientific success will always be a parascientific failure (Boring 1966).

I could see what he meant. If you got to the bottom of some mysterious effect and pinned it down as being some new form of radiation or an error in the method or even fraud, then science had succeeded, but parapsychology had lost. Yet another "inexplicable anomaly" had become "explicable." It seemed that, with its negative definition, parapsychology was doomed to be a shrinking field, always losing interesting effects as soon as they became explicable.

I tackled this head-on in my thesis. I outlined the history of the subject and discussed the way that new theories and methods had tried to get around these problems. I discussed the attacks of the skeptics and the ways in which parapsychology had fought back with improved methods to convince them. But I argued that the only real solution was to find a positive definition of psi.

This we could only get by a better theory. My memory-ESP theory was to be my personal attempt, and my thesis would try to show how this could help ESP become a positive part of "real" psychology. The first long part of the thesis was nearly done.

* * *

It was slow going, and I felt very isolated in our little village a half hour's drive from Bristol. I was glad that once a week I still had to go to Guildford to see my faithful parapsychology students. There they were, every Monday afternoon, asking their awkward questions and demanding to try out dowsing, or Tarot reading, or gazing into crystal balls, as well as doing experiments on ESP and PK.

"What do you think of Uri Geller?" they asked. They always asked that!

"Well," I began, as someone called out, "He's a conjuror," and someone else said, "No, he's not."

In my first year I would undoubtedly have agreed with Beloff (1974) that Geller's "powers" promised to be an exciting new development for parapsychology, but now that hope was all but gone.

"We know that he cheats much of the time," I finally said, "but there have been controlled experiments in which he still seemed able to produce dramatic effects."

"Why do you say 'seemed'?" asked a girl from the back. "Surely he either did or didn't?" And they launched me into finding out about the criticisms of the experiments, until I finally concluded that he must be no more than a very clever conjuror (Randi 1975).

That term I took some of the students on a trip to visit the Paraphysical Laboratory in Downton, Wiltshire. We had been invited by its director, Benson Herbert, to come see what they were doing and even to take part in some ESP and PK experiments.

We took the university minibus early one Saturday morning and drove down to Wiltshire, passing the dramatic monument of Stonehenge on Salisbury Plain and even visiting Salisbury Cathedral on the way. With Tom calling our directions from a crumpled map we found ourselves on a tiny, rutted track leading into gloomy woods. The track seemed to go on and on, getting more and more impassable in the damp dripping woods. Could we really be going the right way? Well, we couldn't turn round, and eventually we came to a house—a reddish, half-derelict looking place, with no signs of any proper front door but with a back door hanging open on lopsided hinges.

We scrambled out of the minibus into the muddy clearing, and suddenly there was a friendly young man to greet us.

"Hello, I'm Howard. Do come in. Benson is busy with an experiment at the moment."

The creaking back door led directly into a tiny dingy room with bookshelves full of journals on paraphysics and endless books and papers on psychical research. Around the edge were a few moldy and decrepit-looking sofas, and in the middle was an upright parafin heater with a tin kettle on top. A trickle of steam added to the foggy atmosphere. Howard bustled off and left us shivering in the damp, hardly daring to sit on the sofas, and wondering whether the kettle might possibly make us a cup of tea.

The lights wavered. "Who'd like to come and help with the generator?" called Howard, and a few of us set off to a rotting wooden shed where a petrol generator with no governor was gamely trying to cope with the varying electrical demands of the latest PK experiment. I began to believe that there really is no money in doing parapsychology!

We did take part in some experiments. Benson Herbert, small and pale and looking as though he had never emerged into full daylight, took us on a tour of the "labs," explaining in his heavy East European accent the array of glass vials full of some suspicious reddish-black fluid, which was apparently part of his "vampire experiment."

In that dingy little place I first heard a tape of "Raudive voices." A Latvian named Konstantin Raudive claimed to have discovered a way to pick up voices from the dead by using a tape recorder on "record" without a microphone (Raudive 1971). He maintained that they spoke in a mixture of languages and gave messages to the living. The one we heard was a message in Latvian from his great-grandmother, assuring him of her well-being. We listened keenly, straining our ears to catch the sounds from among the tape hiss and background noise. I listened again. The tape was rewound and we all listened again. I looked at the others and grinned. Were they hearing what I was hearing?

It was quite distinct. It was the jolly jingle "Johnnie Walker" from a Radio Luxembourg commercial. Did we laugh! It was awfully rude, and we did try to explain that if you hadn't heard it so many times before it might sound like a Latvian grandmother, but we couldn't control ourselves.

Years later, at the SPR in London, Mollie Goldney told me of her own experiences at the Paraphysical Lab. She and I were both members of the Council of the Society for Psychical Research; I was one of the youngest and she the oldest. Once a month or so, we all sat round the beautifully polished but sadly sagging oval table in the library of the SPR, lined with its hundred-year-old collection of books, and argued in intricate detail about the minutes of the previous meeting and whether to increase the subscription by three or only two pounds. Mollie, tiny and white-haired and about eighty, I think, looked up every so often to ask, in a rather loud voice, what was going on.

I had always liked her and enjoyed talking to her, though she invariably forgot who I was. It was on one of these occasions, when the sandwiches and instant coffee came out during our well-earned break, that she told me about her stay at the Paraphysical Laboratory.

"You know," she said, "I had the worst night of my life there! Couldn't decide beforehand whether I should dress for dinner or not. So I took along a few clothes for the occasion. I can't tell you, my dear, the shock when we arrived! And how cold it was! I didn't sleep a wink that night, I can assure you. I wouldn't go there if I were you."

And it certainly wasn't the kind of experience I had anticipated for my students, but, as it turned out, they spent a fascinating day arguing about experimental designs, debating on the nature of life, and fighting with the recalcitrant generator. If anything, I suppose they came back a little more skeptical than before.

* * *

I am afraid that that year the students were getting rather a strange mixture of teaching on parapsychology. I may have begun with great enthusiasm, spawned by Ernesto's successes and the conference in the summer, but by the end of the course I had plenty of skeptical stories to tell them.

One was very important; indeed it concerned that dear old lady, Mollie Goldney, and the famous experiments of Samuel Soal. During the 1930s, Soal, a mathematician at the University of London, began a series of experiments on ESP. His aim was to replicate Rhine's pioneering studies in the United States, and he spent years and years failing to do so. Then finally, through long reanalyses and retesting, he found that one of his subjects, Basil Shackleton, was able consistently to guess the card one ahead of the one being looked at. It was an odd effect, but one which seemed replicable. Soal calculated that the odds of his results being due to chance were one in 10^{35} (or 10 followed by 35 zeros) (Soal and Bateman 1954; Soal and Goldney 1943).

These experiments were often quoted as among the best-controlled and most decisive experiments of their kind (e.g., Thouless 1972), a cornerstone of the evidence for ESP. Indeed they are featured in almost every book on parapsychology I had ever read. But I was now able to tell my students the whole story.

In 1955, G. R. Price, in his well-known attack on parapsychology, had argued that ESP is incompatible with natural laws and that he would rather believe anything but that. Since fraud is commonplace, it was a far more likely explanation than psi. He proceeded to suggest six rather ludicrous ways in which Soal might have cheated, most of them needing at least two accomplices. Then Hansel (1960), the famous Swansea skeptic, suggested even more possible methods of cheating.

Parapsychologists reacted angrily. Soal himself protested that Hansel had produced an "extraordinary hotch-potch of superficially glib assumptions of collusion and fraud" (Soal 1960). It seemed that the critics had at last gone too far and discredited themselves with quite unbelievable accusations.

The arguments went on for years, with one of Soal's agents even claiming that Soal changed numbers on the record sheets (Soal and Goldney 1960). Soal claimed to have used lists of numbers from logarithm tables to determine the order of targets in his experiments. So for years, others searched through these tables to try to prove that Soal had not changed any numbers. But they failed to find the numbers he had used (Medhurst 1971; Scott and Haskell 1974). Finally, Betty Markwick set a computer onto the task. A shy, retiring woman and a longstanding member of the SPR, she had been very impressed by Soal's experiments and wanted to make a last attempt to clear his name. But she too failed (Markwick 1978; 1985).

With laudable determination she kept at the task and eventually, while checking by eye long lists of numbers, found something else. Some long strings of target numbers were repeated. This itself should not have happened but might only indicate a certain amount of carelessness. Soal must have reused previous strings instead of getting new ones from the tables every time. However, much more interesting was the discovery that in some of these repeats extra digits were added. Even more telling was that most of these "extras" corresponded to hits; and, if they were removed, the overall results fell to chance. It seemed that, after all, Soal must have added in the extra numbers to make spurious hits. Yet another great "inexplicable" result was "explained," but it had taken nearly thirty years.

This discovery made quite an impression on me. These experiments had been among the few which had originally convinced me there was something in the laboratory work. Was it possible that all such experiments would eventually succumb to a skeptical explanation? It was with these ideas in mind that I presented my students with the evidence for psi.

One week a boy called Samy put his hand up. Samy had rather embarrassed me because he'd voluntarily taken the course two years running. He had heard all my jokes before, and he knew more about some of the topics than I did. I was ready for a difficult question.

"You know I really don't think you believe in anything any more, do you, Sue?"

I was lost for words. I could never hide anything from them. They never let me get away with anything. Part of me struggled to list all the things I did believe in and compose a suitable reply. But it was no good.

"Yes. I mean, no. I mean, I really don't know anymore." I said at last.

They enjoyed that one.

Fourteen

The Dilemma of Psi

It was in this state of "don't know" that, month after month, I worked on my thesis. From the cold snows of that exceptional English winter, through a spring of working in my new garden, and finally through the summer, I was torn. I had to write up all my own failed experiments but keep on contrasting them with other people's successes. I realized that, whether I liked it or not, my thesis was forcing me inexorably up against that final basic question of parapsychology. Does psi exist or not? I hated not knowing.

I had tried to get away from it, to understand psi in terms of psychology, to test out the conditions that would produce it, and to explore my own role as the experimenter. But here I was, fighting again over that same irresolvable argument, getting ever more critical and ever more aggressive in the face of positive evidence.

That wasn't what I had set out to do. I didn't want to get into an argument in which there are only two sides and neither unarguably right. I had begun because of my interest in memory, because of my out-of-body experience, because of experiences I could not explain and feelings that at times things seem clearer, or better, or more real than "ordinary life." I had wanted to understand a little better what it is like being a human being and to share that understanding with other human beings. But how far had I progressed in understanding any of this? I had to admit that it was not very far. Instead, I was battling over the very existence of psi.

Fortunately I had some much-needed breaks. In April, Tom and I drove to Scotland for the last of our university ski-racing weeks—a twelve-hour trip in a very doubtful car. Our first day was one of those crystalline days, so rare in Cairngorm, when you can see for miles across the brown-and-purple foothills, and the sun shines on glistening snow. I skied with the other racers until my legs screamed and I thought my breath would freeze inside me. For a few brief hours I didn't once think about whether psi exists.

But I never could keep away from parapsychology for long. That night, after a huge supper with a dozen exhausted racers, I set off again, back down to Edinburgh for the third International SPR Conference. I was to give my paper the next morning, to present my dilemma, to ask the audience what they thought I should do with my accumulation of negative results.

Perhaps predictably, most people were sympathetic, but no one had any real answers. However, Carl Sargent intimated that the next day, during his presentation, all would become clear.

The following day we all sat in a warm hall, with snow falling quietly outside, through the excellent and execrable: from John Beloff's paper on why there can be no physical explanation for psi, to something on MICGMOs, which were supposed to sit about in walls waiting to turn into ghosts. At lunchtime a group of us went to the pub, rushing back in time to get a good place for the "show": Carl Sargent, Ernesto Spinelli, and Brian Miller (over from Utrecht, Holland), talking about unrepeatability, experimenter effects, fraud, and the whole basis of parapsychology. It was a fascinating exchange; three committed parapsychologists, well aware of the threat from critics, arguing about whether the telltale signs of psi should convince the doubters, whether we could find regularities in psi effects if we only knew where-to look, whether experimenter effects underlie the whole problem, and above all whether we were making real progress in understanding psi.

Question time was long and heated. We heard it argued that too much fuss was made about fraud. A small amount of cheating goes on in all sciences, and it really shouldn't matter in parapsychology when effects like psi in the ganzfeld are so strong. I wondered then whether one could ever say that cheating didn't matter. Surely in parapsychology we have to be extra careful. But then perhaps if I got repeatable results, as Carl did, I would feel differently.

Meanwhile I was nerving myself to ask a question that had been bothering me all day. I was slightly shaking. I suppose I shall always be nervous about asking questions that people might think silly. The chairman pointed to me. I got to my feet, trying to breath calmly and probably looking quite relaxed.

"Yesterday, I asked why it is that I get no results, and Carl Sargent told me that all would become clear tomorrow. However, all has not become clear."

Carl, my hero, watchdog, critic, and advisor, smiled knowingly from the platform, nonchalantly unwinding his long legs and pushing back a wisp of his ginger hair. He said it was all a question of experimenter effects, of the personality of the experimenter. He could only suggest that I should take a course of psychotherapy!

I sat down stunned, with a mixture of laughter and muttering rippling through the audience around me.

Far more constructive, though partly on the same line, was Ernesto's response. He suggested that I didn't have sufficient rapport with the children in my experiments and that it took a special kind of experimenter to elicit psi. He also suggested other differences between our methods that might explain the different results, like differences in the targets or the disruptive effect of giving the children candy.

For the rest of the day, while trying to listen to interminable papers, I pondered the problem. Were these ideas testable? Should I repeat the child experiments using Ernesto's targets and no candy? That wouldn't change my personality though, would it? Could I do a study comparing experimenters' personalities? But Carl had already done that and showed that successful experimenters were highly extroverted, and so was I. It really didn't add up. Still pondering, I got back into the little car for the long drive up to the mountains and the next day's racing.

I cannot imagine a conference more unlike a parapsychology one than a meeting of the Experimental Psychology Society, but some weeks later I found myself, with others from the Brain and Perception Lab, on a rare visit to Oxford for this select gathering. I found a lot of things to interest me, including several papers on memory and learning. There was also one about vision in rats—rats who appeared to be able to find their way about, even though they could not see. The question was, how were they doing it? I was struck by something. Could it be ESP? Of course, no one suggested this possibility. And I suddenly realized that I would never suggest it either.

And why not? The reason was not that people hadn't heard of ESP or that they didn't believe in it or that they were too narrow-minded or biased. It was because ESP is a totally useless hypothesis. To say that the rats were using ESP would be to add absolutely nothing. ESP is an empty hypothesis. "What a subject!" I thought.

That day I met some postgraduates from Cambridge. All of them knew Carl and had heard about his remarkable ganzfeld experiments. They seemed impressed and convinced that he was onto something. Carl was rapidly coming to stand for everything successful in parapsychology, a success to set against my own lack of results, a success to throw confusion into all my logic.

At lunchtime I slipped away and plucked up the courage to go to see my old tutor, Dr. Mellanby, who still worked there in a laboratory full of animals and glass apparatus. Remarkably she still remembered me.

"Weren't you going off to do that silly psychic stuff?" she asked, handing me a rather murky glass beaker of coffee.

"Yes," I laughed, "I was and I am. I am doing a Ph.D. in parapsychology at Surrey."

"Well, really! I didn't think you were that serious," she paused. "And what have you found?" she looked almost anxious. "Is there really something in it? Have you found any psychic phenomena?"

"No," I could almost see the relief in her face. "I have to admit I haven't. I have spent three years looking for it. I have tried changing subjects, using children, using special training methods, and even using Tarot cards, but all my results were at chance."

"Well, that sounds fair enough," she smiled. "But why do you sound so dissatisfied? Surely it just proves that you did your experiments right. Why can't you just stop now and admit that I was right all along? There isn't anything there to get excited about."

"Oh, it's not that simple," I sighed. "If I could be sure there was nothing there then I'd give up tomorrow. But I can't be sure. And while I am still unsure I have to go on. The real problem now is trying to understand why I don't get results when everyone else does."

"They probably don't do their experiments properly," she butted in.

"Oh, but they do. Or at least some of them do. [I was thinking of Carl, of course]. All those thousands of results can't all be bad experiments." I went on. "No, the latest suggestion is that it is because I don't believe deeply enough, and you need a believing experimenter to get good results."

"What poppycock!" she burst out. "*You* not believing enough!"

"You may laugh," I said, "but do you know I always feel that in the beginning I did believe, and believed strongly, but now even *that* I can't be sure about. You can never really know what your own beliefs were in the past."

"Oh, don't be silly, Susan. If anyone ever wants confirmation that you were once a total, daft, and committed believer, then send them along to me!"

I couldn't help laughing. She seemed to bring a bit of sanity into my attempts at remembering. "You never know, I might take you up on that," I said.

As I went out into the fresh summer air of South Parks Road, I suddenly saw the psychology building in a clear and vivid light. It was as though I was back there as a student, still believing so passionately, riding my bicycle around with posters for Oxford SPR meetings. I could remember so many incidents, so many little details, but it was more than that. For a moment it all seemed real. It was as though I were really there in the past. Then suddenly that feeling was lost. It seemed as though I had, for a moment, been one with a past self. But no amount of trying could bring back that completeness.

An odd thing about that feeling is that I always value it. It has come in all kinds of different ways and often unexpectedly. And it has always left me wishing I could "go back" into past experiences or, perhaps more important, be more *in* the present. I knew, in the way that you sometimes have to trust blindly, that such experiences were important. I wanted to understand them. I had no idea what kind of understanding was required, but I knew I wanted to try.

This was closer to what it was all about. But where had all that struggling after ESP and all that theorizing got me? I may have learned a great deal, but I had not come one fraction of a thought closer to understanding that moment. In this sense, as well as in so many others, my memory theory of ESP was a failure.

My tutor had told me I ought to give up. And she was not the first. Some weeks before, I had been idly glancing through the *Bulletin of the British Psychological Society* when the word *Parapsychology* caught my eye. In fact, it was an article entitled "The 'Royal Nonesuch' of Parapsychology" (Gibson 1979). The author recounted how he had heard "this girl" talking about her wasted research in parapsychology. He likened it to that lovely story in *Huckleberry Finn,* in which the audience of the "Royal Nonesuch" paid fifty cents for a nonexistent show, and then afterward, instead of complaining, they praised the show so as not to look fools and to get their fifty cents worth. Parapsychologists, he argued, were just trying to get their fifty cents worth for their immense expense of effort in a blind alley.

I was incensed: not only at being a nameless "this girl" but at the implication that it was all so simple. If it were, I would certainly give up and not mind looking a fool. But it wasn't that simple. Perhaps there is no ESP, but in that case why do so many people continue to believe there is, and why do other people's experiments apparently go on working? Obviously there was still a dilemma; there were still unexplained positive results. It couldn't all be resolved by running away. While I still didn't understand, I would not give up (Blackmore 1979).

I glanced across the long speckled grass to the great beeches and oaks on the other side of the University parks. At least I felt determined. I may not have any exciting results to write up, but this was what I wanted my thesis to explain. Whichever way you look at it, there is a real dilemma.

* * *

Our house was coming along nicely. Weekends of knocking down old walls and learning to put down foundations were beginning to pay off. With Tom as chief concrete mixer, and me building walls, we were at least beginning to rebuild the garage. We could almost imagine the day when all those tools, planks of wood, old boxes, and filthy rubbish could actually be moved out of the living room. We even had space among all the mess for guests to stay—if they were hardy!

One weekend Julian Isaacs and his lovely wife, Julie, came to visit. Julian was now working on PK experiments for his own Ph.D., and he had a lot to tell me. It was hot and sunny; and, after a quick pub lunch, we took a walk down into the woods to our little local waterfall. Oddly, though the village is only about half a mile away, there are seldom any other people there. It was so that day, and we had the place to ourselves. Julian and I clambered about on slippery rocks in the flickering light of deep beech woods. I pestered him with my usual problem.

"But, Sue," he said, "you're not trying to tell me that you seriously doubt the existence of psi are you? That's absurd. What do you say to my results, or Serena's, or Carl's?" He gave me a penetrating look, spoiled only by his violent wobbling on a tiny stone.

I had time to think. I felt a bit pushed here; that was always the way when it got personal. But neither his results nor Serena's were as yet terribly impressive. It was Carl's that really presented the challenge. "I don't know," I said lamely, "I can't just explain them away, but I don't understand it. Why do you think I don't get results and Carl does?"

"Somehow we have to convince you, Sue." I always rather liked the way people almost made a mission out of trying to convince me. "But I don't know how!"

"I bet you don't. I've been trying long enough! Whatever I do, I don't find any psi. And I really don't think I need to see a psychiatrist either, [Julian laughed] and I can't change my beliefs or doubts at will as if they were some kind of experimental variable."

"I think I've got an idea," interrupted Julian, pausing on a particularly slippery and dangerous rock. He stopped a moment and reached a long leg across to firmer ground. "What you need is a bit of infectious psi. You need to see psi in action. Perhaps it would rub off on you, or perhaps it would force you into believing."

"But that's just the problem, Julian. I can't find any psi to look at."

"Right, so go where the psi is. Go to Carl's lab. It's happening there all the time. He gets about 45 percent hits in his ganzfeld experiments. You'd be bound to see it working." He paused on another rock and glanced across the stream, looking pleased with himself. "Hey, that's a really great idea, you know. You should do it."

I looked at him with a wry smile. It *was* a good idea. It wasn't one I could ignore. Much as I wanted to avoid the awful psi-nonpsi argument, I was in it up to my neck, and this was a challenge, a challenge to everyone's beliefs. "But do you think he'd have me?" I asked.

"Who knows? But you can only ask. Why not write to him?"

"But how could I afford it? There's not only the train fare, but I'd have to stay there too."

"You could try the SPR. I bet they'd pay your expenses for the chance to find out why you're not getting any psi."

A little touch of apprehension came to me. What if I did see psi working there? Well, that's okay, I persuaded myself. It's still not too late to find psi. I could start again with my theorizing. It's never too late if psi is really there.

"Okay, Julian," I said, "I'll write. It *is* a good idea." We waved to Tom and Julie, sitting comfortably high up on the bank. It suddenly felt cold down in the deep shade by the water. Time to clamber up to their sunny spot and make our way home for tea.

I did write to Carl. I told him about Julian's idea and asked whether I might be able to come and observe his experiments in action. Perhaps we could even try some joint experiments? I also wrote to Donald West, the big boss of SPR funding, to ask whether they would consider paying my modest expenses. Then I got back to my thesis.

It was hard and often dreary work, with an old typewriter and lots of retyping to do. I was always finding analyses that needed rechecking. I checked everything at least twice. I began to feel I would never get to the end. Then Tom made me lay out an entire timetable with a dead-line. It was to be September 30, the day my SRC grant ended.

I worked hard. As I had since my Oxford days, I recorded every day in my diary how many hours' work I had done. I timed myself to the minute and forced myself to keep at it, with scheduled breaks for tending the vegetables, now growing nicely in the garden. In July we went down to Devon, to Salcombe, the place that always feels like home. But even there I felt under pressure, working most days and finding myself brooding about psi even on beautiful walks along the rugged cliffs. Then it was back home for more writing.

It was my dear friend Serena who sorted me out. We were all at another conference in London, and both Julian and I went to stay at her house for the night. We talked well into the night, and they really grilled me: Why didn't I believe in psi? What did I believe? How could I reconcile my skepticism with their results?

"You know, you've really changed, Sue," said Serena. "Once you were open to all sorts of things, but now you are just rigid and confined and unbending—stuck."

Me, rigid? Unbending? Was I really?

"And you don't seem to be enjoying it anymore either," put in Julian.

"Right. What's the point of doing it if you don't believe in anything and don't enjoy it?" added Serena.

"But I don't get results!" I shouted. "I bloody well don't get any results!"

At last we were all laughing; late and tired and giggling. In that moment everything opened up inside. I had been putting myself down, blaming myself, seeing myself as a failure, comparing myself with "successes," doubting everyone and everything and hating myself for it. I had put my boredom and even depression down to having to work so hard to finish the thesis. But it wasn't that at all! It was much more important. It was the subject itself. I just couldn't cope with the dilemma of psi. I might kid myself that I was open-minded and detached from the intellectual confusion, but it was gnawing away at my whole being. I couldn't believe in psi, but I couldn't *not* believe in psi either. The concept itself seemed nonsensical, but others kept on finding it. No wonder I was confused; it was the subject that was confusing, and the more open I tried to be to it, the more confusing it was. I suddenly appreciated, deep down inside, how very, very hard it is to have an open mind.

I laughed and laughed and laughed. I went outside in the middle of the night, and the streets looked brighter and "realer" and better, and the stars seemed cheerful and distinct. The dilemma hung in the sky in all its opacity. I hadn't found any solution, but then, after all, I knew there wasn't one. Not here, not now at any rate. What I had done, much too late (but better late than never) was to laugh at myself. Thank goodness for friends who can point out the obvious!

And I did get the thesis finished! On September 30 at 11:30 P.M. I dragged the last sheet out of the typewriter and shouted wildly for Tom. While he went for the corkscrew, I ran myself a hot and bubbly bath. "I've got to read you the last bit," I shouted. Poor Tom! He proudly opened the bottle of Chateau Haut St. Lambert 1973 that we'd brought back from France, and I subjected him to my closing thoughts:

And what of the experiments reported here? Are the negative results due to an inadequate experimenter, poor experimental design, or some other factor inhibiting the appearance of ESP? Or are they to be seen as the natural consequence of collecting large amounts of random data in a world without ESP?

It might be thought that these results would lead me to the latter conclusion. But in fact the negative results of one person's research have remarkably little bearing on the overall picture, and that overall picture is far from clear. Reluctantly, the only answer I can give is that I do not know.

"That'll do," said Tom. "Cheers!"

Fifteen

Disappointment in Cambridge

One Thursday morning in late November I took the train to Cambridge with no inkling of the kind of week I was in for. Everything had been organized. Donald West and the SPR had happily agreed to pay my expenses, and Carl had welcomed the idea with far more enthusiasm than I'd dared to expect. He even seemed to relish the prospect. "We can," he wrote to me, "make a last determined attempt to shake some sense into you."

It was therefore with excitement and anticipation that I cycled through the familiar streets of Cambridge to the Psychology Laboratory. If I had expected anything, I suppose it was one of two possibilities: Either I would find some fatal flaw in Carl's otherwise impeccable experiments and so be able to "explain away" his results, or I would find nothing wrong, find lots of psi, and so have to admit that it did exist. Either would be somewhat traumatic, but in either case I would be closer to knowing the truth about psi.

I must admit that I was a little worried that my skeptical presence might inhibit all signs of psi, then I would be able to learn little or nothing. But I just kept hoping that this would not be the case.

To my great excitement, it wasn't. Indeed the results I observed were quite outstanding. Altogether I was there for thirteen ganzfeld sessions, most of which formed part of ongoing experiments (Ashton et al. 1981; Sargent 1980; Sargent et al. 1981). In some of the sessions I stayed with the experimenter, in others I went with the agent or was agent myself, and in one I was actually the subject. In these thirteen sessions, no fewer than six produced direct hits; that is, the correct picture was chosen from among the four choices.

However, there was nothing so clear-cut about the rest of my observations. It is perhaps some reflection on the difficulty of the issues involved that many years later they remain unresolved. For that reason I cannot describe in any detail what took place, the observations I made, the notes I took, and the problems I encountered. I can only say that I found a number of errors in the way the experimental protocol was followed and the randomization procedure carried out. The question then became, were these errors serious enough to cast doubt on all the significant findings in Cambridge, or were they just minor hiccoughs in an otherwise watertight procedure?

I failed to answer that question. In spite of many hours spent observing the procedures, by the end of my week there it was not at all clear how the errors in the randomization, or the failure to follow protocol, had come about.

Fortunately the whole week wasn't spent in the laboratory. One evening I went to a meeting of the Cambridge University Society for Psychical Research; a perfect way to forget all about the experiments. We were supposed to be making posters for the lecture I was to give later in the week, but it was just like old times in Oxford. The posters were a shambles; we larked about in a gloomy basement room, scrawled with felt pens, and drew silly pictures of people zooming out of their bodies and floating about in the clouds while we drank endless cups of coffee until three in the morning.

The lecture, of course, was to be on out-of-body experiences, and I was excited about giving it. The year before, I had been invited to give a lecture to the SPR in London. Eleanor, the secretary, her pen poised over the lecture list, had asked me what I would like to speak about.

"Well, I suppose I could talk about my memory research," I said.

She involuntarily made a face, and then very politely suggested that, perhaps since I had spoken about that at the conference, I might think of something different. I laughed. I didn't mind if people thought the memory work boring. I suppose it was. But what could I talk about?

"But I don't know enough about anything else," I said rather lamely.

It was then that my fascination for OBEs began to surface. I hadn't done any research on the subject, but I had never forgotten my own experience and would love an excuse to learn more about the topic.

"How about OBEs then?" I asked.

"That sounds much more interesting," agreed Eleanor, already writing it down on the list.

And so it was that I spent weeks reading about OBEs and presented my talk to a full lecture theater in Kensington Central Library.

Afterward I was asked to write up the lecture as a pamphlet (Blackmore 1978) and was asked to give lectures like this one in Cambridge.

Another evening I went to dinner with Donald West. A criminologist at Cambridge and subsequently professor of criminology there, Dr. West was a quiet and inscrutable man. Nearing sixty, he was short, with soft gray hair, a calm unmoving face, and a rather formal manner. He administered the Perrott-Warrick Studentship. Indeed he must have been among those terrifying interviewers I had when I had applied all those years before. He was a past president of the SPR and very much respected by psychical researchers in Britain and abroad. It was he who had arranged for the SPR to pay my expenses and he who would be expecting some kind of account of my findings.

I had always been rather in awe of Dr. West, but I was beginning to find him gently human under the very British formality, and that evening did much to break the ice. He lived alone in an old house in a village outside Cambridge. He welcomed me there with a drink, cooked us both dinner, and served it to me on the shiny dining table in a room full of books and antique furniture. Over glasses of wine, we talked at length about parapsychology, the importance of Carl's research, the problems of psi, the lack of funding, and the pitiful progress in the field. He even encouraged me to apply for the Perrott-Warrick Studentship again; advice which I was determined to take.

But this was just one ray of hope in an otherwise gloomy week. When I humped my bike back onto the train for Bristol, it was with none of the hopeful enthusiasm with which I had arrived such a short time before. I had naively expected that that week would clear up my confusion and resolve my doubts about the existence of psi one way or the other. Instead, it had only made them worse.

One look at my face and Tom threw his arms around me in sympathy.

"I think you need a very large gin and tonic," he said.

"How right you are," I replied, slumping down in the rocking chair by the warm kitchen range. I put my feet up on the untidy pile of firewood that was shedding its bark and woodlice onto the floor around, and Tom pulled out the ice and cut up slices of lemon. "I can't tell you how glad I am to be home."

It was nearly Christmas. I was soon busy making our annual Christmas card, putting up decorations, and packing up parcels. I was also preparing the last of the tables to go into my thesis. I thought ruefully of that long time ago in September when I had "finished." And I was still adding the finishing touches to the final typed version. Still, it was almost done.

All of it took my mind off my problems: First, the Cambridge episode was hanging in my memory as a big lump of something I didn't want to think about. For a time I was still hoping that, with Carl's help, we would be able to track down the source of the errors. We had planned a further visit, and Carl seemed confident that we would be able to get to the bottom of the problem then. Hopefully, I tried to fix up a firm date to go back to Cambridge. I wrote to Carl, and then finally telephoned him. It was only then that Carl asked me never to return to his lab again.

Disappointed, I nevertheless hoped that at least some sort of explanation would be forthcoming. Since the SPR had paid for my visit, I had to write up a report of what I had found for them, and this I did straight after Christmas (Blackmore 1980d). Carl said that he would write his own version of what had occurred so that everyone could read both sides of the story. I thought that this might lead to a resolution, and I anxiously awaited Carl's version. In the meantime I just tried to put the problems out of my mind since there was nothing I could do to solve them.

Second, I now had to answer a more immediate and personal question: To put it simply, what was I going to do with my life?

In some ways the decision was easy. I still didn't know whether there was ESP or not, and my recent experiences had only made that problem more complex. I still didn't understand all those strange experiences and phenomena. So my original motivations had never been satisfied. I still wanted to find out. I still wanted to spend my life doing parapsychology. But how was I going to fund it? I knew I couldn't get a job in parapsychology; there weren't any in Britain. I would be happy with a small grant, but even that seemed a remote possibility. I might be able to apply for the Perrott-Warrick Studentship for the following autumn, as Dr. West had suggested, but that was nearly a year away.

In that wonderful way in which opportunities seem only to arise when you are looking for them, one landed on my doormat. But could I actually take it? It was a letter from Brian Millar at the Parapsychologisch Laboratorium in Utrecht, Holland. They had a small amount of money left over between appointments, he wrote. It was enough for a part-time research job, two days a week for four months. Would I like it?

Would I like it? I would love it—a new country, a real parapsychology lab. But I was married, we had our house to worry about, the garage half built, the decorating not done. We had even been talking about starting a family soon. It was also a bad time to leave Tom. He was on short-term grants, with one about to run out. I was worried about what he would say; and, to tell the truth, I didn't want to "ask" him if I could go. It wasn't up to a husband to "give permission." I thought I should decide for myself. I told him I didn't think I could go. It was so little money and at such a bad time.

Tom was annoyed, but only because I was being so pathetic.

"Why on earth do you keep on about it?" he said in exasperation. "Of course you should go. It's a fantastic opportunity. You'd be crazy not to."

"But it's four months. You'll have to build the garage and look after everything by yourself." It sounded silly when I said it. Of course he'd manage, or he'd not bother. It didn't matter.

"Ring Brian and ask him more about it, if you're so worried."

"Ring Holland? We can't afford that!" I laughed when I saw the look on his face. I was stupid. I picked up the phone.

Within two days it was all settled. I would go to Utrecht in the middle of February. Brian would find somewhere for me to live for the four months. Tom said he'd drive over with me.

The final stages of my thesis were struggled through with increasing enthusiasm and impatience. I numbered the pages, prepared the index, checked the tables, and finally began photocopying the obligatory four copies. Even that took longer than I could possibly have imagined, 389 pages, four times! As a final gesture to I don't know what, I drew a little cat and an even smaller mouse on the bottom corner of the very last page. Then, I took it all off to the binders.

When I collected it a few days later, I was suddenly filled with a terrible disappointment. There it was, in the back of our ancient yellow van, four identical huge blue volumes, beautifully bound, with neat gold lettering on the spine. Was that all? Was that it? The entire result of all those years of work? I felt I ought to be elated, but instead I was let down and just glad it was over. I took it on the train to Surrey and handed it in with relief.

Miraculously there was yet another opportunity in store for me. I went increasingly often to the SPR in London, where I attended dreary meetings of the library committee but enjoyed the chance to talk to Eleanor, the secretary, or to borrow some new books from the library. One evening I was drinking tea with Eleanor in her office, when an older member of Council, whom I knew only slightly, took me aside.

"We've been thinking," he began. "It is the SPR's centenary in two years time." I knew that well enough, the whole Society had been talking about it for months. "We thought it might be a good idea to start a series of books, a sort of SPR centenary series. We could cover several different subjects and then build up into a complete series if there was the demand. I've spoken to some publishers and I think we might have a contract soon." I wondered what on earth he was getting at. "We wondered whether you would like to write one on out-of-body experiences."

"Oh, I'd love to," I burst out. I was so surprised. "Do you know I've been vaguely thinking about doing that for years. I am sure I never would have got around to it. But it's just what I'd like to do."

I sat through the committee meeting with my mind elsewhere. Somehow, like the Tarot cards and mystical experiences, the out-of-body experience had always seemed a bit too "far out" to devote my research to. But in a way it was the thing about which I cared the most. After all, it was my own out-of-body experience that had really set me off in the first place. It was failing to understand that experience that had always spurred me on. Now I was going to write a book about it. I would make it the very best book I possibly could.

I ran, as usual, all the way to the station and onto the platform. As I sat down in the half-empty train, my heart seemed to be beating unusually fast and sounding unusually loud, but I dismissed the vague apprehension that something was wrong. Suddenly the prospects for 1980 looked so much better.

Sixteen

New Research in Holland

Very early one cold Friday morning in February, Tom and I drove our van onto the cross-channel ferry that would take us to Calais. It was a long drive to Utrecht—from the dusty and relaxed towns of France, through increasingly tidy Belgium, and into smart, clean Holland with its flat, flat countryside and handsome steep-roofed houses.

Ahead of me was something totally unknown. Tom and I tried to imagine where I would be living, what sort of room Brian would have found for me. Tom thought it would be in a modern block and very plain and dull. I thought it would be in an old city house in an interesting attic. The nonexistence of precognition suddenly seemed to be the only possibility. I really couldn't predict.

And neither of us was right. I wasn't to live in Utrecht at all but in the expensive nearby town of Bilthoven. There, my landlady was waiting for us with tea all laid out, in a large, typically Dutch house, set in a wonderful garden full of pine trees. The garden, she told me in perfect English, was where they had buried all their money during the war, when they had practically starved under German occupation. Now it was full of little wooden nesting boxes and fluttering birds.

After tea and cakes she took us to my room. It was large, square, white-painted, and light. To the left a great wide window looked out past pretty curtains through the pine trees. In front of the window stood a round table with a checkered cloth and a welcoming vase of great pink tulips. To the right was a narrow bed, all made up, with a colorful counterpane, a lamp beside it, and a little rug. I even had my own kitchen. I loved the room straight away.

Tom and I had all weekend together to explore Utrecht, wander around the marketplace, eat deliciously novel Indonesian food, and realize how frightening it was to contemplate being apart for so long—when we took each other so very much for granted. Then at 5:00 A.M. Monday morning, I ran, still in my nightie, out into the road to wave goodbye.

When I awoke again at eight it was to a new routine and a new life. The van had brought my bicycle, and now I cycled every morning the six miles to the city. The Parapsychologisch Laboratorium of Utrecht was high up in a dreary building over a large department store. But there, in the orderly lab and offices, were parapsychologists. The head of the lab was Professor Martin Johnson, a Swede, well-known to parapsychologists and long the holder of the only Chair of Parapsychology in the world. There was Jerry Solfvin, a soft-spoken, dreamy American with the gentlest of manners and widest of smiles. There was Sybo Schouten, the only Dutchman, who was rumored to keep the entire place together by scheming for university funds. And finally there was Brian Millar from Scotland. To my intense relief everyone spoke perfect English. Not so happily, I discovered that there was rarely anyone there. Martin was often lecturing abroad. Jerry and I only overlapped for a short time there. Sybo was busy with committees and administration, and Brian appeared at somewhat irregular times.

My first day Brian came in at about 4:00 P.M. He told me this was in my honor. He didn't like daytime. He usually came in about 5:00 P.M. so as to see anyone he needed to, but his working day began then and lasted deep into the dark, when no one was around.

However, Brian did me an even greater honor. From then on he came in earlier and earlier, eventually making it in by midday. Then every lunchtime we went out to a little restaurant next door and argued long and hard about psi.

"I get the impression," said Brian through a mouthful of soggy french fries, "that you are getting more and more skeptical."

"Is it that obvious?" I replied, wondering how someone in a different country could get an impression at all. "It's not as though I'm a complete disbeliever. I mean, that wouldn't make sense. You can't say that psi is impossible or can't exist. It might exist, for all I know. It's just that the whole idea of psi doesn't seem to get you anywhere. It's not only that I never seem to find any but that the whole concept is negatively defined and—well—useless!"

"It's not that useless," said Brian. "What if you found some in an experiment tomorrow? Or, more important, what about theory? If we had a good theory of psi, then you couldn't say it was useless, could you?"

"But I've never seen any good theory of psi, have you?"

"Of course I have—the observational theories [Millar 1978]. That's where the future of parapsychology lies. That is, I am convinced, the only hope. In fact," he said, almost defiantly, "I would go so far as to say that if the observational theories (OTs) don't work, then I will be finished with psi."

"Oh, Brian," I sighed, "you'll have to start at the beginning. I never did understand Harris Walker's ideas, and I am quite confused by Schmidt's retroactive PK" (Walker 1975; Schmidt 1975).

Brian's face lit up. He was good at explaining, and it was the greatest joy for me, after years of working on my own, to have someone to explain something new in parapsychology to me.

The basic principle of the OTs is that all forms of psi are essentially retroactive PK. Take the example of simple PK: imagine someone sitting in front of a computer with two lights on it, trying to make the red one come on more often than the green one, while the computer randomly lights one or the other. Traditional views would say that some "force" or "energy" or "effect" comes from the person and "causes" the red light to come on. The OTs turn the whole thing inside out. They say that the psi event occurs at the time of the observation. When the subject *sees* the red light come on, then and only then a PK force acts *backward in time* to influence the system to turn on the red light. In other words, it is *retroactive.* It all happens at the moment of feedback.

"But hang on, Brian. I don't understand. Do you mean that everything starts at feedback? There is no psi until then?"

Brian nodded.

"But then if I didn't look at the lights, it wouldn't work!"

"That's exactly right," said Brian. "That's the beauty of the OTs. They are testable. By manipulation of the feedback conditions, you should be able to affect the PK. And you can do experiments on that."

"But wait a minute." I had pushed my last few chips away by now; this was getting interesting. "I was thinking you could do an experiment with and without feedback. But you can't. If no one gets feedback, then you can't know the results of the experiment. No one can look at the results because that would be feedback too. So you can't do it."

"Exactly," grinned Brian, and he began to explain. "You can vary who looks at the results and when. In fact," he said, "Dick Bierman, in

Amsterdam, has done just that and found differences. I must take you there to meet him one day," he added.

"Oh, but now I'm even more confused. I have been assuming that only one person ever looked at the red and green lights, but what if other people looked too?" I was struggling here and Brian was smiling happily. "And wait a minute. What counts as an observation? I mean if you write down all the lights as 1s and 0s on a data sheet and look at that, does it count? And what if more people look at it? And what if——"

"You talk too fast!" laughed Brian. "Start with the first one first. We don't know what counts as an observation. That is something we have to find out."

"The cat might glance at the lights," I butted in, "or what about a fly sitting on the computer terminal?" I paused. "Even worse, what about the published paper? When people read that it was significant, does that count as an observation?"

"That," continued Brian, "is the important thing and what everyone was worrying about now, that is, how the addition of observers works.

"The question is: If a hundred people observe the same results, are the effects cumulative? Or does only the first one count, or perhaps do they add up in some rule-governed way? The interesting question is whether you can protect the results against future observers. You see, you might have a powerful psi source—someone who could look at the lights and get the red one to light all the time, but then other people in the future would look at the results and get feedback. If they were just ordinary people, not psi-sources, or if they were skeptics, then they might wash it all out. So if we publish our results, we must worry about all those future observers in the years ahead. This," Brian concluded, "explains why psi is so elusive. You can't screen it against the effects of future observers."

"Mmmm," I muttered. Brian had given me an awful look when he'd mentioned skeptics. I was busily imagining my own skeptical influence reaching out by retroactive PK and doing untold damage to the entire future of the universe—a horrible idea. But this really was fascinating stuff, and so much more interesting than it sounded in the journals. "So then you ought to be able to do an experiment in which you didn't let future observers see it——"

"Precisely," Brian nodded enthusiastically. "It is the ultimate experiment. Data destruction. You, the experimenter, can be the only one to see the results."

"But that's preposterous, Brian." I stopped a moment. "It's like alchemy. You mustn't tell. Perhaps all those occult traditions are based on that idea. Psi only occurs in restricted data. It's like. . . ."

Brian was fiddling with his knife and fork and smiling. He was obviously as delighted as I was to have someone to talk to at last.

"Come and have supper with me this evening," he suggested.

It was a strange evening. Brian lived in a sort of outhouse in the back of Sybo's garden. Damp but cozy, it was lined with pine panelling and littered with cushions, dirty cups, books, and orderly heaps of paper, like a workaholic's sauna bath. Brian cooked me dinner, and we sat by candlelight on a wooden bench and took up the threads of our argument.

"You've really set me thinking, Brian. It's always the way. Just when I am despairing of psi, something comes along which makes me think it just might be possible."

"So you like the OTs?"

"Oh no, not so fast. I still don't understand. When you say the effect work backwards in time, I get a bit confused. Let's say the red light comes on. Then the psi, whatever it is, goes back in time, to the moment of decision. Then—oh, but you can't say *then* if effects are going backwards. The person sees the red light. The psi works backwards to affect the computer's decision. The computer lights the red light. So the person sees the red light. It is a kind of like a closed loop, isn't it? There seems something wrong with it."

"Aha, that's what some people say. You should read Steve Braude's critique of the observational theories (Braude 1979b). He thinks you can demolish them all because they imply a closed causal loop."

"And don't you agree?"

"No, not at all. It's just a different kind of loop from normal causation. The information is input at the moment of feedback rather than at any other stage in the loop. I don't think it is a problem at all."

I would have to read that paper. I knew Steve Braude was an American philosopher. I also knew that he played the piano, for at the last P.A. Convention all the people who knew him went off to hear him play. But I'd not read any of his esoteric work, and at that stage I'd never met him.

"Can I cut your hair?" asked Brian.

"What? Are you serious?" I now recollected that I'd seen various books about hairdressing around the cluttered room. I was never much bothered about my appearance and couldn't afford hairdressers.

"Well," I hesitated only for a moment, "all right."

It seemed mad enough to try, so Brian cut it with extreme care and infinite slowness. He snipped and clipped and fiddled and tidied and did a very nice job.

"I used to have very thick hair," I moaned. "But now it must be old age. It's all starting to fall out!" It was true, and as I made my way home, with my new hairstyle and a head full of ideas, I had a moment's worry. I hadn't been feeling too well lately; my heart raced, and I felt dizzy if I cycled too fast into town, but I thought that perhaps it was just the excitement of this wonderful new job.

* * *

I had plenty to do and seemed to have lots of energy to spare. Brian was teaching me to use the (by today's standards) cumbersome word-processor on the main computer. The *European Journal of Parapsychology* was produced in Utrecht. I wanted to write up all my thesis work, and if I put it straight into the computer it could go directly into the *Journal*. It was so quick compared to a typewriter, and I knew exactly what I wanted to write. So within a month or so, I had written three papers. Even if no one read my thesis, the results would be published elsewhere (Blackmore 1980a, 1981a, 1981b).

Still, it was odd how I seemed to have so much energy. I slept less than ever before and found myself reading journal articles late into the night and waking early for a stint at writing. On weekends, if I wasn't working, I went out cycling or walking or even oil painting, a pleasure I had long neglected.

I was also getting involved in the lab's plans for a ganzfeld experiment. Martin Johnson and Brian had both, like me, been impressed with Carl Sargent's results and now wanted to try to replicate them in Holland. They had even tried to get Carl to come over and help them set it up, but Carl had said that he could not come. Since I had been to Carl's lab and I knew his methods, I was the next best thing.

Apparently they had heard about my visit, and they wanted to know everything. Who were his subjects? What did they lie on? Was it a red light or a plain one? Were the targets colored? Were the experiments done properly? Was I convinced the results were due to psi? What else had I found? I answered them all as best I could, and naturally I felt I had to tell them about the errors I had found. It was clear they thought Carl's experiments very important, and this made it all the more important to replicate them.

We found Dutch- and English-speaking experimenters, volunteer subjects, lights and ping-pong balls, and a room to work in. Within a couple of weeks our ganzfeld experiment was underway, and the results were beginning to come in.

Martin Johnson called Brian and me into his office to hear how the experiment was going.

"By the way," he said, "I thought you'd like to know that J. B. Rhine died last week. I just got this letter."

I was rather sad. I recalled that day in Durham when he and Louisa had welcomed me into their home and given me such encouragement. They had set "scientific parapsychology" in motion and steered it through all kinds of crises. Now he was gone. In a way it marked the passing of a long phase of parapsychology. Now *we* were the researchers who had to fight today's problems. And what were those problems? Still, after fifty years, we were grappling with the very existence of psi! I grimly wondered what J. B. Rhine would have thought of our current efforts and our persistent doubts.

This question of the existence of psi was continually nagging at me. I tackled it in my mind from every point of view I could think of. It occurred to me that the only thing to do with any hypothesis is to test it. Now I had a new hypothesis: perhaps psi did not exist. Could I test that?

It is an interesting question, and in a way the answer must be "no." One cannot prove the nonexistence of something negatively defined. But then *proof* is not what is meant by testing. Most testing of hypotheses is a question of drawing predictions from the hypothesis and finding out whether they hold or not. If they do, you progress; if they don't, you have to modify the idea. The most valuable predictions are those which clearly distinguish between one theory and another. Could I draw any predictions from the hypothesis that psi does not exist?

One idea was to tackle the "no smoke without a fire" argument. A persistent suggestion is that there must be psi because peoples in all ages and cultures have believed in it. But perhaps there were reasons people should believe in psi even if it doesn't exist. If I could find these out, I would be closer to an answer, but it was not something I could tackle yet.

I tried a different line of thought: Why should there be so many successful experiments reported if there were no psi? One answer, apart from fraud, error, and the like, is selective reporting.

One of the arguments against the evidence for psi has always been that only the good results are published. If a hundred experiments are carried out, you will expect—by sheer chance—that about five will give results "significant" at the .05 level. If only those five are published, and the other ninety-five forgotten, the published evidence will be quite unfairly biased. It seemed feasible that this selective reporting accounted for much of the significance reported in the literature.

This is a problem common to many fields of science, but like so many problems, it looms larger in parapsychology. Indeed there have often been criticisms that the parapsychology journals will accept positive results in preference to negative results, thereby unfairly biasing the published work and putting pressure on researchers to "come up with something" at all costs. It was to counter this that the *European Journal of Parapsychology,* edited in Utrecht by Martin Johnson and Sybo Schouten, developed a very unusual publication policy. In every issue the editors explain that priority will be given to papers for which the authors have submitted details of their experimental design and proposed analyses *before* they actually carry out the experiment. This way the papers can be judged on the quality of experimental design, rather than on whether the results are significant or not.

Of course some people have argued that it isn't really a problem at all: There are a few experiments with results so staggeringly unlikely to be chance that selective reporting couldn't conceivably account for them. But of course this argument was used for Soal's experiments, and where did that stand now that he had been found a fraud?

It was an interesting problem, and I had an idea. Card-guessing experiments are easy to do, and one could imagine hundreds of people doing hundreds of experiments and no one ever knowing about them all. But ganzfeld experiments weren't like that. I realized it was very unlikely that many ganzfeld experiments would be done that couldn't be tracked down. First, ESP-ganzfeld experiments had begun only seven or eight years before. Second, they were very time-consuming and arduous to do. Third, they needed quite a lot of setting up. Anyone contemplating doing one would surely get in touch with others who had done them before.

So, I thought, I might be able to track down virtually all of the ganzfeld studies ever done. Then I could look at the results of the published ones versus the unpublished ones. If selective reporting were an important problem, then I would expect far more significant results among the published studies. The unsuccessful studies would be the ones buried in a drawer and forgotten about.

It was a plausible and feasible idea and something I could hope to complete during my short stay in Utrecht. So I set to work making up a simple questionnaire. I asked each respondent to say whether he or she had ever done any ganzfeld experiments and then to give brief details of each experiment, including any that were stopped in progress, aborted for any reason, completed and not published, or published. I included a list of all published studies I knew about and asked them to give the names of any further researchers they knew who might have done a ganzfeld study. I got the list of PA members and sent out the questionnaire to anyone who I thought might conceivably have done a ganzfeld study.

While I waited for the results to come in, I set about analyzing just how successful the known ganzfeld work really was. Carl had told me that the replication rate was far better than anything in ordinary psychology and that this just proved what a fuss people made about nothing when it came to parapsychology. If it weren't for their resistance to psi, they would have accepted the overwhelming evidence from the ganzfeld years ago, or so said Carl. He had estimated that 58 percent of ganzfeld studies were successful.

I went to the library, thinking it would be an easy matter to look up all the ganzfeld studies and count the successful ones. Almost as soon as I began, I realized the problem. What was to count as successful when so many analyses had been done? How could you compare one study with another when different labs used different methods of assessment? Did you count a study with three parts as one, or as three, experiments?

It turned into a terrible job, but in the end I decided I could make a rough estimate. To my surprise it came out exactly the same as Carl's. I reckoned that for thirty-one experiments, the successful replication rate was 58 percent. This is very high. If selective reporting were responsible for the whole effect, there would have to be thousands of unreported ganzfeld studies. This surely couldn't be so, but as soon as my questionnaire came back, I would be able to make a good guess as to just how many there were.

In the meantime I got a letter from John Beloff. He was to be the external examiner for my Ph.D. and was suggesting a possible date for my viva, or thesis defense. In two weeks time I would return to England—to get my Ph.D. or not.

Seventeen

The Illness Catches Up With Me

"I really must take you to Amsterdam to meet Dick Bierman," said Brian for the tenth time. I was somewhat reluctant. As always, I felt I had too much work to do to go off on a trip. But then, I persuaded myself, this is work too. So I agreed, and early (well, early for Brian) one Thursday morning we set off to drive to Amsterdam.

"What's Dick like, Brian? Does he speak good English? Will he mind us coming to visit him?" I asked.

"Oh, you'll like Dick," he replied, taking his eyes dangerously off the road. "But you watch him. He's always after women!"

I couldn't help laughing. Brian always seemed to see everything in terms of love or sex or intrigues of various kinds.

"Don't be silly, Brian. I'm married and more interested in the observational theories than in men."

"Yes, I know." He made a wry face, looking at me almost accusingly. "And yes, he does speak good English." I certainly didn't speak much Dutch!

We got lost several times on the way. I remembered the first time Brian had offered me a lift home from the lab when I was in a hurry, but had forgotten where he'd parked his car. It took us hours to find it in the winding streets of old Utrecht. Now he was negotiating terrifying, tram-filled Amsterdam with the same randomness, until suddenly we were there, in a tiny one-sided street of tall houses by a tree-lined canal. The last house was Dick's.

We let ourselves in and climbed three long wooden staircases, where we were met by numerous friendly cats, to the very top. Through a large space, like a classroom, there was a little door, and there, in the warmth of a tiny room, surrounded by humming computers, was Dick. He was small and very thin, with slightly thinning brown hair and dark eyes. He looked much older than I had expected, though I suppose he was only ten years older than I. I felt a little awkward as Brian introduced us. I was longing to get into discussions about the OTs but didn't know where to begin.

"What do you do with all this computer set-up?" I asked.

"Oh, all my experiments are run here," he replied. "Let me show you." He did speak good English, with a heavy but rather pleasant Dutch accent.

A quick flip of a few switches, some rapid typing, and some instructions appeared on a screen.

"Try it!" said Dick. I took the proffered seat at the terminal and began. My task was to make a spot move out of an enclosure, in one direction or the other. I got quite engrossed, though I wasn't very successful.

"Is this controlled by a random-number generator?"

"Yes, I build them myself. All this works on an Apple II computer. Several other parapsychologists have them, and I start to supply random number generators for other people too."

"You mean you'll all have similar systems and can share programs and compare results?" He nodded. "And how does this relate to your other work?" I went on. "Brian tells me you are working on the observational theories."

"That's right. I am interested in checker effects. On the observational theories what's most important is who looks first at the data, and of course it can be computer-generated data.

"I did an experiment with Debbie Weiner," he said. I remembered Debbie well from my visit to Durham. "We split in half the data from one experiment. She checked one half and I checked the other, and we got significant differences" (Weiner and Bierman 1979).

"You mean that because you were observer for some and she for others, that made the difference?" He nodded. "But what about the actual subjects in the experiment? They were the first observers, weren't they? Shouldn't they have—but hang on—how do you think the summation of later observers works? Does everyone have an equal effect or what?"

"Ah, that's the question. But this is a method by which we might be able to find out."

We had lots of tea from a Chinese pot with a broken spout, and we sat on well into darkness in the tiny warm room. I was fascinated by the OTs, but I also wanted to get back to writing my paper at home. However, Dick had other ideas.

"Time for the pub!" he said. "I would like to take you both out to dinner. You haven't seen much of Amsterdam, Sue?"

"No," I admitted and for once was glad that I'd been forced away from my work. We drank endless glasses of Genever—Dutch gin—in an endless series of wonderful Amsterdam bars. Then finally Dick took us to a crowded restaurant with large round tables where people who didn't know each other squashed together into any space they could find. Through the noise and smoke we carried on with our discussions. We were getting very used to our three-way arguments about the nature of psi.

While we waited for coffee, Brian excused himself, and Dick and I were alone at the noisy table. I looked up at Dick, his eyes slightly squinted against the light. In that space, the entire afternoon was turned inside out. Sitting beside me, his fingers burning through the back pocket of my jeans, was someone I had known all my life.

When Brian returned, we had barely moved. But Brian took one look at us and turned white. As I stared back at him in surprise, he reached over, grabbed his mug of beer and, with sudden fury, tipped it all over Dick's hair. For a moment I just sat there, speechless. Then I burst out laughing as Dick carefully wiped the beer from his clothes and polished the table in front of him.

As I climbed into Brian's car, somehow out in the street again, Dick leaned across.

"Where do you live?" he whispered. I told him the address in Bilthoven. "But where is that?" I told him roughly where it was, and then Brian was revving the engine. "Oh, God," I thought, "I do hope Brian hasn't had too much to drink."

We got lost again. Very lost. And it was about 2:00 A.M. when we finally arrived back in Bilthoven. Brian was furious. He'd warned me, he said. How could I?

How could I what, I thought? What had I done? Nothing. He slammed the door after me, as I tried to say a friendly goodnight. He was so furious he didn't even see what I saw. Parked across the drive was another car. I knew I'd seen it before—outside Dick's house! I didn't know whether to be delighted or furious, but one thing I was determined about—I wasn't going to get entangled!

* * *

The next day Brian and I were back at work on the ganzfeld experiment. Enough sessions were completed to give us a good idea of how the results would turn out. It was becoming increasingly obvious that the results were more like mine than like Carl's. This experiment was not going to be the successful replication of the Sargent work. It was going to be another chance result. Of course we tried not to prejudge the conclusion before the results were in, but it was increasingly obvious. So Carl's results were still the exception, at least as far as European research was concerned.

My questionnaires began to come in. I must admit that I had had an ulterior motive in this study. I had wondered whether people would be willing to share their data with others, to provide information about their work, and to make the effort to dig out old results. I thought that if they were trying to conceal unsuccessful experiments (as was often implied by skeptics), then they would not be very forthcoming. However, my fears proved quite groundless.

Almost everyone replied. Many wrote long, long letters describing their unpublished experiments in detail and offering more information if I wanted it. Several people told me about others who had done ganzfeld research and provided me with names and addresses so that I could follow them up. There was no sign of any coverup going on here, no obvious hiding of data, no secretiveness. It was very encouraging.

But my main objective was to find out how serious the selective-reporting problem was. First, how many unpublished studies were there? And second, were they more or less significant than the published ones?

I eventually tracked down nineteen studies which had been completed but not published. Of these, seven provided significant results. This success rate was less than that in the published papers, but the difference was not large. There might be a slight tendency to report significant outcomes more often, but it wasn't a clear-cut effect. Perhaps more important, there were certainly not enough unpublished nonsignificant studies to make up for all the significant ones. Of course I may have missed some, but it couldn't be more than a few, and that would make no real difference to the argument.

I therefore concluded that selective reporting was not responsible for the successful replication rate of ganzfeld studies. The apparent success of the technique had to be attributed to some other effect—

whether psi or something else—but not to selective reporting (Blackmore 1980e).

But I am jumping ahead. Before all this was completed, I was traveling back and forth to England on the Magic Bus, that extraordinarily cheap mode of travel full of cannabis smoke and noisy young people who didn't encourage much sleep on the overnight crossing. My first trip back was for my viva. The day I left Utrecht, I found a red carnation on my desk: a good luck present from Brian.

Dick drove me to the bus station, and I set off "home," full of strange fears and confusions. How would it be seeing Tom again after all this time? How would my viva be? Would I get my Ph.D.? Was it just worry, or wasn't I very healthy?

I had to think about this one. It wasn't like me to worry about things. And my heart still seemed to be beating too fast. I'd even asked Brian about it, but he thought it was nothing to worry about. I made up my mind I would see my doctor in England. The National Health Service, for all its faults, is wonderful. I knew I could get any medical attention I needed entirely free, whereas in Holland I would have to pay. I would definitely see my doctor while I was there.

I arrived at Surrey, exhausted, but in plenty of time for my viva, and I made my way to the office outside Professor Lee's room.

"Oh, Sue, how thin you look," said all the secretaries in the office. "How's Holland? What's it like being back at Surrey?" They kept my mind off the coming ordeal quite effectively.

Very soon Terence Lee and John Beloff arrived, obviously back from lunch together (where they had obviously been talking about my thesis) and strode through the office to Terence's room without a glance in my direction. I was terrified. I knew them both well. Were they avoiding my gaze because it was all going to be so bad? Why was I still having to wait?

A few long minutes later, John Beloff appeared in the doorway, formally dressed. I got up to smile at him and say hello, but he looked straight ahead. "We are ready to receive the candidate now," he announced to no one in particular. With a terrified look back at the secretaries, I crept in behind him, not knowing whether to smile and be friendly or sit down and keep quiet.

Then they began: question after question on the details of my experiments, the references I hadn't got quite right, the arguments they didn't understand, the details I had left out. I enjoyed it. It was like exams at school, which I had always loved though never dared to admit the fact. I loved the pressure, the intensity, the challenge to think hard and fast. I can only remember two things about my viva. At one point, John Beloff's formal pose was broken by a real laugh when I proposed something that he said knocked everything his life's work stood for! He really challenged me on the question of dualism, which he thought I dismissed far too easily. And then after the shaking, nervous hours were over, I remember him saying, as he gently rubbed his chin, "Mmmmmm, a noble work, a noble work. That will be all, thank you, Dr. Blackmore."

I crashed out into the office again, still not sure whether I had got it. They had said something about some small changes I had to make in the text, but that was all. Was that it? Had I got it?

"Well, what happened?"

"Tom, Oh, Tom, it's a——"

"Have you got it?" persisted Tom, who had just driven up from Pear Tree Cottage and looked worse than I felt.

"I think so, I——"

"What do you mean, you think so? You do look thin."

"Oh, Tom, yes, I think I have."

"Well done." Everyone was congratulating me, and I burst into tears. It was all too much: seeing Tom again, being back in England, feeling peculiar. But we had a lovely evening. My parents invited Terence Lee to dinner, and we all drank to my Ph.D. My father was obviously very touched. In his own way, he had worked for that, for me, for very long. He was very proud of his daughter—Dr. Blackmore.

The next day Tom and I drove home. Tom wasn't too pleased with me in spite of the Ph.D.

"You look awful," he said. "You are so thin. Have you been getting no sleep, up every night with Dick Bierman, I suppose?"

"I haven't," I protested quite truthfully, but I did feel odd. "I think I ought to see the doctor."

"You do that," said Tom, "first thing in the morning."

* * *

I sat there in the waiting room, counting my pulse. If it were 72,

Doctor Spurling would surely laugh at me! But I was just sitting there, and it was 110.

"Good morning," I began tentatively, when my turn finally came. Martin Spurling was renowned for chatting to his patients. It made for a good doctor but an awfully long wait. "I'm afraid you might think I'm silly, and there may be nothing wrong but——"

"You're looking thinner," he interrupted. "I hope you haven't been dieting."

"Don't be silly," I was relaxing a bit now. "You know I wouldn't do that. Actually I've been eating more than ever before." I recalled the night the previous week when, after dinner with Brian, Dick had appeared and wanted to take me out to eat. I'd eaten two huge dinners within a couple of hours! "It's rather weird eating so much and getting thinner," I said.

"Hmmm," said Dr. Spurling, "so what's wrong, then? It sounds rather nice to me!"

"Well, it may be nothing, but my heart seems to be beating faster than usual and ——"

"And don't tell me," he broke in, "you've been feeling hot, sleeping without blankets, full of energy, hair falling out?"

"Exactly! How do you know? What is it?"

He was really laughing, "Are you having me on, Sue? I know you did physiology at Oxford." He saw my surprised face. "You're not having me on!"

I was thinking now, why hadn't I tried to diagnose it myself? It was my metabolic rate. It was higher than it should be, burning up more fat, using up more oxygen, everything going faster.

"What controls the metabolic rate?" I asked.

He was enjoying himself. "Do you really mean to tell me that you have all the symptoms and you still haven't guessed what it is?" I nodded dumbly. "You've got thyrotoxicosis. It's a hyperactive thyroid."

I could have kicked myself. I should have known, of course. The thyroid gland produces a hormone called thyroxine which controls the metabolic rate. Too much thyroxine meant too high a metabolic rate. I was burning myself up. No wonder I was eating so much and getting so thin. No wonder I had so much energy. Why weren't people like this all the time, I wondered? It seemed rather better than normal in some ways.

But I wasn't banking on the progression of the disease. An excess of energy is fun, but the shaking and weakness that became more and more pronounced later weren't. Nevertheless, I was given some drugs to control the hormones and set off much relieved back to Holland again.

Everyone I knew in Holland was concerned about the horrors of powerful modern drugs. They said that what I was taking would interfere with my whole system and do untold damage to my very being. I should have homeopathic remedies and gentle treatments. When I told Dick about it, he immediately said he'd take me to meet Gerard Croiset. He might be able to heal me.

I was fascinated to meet Croiset. He was well known to parapsychologists as a controversial "paragnost." He claimed to have solved murder cases and found numerous missing persons in cases when the police had given up hope. However, he was now concentrating on healing work.

He lived in an ordinary, pleasant, and Dutchly tidy little house. He was tall and gray-haired, stood firmly erect, and wore a bright bow tie. He showed us slides depicting the cases he claimed to have solved and explained his theory of the paranormal. Then Dick asked him about my illness. To anyone who didn't know me, I am sure I didn't look at all ill. He studied me for some time, holding his hand gently to his forehead.

"It is an allergy?" he concluded. We said nothing. "There is something wrong with the blood. It all stems from the liver. And there's something wrong with the gall bladder too."

"But can you help?" asked Dick.

"Yes, most certainly I can," exclaimed Croiset, "but you will have to come regularly and it will take about three months."

We thanked him for seeing us, and I said I would let him know if I needed his help. It was interesting; I had begun to suspect I was allergic to those drugs I was taking. Had he seen me scratching surreptitiously, asked my skeptical half—and he hadn't mentioned hormones.

It was also interesting that he said it would take three months. I had already talked to an acupuncturist about the thyrotoxicosis, and he said it would take him three months to cure me. I felt I ought to try these alternative routes to health. After all, I had spent enough time learning about fringe medicine and alternative therapies. But I never did. As it turned out, I didn't have three months.

On my next visit back to England, I told my doctor about the allergy. Over my protests, he sent me to see the surgeon at the hospital in Bath. I didn't really want to have an operation if there were any other treatment.

The surgeon was kindly and intelligent and definite. He patiently explained the progression of the disease, the problems of the various drugs, and that my thyroid gland simply had to go. When I had taken it all in, I agreed with him. When I said I was off the next day on a bus to Holland, he nearly had me admitted right away. But I needed one last trip back. I had to complete my research there, finish the papers I was writing for that year's P.A. Conference, and pack up my much-loved room.

Before I went, I had a very special treat. I had to go to the SPR one day for a meeting, and quite by chance Eleanor, the secretary, asked me whether I had ever met Rosalind Heywood. I said I never had but would love to meet her. It was her book that had set me off in the first place. Indeed I didn't even know that she was still alive. Eleanor telephoned her straight away and arranged for me to go to tea.

Rosalind Heywood lived in a beautiful old house in Wimbledon, with spacious, elegant rooms and a lovely flower-filled garden. She was elderly, slow-moving, and white-haired, but her eyes shone brightly. We sat across a low and lustrous antique table, and I crunched my way through piles of dark chocolate biscuits, while we drank china tea from finest tea cups. She entranced me with stories of how she had taken mescaline long before it ever became popular. She had once seen the ghost of Whateley Carington, whose memory theory I had struggled over so long ago, and she talked about the old days of the SPR when Soal was doing his infamous research; Eric Dingwall was in his fighting prime; and there were high hopes for psychical research becoming an accepted science. Before I left, she took my hand and read my palm for me—"a well balanced head and heart line"—she declared. Like Louisa Rhine two years before, she declared she could see no reason why I couldn't get good results in my ESP experiments.

I walked very slowly back to Wimbledon station. My hands were shaking a little more every day, and I seemed able to walk less freely. Was it my imagination, or was I thinking differently too? Certainly Tom had accused me of being irrational and emotional. I worried more too. It wasn't like me at all. But then what was me? "I" wasn't some psychic, mysterious, fluid something; "I" wasn't some nebulous, etheric, or astral substance, nor some unchanging soul or spirit. I had to be a product of my body and brain. It made perfect sense that when body and brain were sick, I would change too. I realized then the very frailty of my concept of my own self, my own personality. Just a little extra hormone and "I" was quite profoundly changed. Perhaps "I" wasn't even there any more. "I" was some new person. It was the same old problem that always haunted me when thinking about memory. How much of myself could "I" remember? Who was remembering whom?

Before I got around to writing to Rosalind Heywood to thank her for having me for tea, she died. If ever I wished I had never got started on parapsychology and had never read her book in the first place, I took it back when I met her. Her theories and explanations didn't solve the problems, but she was not content with such theories either. She had spent her life fascinated by human experience and died, I imagine, just as baffled.

Eighteen

A Time for Reassessment

I had plenty of time to think as I lay in my hospital bed. I was to rest for three days to prepare for the operation, all at the expense of the state. I was free to sit out in the May sunshine, or sleep, or walk about. Characteristically, I had a stack of work with me, but I was weak and shaky, and my eyes got tired quickly. So instead, I set myself to wondering. What was I really trying to understand? Had I got anywhere in doing so?

There were two threads to my tangled thoughts. One was all about psi. Where was it? What was it? Did the whole idea of it make sense? The other was all about memory and experience: strange feelings, odd thoughts, difficult to put into words. It was all to do with the longing to remember and with the nature of self and the way it changes. Why was "I" so dependent upon my ability to remember? Who or what was "I" anyway?

Were these just childish questions, I wondered, the sort of things I might have asked myself at age thirteen and never answered—could never answer because they were fatuous or unanswerable or based on some kind of mistake? Moreover, did they have anything to do with psi? I was just beginning to suspect that they did not, but where would that line of thought take me?

Clearly I had a lot of thinking to do. Fortunately, I was getting better at mental discipline, and I no longer found it at all hard to work. After many years of practice I could set myself to thinking out a given problem and keep at it for a considerable time. It was part of the same skill that is trained in meditation, that made it possible to sit and not to let stray thoughts drag my awareness to and fro. The same discipline helped in "just sitting," in controlled imagery, or in thinking persistently. Lying there in hospital, I thought. I tackled these questions, one by one, again and again, pinning my awareness on a rambling crack in the pale green ceiling.

At first, I had thought that psi would appear more or less to order.

I sought it first in my memory experiments. Then, when those failed, I listened to all the suggestions. I tried different conditions, different kinds of subjects; I used young children; I tried the ganzfeld. I had even considered the relevance of my own beliefs and tried experiments I believed would work. When I had finally given up finding any psi for myself, I looked into other people's experiments. There, it seemed, the harder I looked, the less psi I found.

So was there no such thing? I had certainly become increasingly skeptical and even set about trying to find ways to test the skeptic's hypothesis, but I still didn't totally disbelieve. I was almost prepared to believe that psi simply did not appear in the laboratory experiments, but what about the "real world"? Surely psi was there, all around us. There were poltergeists and hauntings; there were spontaneous psychic experiences of all kinds. Above all, there were out-of-body experiences (OBEs). Admittedly my own had shown no signs of psi, but I had read innumerable books that proclaimed the psychic side of OBEs.

I had always shunned working in "the field." Experimental work was what I was trained for, what I liked, and what my theories always seemed to lead to, but now the challenge seemed to be "out there." The last hiding place of psi had to be in these experiences outside the lab. I was going to have to tackle them. It was appropriate that I had to write a book on OBEs. That was where I should start. Perhaps there I would at last find a clue to the nature of psi. I was glad to put that thread aside, with some hope and determination.

The other thread was far more knotted and tangled. It had started as part of the first but was rapidly taking on a life of its own. I struggled to sort out what the questions really were.

As I stared at the distant ceiling, I was suddenly back in Holland, the hospital quite forgotten. One glorious spring day Dick had taken me up to the north of Holland, through the land of dykes and re-claimed fields, flat and wet. With biting clarity I could relive that day: Dick and I were lying on a bank, our backs wet with dew, our feet nearly reaching the puddled field, the smell of squashed leaves around our faces. Across the water, horses rolled in the mud, and a farmer cycled by just above our heads. It was a magic day.

I even wrote a poem. It just flowed out of its own accord. It was as though I had not created it, as though I were just a vehicle for its expression. Wasn't that what mediums always said about their psychic pronouncements? Again I hit that connection—psi and these experiences. But might it be a false lead, a spurious similarity? Could it be that "psychic" visions and creative acts spring from the same source— human imagination? The notion of psi, it seemed, explained nothing.

So why were things sometimes so different, so clear? What was clear? Why did "I" feel different then? What had changed? I didn't seem able to answer any of these muddled questions. I couldn't even begin. However, I could at least start by listing some of the times I felt were like that.

Meditation was one. It can be clear and real, as though oneself is more alive than ever before. Being in love is just like that—clear and sparkly, and "real." Odd moments like that come for no reason sometimes, "out of the blue" things seem more immediate, colors more colorful and light brighter. Creative work, painting, or writing can spring from that special quality. Certain drugs can induce it too. Could such a list give me a clue? I didn't really even understand what it was I wanted to know—I only knew that it felt important.

The arrival of the dinner trolley broke into my thoughts—faggots or fish to choose between. The hospital food left much to be desired, but I was still ravenously hungry all the time. And this was my last meal before the chop.

It was a long time before I could get back to my thoughts and fix my eyes once more upon that helpful crack and that list of special experiences. Perhaps the simplest were the drug-induced ones. I tried to remember my long-ago experiences with LSD.

Back in Oxford, John and I once took a "tab of acid" first thing in the morning and spent the day walking through rough fields and along the riverside. Our progress was unbelievably slow. Everything was so very interesting. I had hardly finished looking at a particularly fascinating blade of grass, when a grasshopper grasped my attention, and I spent twenty minutes crawling after it through the meadow.

It was in this wonderfully enlarged state that we found ourselves beneath a tree that stood proudly beside our path. The scene was thoroughly English and picturesque. The small damp meadows around us were full of flowers, and the path meandered pleasingly into the distance, loosely following the river Cherwell. The bark of the great tree was riveting: a thousand different shades of brown and grey and blue and green; a thousand different lives lived beneath it. Then there were the roots of the tree, sinking thirstily into the ground. And then there was the ground. I leaned my back against the tree, feeling every knobble of the well-examined bark through my back and watched the ground. It was an expanse of trampled mud, long since squelched by cows before it dried; now hard and knobbly. There were pockets of deep shade, and pale, dried crumbly pieces. I watched it for ages in rapt fascination.

Then gradually a very old man came into view. He was following the same path and slowly, with the aid of a walking stick, approached "our" tree. I tried desperately to look "normal," wondering what on earth normal people did who were not tripping on LSD. I stood there trying to look purposeful and slightly cross.

The man approached. He leaned toward me and, in a crackled voice, called out, "Young lady, would you be so kind as to guide me across this mud? My eyes are weak and I cannot see the path in this light."

I froze for what seemed like hours. Was this real? Was I hallucinating? I knew this expanse of mud like the back of my hand. And now here was someone asking to be taken across it. But people didn't usually ask to be led across patches of mud, did they? I looked out across my space. The light was indeed tricky, dappled by the leaves of the great tree.

"Certainly," I replied, a hundred years later, "Take my arm." And I led him slowly and carefully across to the place where the path became clear, and the light distinct. He leaned heavily on my arm and thanked me profusely when we reached the other side. I stood and watched as he slowly made his way round a bend in the river bank, never looking back, concentrating on his task.

I ran back to my tree, rejoicing in my easy stride, the tears pouring down my face; a face which felt like rubber, as though the tears were touching someone else's skin.

"Was he real?" I whispered.

John was laughing and laughing. "I think so," he managed to say.

"But why should he need to go across our piece of mud? I don't understand. People don't usually ask to be helped across pieces of mud, do they?"

"Well, perhaps you dreamed him up," said John helpfully.

"But you saw him too, didn't you?"

"Well, I might have dreamed him up too, you know."

"Don't be silly, John! I mean seriously, how likely is it that just when you know a piece of mud really well, someone comes along and wants to go across?"

"About as likely as this piece of grass," said John, holding a well-chewed squishy blade up to the sun.

I felt like Carlos Castaneda, the sorceror's apprentice, asking stupid questions of his teacher (Castaneda 1968). I thought a lot about that old man. And he *was* real. I saw him some days later in the University Parks, still walking slowly and carefully and leaning on his stick.

The crack in the hospital ceiling reappeared, like a fade-in in a film. Why was it so hard to remember these altered states? I felt tired from the effort. And that was always another fascination for me. It is so very hard to remember. Psychologists call it state-specific memory. The drunkard may hide a bottle of something when thoroughly drunk and when sober forget all about it. Only when he is next inebriated can he find his hoard again. It is similar with other altered states, like dreams. You can wake up feeling as though you are deeply immersed in a complicated story, and in a second it is all gone. So what has changed?

Gradually a more definite question was forming itself in my mind. I was really asking, "What is altered in an altered state of consciousness?" I realized that the answer was very far from obvious. It did not help to say that "consciousness" was changed, when we had no clear theory of the nature of consciousness, or even any agreed-upon definition of the term. And "state of consciousness" was similarly ill-defined. No, there really was no obvious answer. Pehaps this was the question I should try to tackle.

Related to this is the idea of state-specific sciences. Charly Tart, whom I'd met in St. Louis at the P.A. Convention, had tackled the question of how one could investigate altered states from within. He concluded that the thinking and logic used in altered states can be quite different from normal logic and reasoning. One might therefore need quite different sciences to operate within altered states of consciousness. One could imagine scientists able to move into different states and communicate their findings to each other, but because of state-specific memory it might be impossible to remember accurately what had happened when back in the normal state. The communication would therefore also be specific to the altered states.

I had loved the idea ever since I first read Tart's paper (1972) years before. It took the altered states as something worthwhile in their own right, the altered logic as being valid in its own terms. I had shared Tart's hope that state-specific sciences were possible and might soon be with us. However, the more I thought about it, the less plausible it seemed. The years went by, and Tart published nothing new on the subject. There were no revolutionary papers written from within altered states. I was beginning to think that the whole idea was unworkable.

But the idea of state-specific memory stayed with me. I often wondered whether telepathy might be like trying to remember your childhood. When "I" now remember things that "I" did at age five, whose experience am I recalling? Could it be like recalling someone else's experiences? Like ESP? And there I was, back to the same old idea—psi and memory. These were among the ideas that had prompted my "memory theory of ESP," though I now suspected they were misguided. I had even once done a little experiment to see whether the age of people's earliest memory was related to their psi ability. But of course nothing was related to psi ability—or so I found. So where had it got me? At least I could answer that one easily enough—absolutely nowhere!

Both my threads of thought had got me nowhere. Psi seemed ever more elusive and less and less relevant to the most interesting questions about human nature. Nevertheless, I was still hopeful. I was going to study out-of-body experiences.

* * *

"Excuse me, Dr. Blackmore?" I looked up to see a kindly nurse beside my bed. "It's time to take you down to theater now," she said.

They heaved me onto a trolley and wheeled me along echoing corridors, of which I could see only the ceilings and the bottoms of signs with the names of the wards on them. Then they swung me round into a small preparation room full of tubes and bottles on high shelves. The anaesthetist loomed above me.

"They're waiting for you in theater now," he said. "I'm just going to put this needle in your arm. Then I want you to count to ten, though I don't suppose you'll get very far!" He laughed, not unkindly.

I had been looking forward to this. The day before I had suddenly realized I could do a little experiment. Lots of OBEs occurred when people were under anaesthetics or having operations. Perhaps I would have one! When Tom next came to visit me, I asked him to place a number, randomly selected and written very large, on my bed at home. If I had an OBE I would fly across the countryside, back to Pear Tree Cottage, and look at it. As the needle went in, I plucked up my courage and hoped!

"One, two——" I could feel myself disintegrating, disappearing, going under. "Thr—-"

I was back in the ward. Everything ached. My arm throbbed from the drip in my wrist, my neck hurt from a vast ziplike row of clips from one side to the other. I tried to swallow. No OBE. A general anaesthetic and no OBE.

The operation was successful and my neck remarkably quick to heal. The next morning at breakfast I helped myself to three sausages, a heap of scrambled eggs, five rashers of bacon, tomatoes, and a pile of toast and found I couldn't eat them all! I was obviously getting better already. I even felt more like my old self again—whoever that was. Within a week I was back home, my enforced rest over.

I had to get better quickly. A few days later I had an interview in Cambridge for the Perrott-Warrick Studentship. It was seven years since that first failed attempt—and how much I had learned in the meantime. Most important, I now knew that I would only stand a chance of getting the grant if I had somewhere to work.

One night Tom and I had been invited to dinner with Richard Gregory. Richard always had interesting parties. They might bring out furious arguments on the feasibility of artificial intelligence or turn into pun-telling sessions or competitive games with plastic toys, but they were never dull. During this one, I believe, I talked too much and too loudly and argued too vociferously—though about what I cannot recall. Nevertheless, I plucked up the courage to interrupt Richard's joke-telling.

"Richard, can I ask you a question?"

"Of course." Richard had an amazing capacity to switch in no time between any number of modes of thinking.

"I would like to apply for the Perrott-Warrick Studentship, but I need somewhere to work if I got it, and——"

He immediately began asking me sensible questions about how much money was involved and what sort of space and facilities I would need.

"I could share Tom's room," I explained, "so I wouldn't need to take up any space, but is it possible at all? What would I be? I mean I wouldn't have a job or anything, and I wouldn't really be a student. Can you just have people hanging around doing research?"

Richard grabbed my shoulders with his vast long arms. "For you, anything is possible!"

"No seriously, Richard, can I?"

"Seriously, Susan, yes." He held me out, like a doll, at arm's length. "We can make you a visiting research fellow or something like that. You apply!"

And so I had done. Now, feeling just about able to walk from the house to the car, Tom was going to drive me to Cambridge for the interview.

This time it was quite different. I took Tom to meet some of the friends I had made during that fateful week in Cambridge the year before. We stayed in a wonderful ancient room in Trinity College, where the feather mattress on the four-poster bed forced us together into one great hollow in its well-used middle. We had an improvised breakfast of toast cooked on an electric fire, with Bernard Carr and Julian Isaacs, who was visiting too. Then they all sent me off with encouraging advice and many good wishes.

This time the table full of electors didn't look so daunting. I knew Donald West quite well by now, and the others looked quite human. The bishop, John Robinson, whose reputation was great, came closest to terrifying me, but actually he was charming and kept saying that really he didn't know anything about psychical research!

In answer to their questions, I explained that I wanted to study out-of-body experiences and that I hoped to work at the Brain and Perception Laboratory. I said I had so far failed to find any psi in my experiments, but I now wanted to study it in "real life." I would be doing surveys and experiments to try to find out who had OBEs, under what circumstances, and whether there is any psychic component to them. I felt quite relaxed and chatted happily with them all.

It was only outside the door that I felt nervous. Suddenly it was all catching up with me: the illness, the tension, the fear for the future.

Here I was doing this stupid subject, having never found any psi, and still with this crazy ambition to become "a famous parapsychologist." My only hope for carrying on with my research was getting this grant, and I might well not get it. What would I do then? I would hate to give up research. I really didn't want to have to think about it. I fell gladly into the van and slept all the way home.

Nineteen

Back to My Own Experience

I went to the obvious place to recuperate: Salcombe, in Devon: the place which, far more than anywhere I have actually lived, feels like home.

Salcombe sits on the mouth of a convoluted estuary. Once a fishing village and now a small town, it is swarming with tourists during August but peaceful and delightful the rest of the year. There are sandy beaches, like the one where I first read Rosalind Heywood's *Sixth Sense* and pined over seventeen-year-old boys. There are wild, rugged cliffs, with paths along the rocky edge, and the ominous shapes of distant Dartmoor inland.

I had first been taken there at the age of six weeks. In those days we owned an old house high on the hill, where the wind never stopped blowing and terrifying molds grew on the walls of our children's room and turned into monsters when the grownups turned off the lights. The wash wouldn't stay on the lines without ten clothespins apiece, and the salt in the salt shaker would never come out of the holes. When I was twelve or thirteen I used to get up at six in the morning and walk on the cliffs until breakfast time.

My parents had now bought a different house, safely down in the town out of the ferocious winds but looking out toward my favorite cliffs. I took up my old habits again now and went walking on Bolt Head. There I longed to remember how I had felt at age twelve. Perhaps it was just a sign of my clinging to myself, but I was endlessly frustrated at not being able to remember—not being able to "be" that previous me anymore. I even felt I wasn't really anybody anymore. Those hormones had totally confused me. I was irascible and uncertain, afraid of being an unfamiliar person, and even my own reactions surprised me (and terrified and annoyed Tom). So it was good to be out in the wind and salt spray, walking myself back into shape, remembering myself.

Tom stayed a few days and then, having to get back to work, set off in the van one morning at six o'clock. I got up to say goodbye and leaned out of the wide windows overlooking the sea to watch him go. It was a misty morning. The sun was already high but barely visible up the shrouded estuary, glinting weakly on the hundreds of moored boats. Out to sea there were fog horns still sounding and fishing boats making their way back in, followed by hordes of screaming sea gulls. I couldn't go back to bed. By 6:15 I had started my book.

I arranged a little table in the Georgian bay window and laid out the few books I had brought with me. I put my typewriter in the middle, wound in the first sheet of paper, and began. The first bit was easy. I had to define the out-of-body experience. "An OBE can initially be defined as an experience in which a person seems to perceive the world from a location outside the physical body," I wrote. And then I thought a bit. Perhaps it wasn't so easy after all. "This sounds simple enough," I typed on, "until one gives it a second look. Do we normally seem to perceive the world from inside our body? Is this then an 'in-the-body experience'? If we imagine a distant scene, or dream of flying over far places, does that count? Perhaps that would not be 'the world' but some imagined world. But where is the line to be drawn between imagination and perception?"

No, this really wouldn't do. I was just asking a whole load of questions, and I couldn't think I was really going to answer them. I looked out at the blue water, its color now rapidly emerging from the mist. I decided to start somewhere more concrete. What about a good example of a typical OBE?

I began hunting through books. I hated this part of the job the most—looking for things. I liked the writing, not the searching. And I really couldn't find an example that demonstrated everything I wanted to show. I needed one that would have all the special characteristics that I had experienced all those years ago. But I couldn't find it.

Eventually, I put Chapter 1 aside and tried to begin somewhere simpler. I began on the history of the experience and its appearance in cultures across thousands of years and thousands of miles. I got out the classic books by people who had written about their experiences, and I wrote about those. I looked up cases of spontaneous OBEs and wrote about those. This wasn't so difficult, I began to think.

That night Tom rang. "I've got something to tell you," he said, in a totally expressionless voice. "When I arrived back at Pear Tree Cottage, there was a letter from Cambridge."

"Well," I almost shouted, did you open it? What did it say?" Tom was so good at concealing things!

"It's all right," he laughed, "you got it."

I had got the Perrott-Warrick Studentship! From October on I would no longer be in limbo. As the Perrott-Warrick Student, I would be doing research on OBEs at Bristol University. It was a tremendous relief. When he next came down to Salcombe, we had a huge seafood dinner to celebrate.

Soon I was back home again; regaining the strength to dig the garden, work on the still half-built garage, and deal with the problems of an old house. I worked with increasing enthusiasm. For a start, I read up on all the survey work on OBEs. OBEs are quite surprisingly common. Previous surveys showed that something like 20 percent of people questioned claim to have had an OBE at some time during their lives (Green 1968; Haraldsson 1985; Irwin 1980; Palmer 1979).

Most interesting is the fact that the people who claim OBEs don't seem to be obviously different or odd in any way. For example, they are not more often male or female, older or younger, more or less educated, especially religious or atheistic, or anything else. It rather seems as though it can happen to anyone. Perhaps I could find out more about this too. I was looking forward to starting more research.

I had already done one small survey; in Guildford I found that only 8 percent of my students claimed to have had OBEs. Indeed, I was hoping to present the results of this survey at the P.A. Conference later that summer in Iceland.

My figure was so much lower than that found in other people's surveys. I wondered whether perhaps I had got closer to an accurate figure because all my students knew quite a lot about OBEs. Possibly the respondents in other surveys had misunderstood the question. This was something I wanted to test immediately, and I began planning new surveys to carry out when I had my studentship.

It is funny how quickly things can change. Perhaps it was still the weakness and instability left over from my illness, although I couldn't tell. In any case, a few days later I got another letter, saying that a paper I had written on my Tarot experiments had been rejected by an American journal. Being a parapsychologist didn't seem so much fun after all. What on earth was the point of all this hard work if no one even wanted to hear about the results?

But I didn't want to stop. I realized that my fascination was because of my own OBE. It was this experience that formed the whole basis for my questioning. It had to be *this* experience which started my book. Only if I could contribute to understanding that experience could I call my research a success.

But writing about it was tricky. For a start, it had been at least partly drug-induced. If I didn't mention that, it might cause problems, not to mention that it would be dishonest. I would also sound very childish if I wrote about it. It would make me sound like a "weirdo." Was it the sort of thing real scientists would write about? In the end I decided that I just had to tell the truth and hope for the best. After all, it was exactly what I was trying to explain.

It was a useful task. I had to think hard about what I had experienced in those two or three hours back in 1970. Fortunately I had written a detailed account of it only a couple days after it had happened. I read and reread that account and tried to imagine myself back inside it. What had it really been like?

I cast my mind back to that evening, my first term at Oxford, sitting cross-legged on the floor of Vicki's college room, with Kevin asking me, "Where are you, Sue?" It is in any case a weird question. But why, on that occasion, did it propel me into that out-of-body state? Could I answer that question?

I fought with my memory again and remembered that after seeing my own body down below I began to travel around the room. It all seemed quite real and quite natural. I could see my body sitting on the floor, and "I" seemed to be another self up on the ceiling.

"Can you fly around?" asked Kevin's calming voice from down below.

"Yes, I can go anywhere I want," answered a second voice. The odd thing was that I could actually see my own mouth opening and closing down there on the floor. It seemed to be giving sensible replies but equally seemed to have nothing to do with me at all.

"But I'm joined to the body by a cord," I added.

It was true. There was a wonderful glowing grayish-white cord snaking down from my tummy "up here" into the head "down there." I wondered whether I could move it and began to reach out a hand to touch it. But before I had even begun to move the hand, the cord moved. I didn't need the intermediary hand. Just thinking about it made it move.

This led to an important discovery: that in this state anything was possible by thought alone. Even while it was happening I realized that this must be what the occultists called the "world of thought" or "astral world." Some even referred to it as the "world of illusion." I did reach out a hand, and then with a leap of pleasure, reached out two hands, and three, and half a dozen! I could have twenty hands, I could fly and float and change shape and move just as I liked.

"But can't you go anywhere else?" asked the matter-of-fact voice of Kevin.

I realized then that I need not stay in the room, and I set off, the cord flowing out wildly behind me, across roofs and streets and towns and cities and right across the channel to France. There I saw a star-shaped island with a hundred trees. And something inside me reckoned that this must be someone's idea of an island: a "thought form" on the astral plane, or just an idea of my own made manifest in this odd reality.

It was exactly as people had so often tried to describe it in books. And I suppose I shall fail, as they have before, to convey just how real it seemed. I can only say that when I became a flat brown pancake rippling and surging with the waves on the ocean, it felt real. It felt as real as any other experience ever felt—perhaps more so. I knew quite well that my body was sitting back in Oxford with my friends, that it was chattering away, telling them all about my adventures as fast as it could, but "I" was really here, on the surface of this cold, oily-black water.

On one of my two visits back to the room and to the sight of my own body (was it really mine?), I decided to try to get back in. I was getting tired and just beginning to fear that getting back to normal might be a little difficult. I looked in at the window. I could see the three of us sitting there. Vicki was looking rather annoyed. I felt sorry for her, having this chattering and unstoppable body keeping her awake at one in the morning, shouting with excitement, and waving its arms about. It was definitely time to get back in.

I moved easily into the room, but nothing seemed to make much sense. I struggled to make myself smaller and to fit into the body, but I overshot. Suddenly I was getting very small. Indeed I was so small that

I could crawl about inside the body and look out through the semi-translucent toenails, a wonderful experience which had me chuckling and giggling.

But, back to business, I had to get bigger, and again I overshot. This time I just began to grow and grow. And because it was pleasant I didn't try to stop it. I let myself get bigger and bigger, and bigger and bigger. I could feel myself in two parts, the warm soft airy part above, and the cooler, slightly unsettling sensation of sinking into the earth underneath. As I expanded, Vicki and Kevin became a part of my inside, and then the whole room, the town, the world and all. I just went on getting bigger and bigger. Even at the time I was grappling with my primitive ideas of physics and cosmology and wondering what on earth I would expect to find, I remembered the "visions" of the early Theosophists who had "seen" in graphic detail all the (since superceded) models of the inside of atoms and chemical bonds. I could laugh even then at my own cosmology. But how real it seemed!

Eventually I seemed to have expanded as far as it was possible to expand. It was as though "I" had filled up everything there was to fill. I had accelerated faster and faster until I could accelerate no more. Then it became impossible for me to have more hands or to change shape or to do anything, for all of me was expanding at the maximum speed. Time seemed no longer to have any meaning at all. Everything simply was.

Then out of that silence came Kevin's sensible voice, "Isn't there anything further, Sue? Is that all?"

No, it couldn't be all, I thought to myself, there had to be something further. And as I thought this, in the way of my thought-created world, another entire view opened up. There were great white flowing clouds, moving and shimmering, and between them (or at least that is as close as I can get to describing it) was a gap through which I ardently wanted to climb. However, the faster I tried to climb up the yielding clouds, the faster I slipped back down. Then, with an immense struggle, I glimpsed over the top. There, spread out all around was an endless plain. And gazing at me with some kind of amused acceptance was some vast being or some hundreds of vast beings. There was a deep sense of familiarity to all this. It felt like some kind of coming home, strange though it was.

I stammered to myself (and I suppose aloud as well): "Wherever you go, there is always something further." I hoped that repeating the words would save the experience from disappearing in my memory forever. With that, it was obviously time to come back, but I had no idea of what a struggle it would be and how long it would take. Some time later I was still repeating to myself, "I must go behind the eyes and look out through them. If I want to go anywhere I must take the body with me." It wasn't easy.

Now, nearly ten years later, it was hard not to feel that this was all childish, pseudo-occult nonsense. But if I were honest I had to admit that it seemed "real" and that it had a profound effect on me. I also knew that I was not alone. There were books full of accounts of similar experiences (Green 1968; Muldoon and Carrington 1951). Some people were frightened, some excited, some took it all for granted. But one thing was clear: These experiences had profound effects on people, happened surprisingly often, and could not be explained by any current scientific theorizing.

Superficially, the situation was much like that with ESP. "Real" psychologists either scoffed at the experiences or paid no attention. Parapsychologists were interested, but they had no adequate theory. This was what I had to show in the book.

The most popular "theory" was the doctrine of astral projection, that old favorite on mine. According to the Theosophists, man does not have one single body. The physical is just the lowest manifestation of our being. On higher levels are the etheric body, astral body, mental, causal, and spiritual bodies, all of which have increasingly subtle vibrations and fewer restrictions. The astral body is rather special because it is the "vehicle of consciousness." Under certain circumstances, it can leave the physical body and travel at a distance. This is what is known as "astral projection" (Blavatsky n.d.; Muldoon and Carrington 1929).

As I studied these ideas, I became more and more aware of their shortcomings. The most important problem was the nature of these other worlds. It was reminiscent of all the arguments over the mind-body relationship. If the astral world were, as some authors seemed to maintain, a kind of extension of the physical, then it would have to do some truly extraordinary things. Its eyes would have to see physical objects, and this would mean picking up light from them (or perhaps some other kind of energy). But this would necessarily entail interacting with the environment, so the process should be detectable. As one scientist put it, we should expect to see floating eyes, but we don't (Rushton 1976). Also the world of the OBE just isn't like the physical. It is fluid and thought-affected; it differs from the physical world in many details, like the red roofs I saw in my travels that turned out to have been gray when I checked the next day, or my layout of Oxford city which didn't correspond to the map. Clearly the astral world wasn't a true replica of the physical.

Alternatively, other authors implied that it was entirely thought-created, but this brought on even worse problems. If all the thoughts making up this world came from the same person then it would all be imaginary and there would be no sense in which anything traveled or any psychic events occurred. This would be quite possible, but it wouldn't in any sense be astral projection.

On the other hand, if it were a world made up of the combined thoughts of many people, then it had to be explained how the thoughts of one person could be correspondent to those of another. If I traveled in the astral, would I see mostly my own thoughts or equal amounts of everyone's? Were "stronger" or "clearer" thoughts any more effective? How, indeed, could any sense be made out of the idea of combining separate people's thoughts? It was back to all those old problems of the units of ideas and of similarity that had helped me to reject my memory theory of ESP. I felt that they were just as damning here. I could not make any real sense out of the notion of astral projection.

The alternatives were rather feeble. There were parapsychologists who argued that the OBE was "imagination plus ESP," but that got us nowhere. ESP, as I knew so well by now, is a nonexplanation, and "imagination" is just a word that can cover almost anything. So that "theory" was vacuous.

There were a few attempts at "psychological theories." The most important was John Palmer's theory, which viewed the OBE as one result of an attempt to reintegrate the body-and-self image when it has been threatened (Palmer 1978). This theory left the door open for psychic events to occur but did not actually explain how they could.

Finally, there was a kind of nontheory everybody liked to poke fun at, that the OBE is "just imagination." Evidence was always being put forward to prove that it could not be "just imagination." This began to irritate me more and more. It is saying absolutely nothing to say that something is "just imagination." And clearly the OBE was not "just imagination" in the sense that it feels quite unlike just imagining being out of the body. Imagination it certainly might be—but it was not to be dismissed without further explanation.

There are several other theories too, but they all converge on one important question, "Does anything leave the body in an OBE?" This had to be answered before I could get any further with theorizing. With this question in mind, I started to look into the evidence.

As the summer wore on, and the tangled garden fought back with its spreading bushes, rampant weeds, and finally those delicious home-grown vegetables, I ploughed through the journals, trying to find out just what the evidence was like.

Then one day in July, I was out in the sunshine earthing up the rows of potatoes, when the phone rang. Tom was under the van and couldn't easily drag himself out, so I quickly wiped my muddy hands on the grass and grabbed the receiver. It was Martin Johnson, from Utrecht. The P.A. Convention in Iceland was the following month. Martin was organizing a group to go from Europe together and needed to know whether I would join them. I asked him how long I had to decide. It was only a few days.

I walked slowly out to the van, sitting lopsidedly in our gravel and weed drive. I had to talk to Tom about it. We just didn't have the money, and I felt terribly guilty at the idea of going off, on our joint finances, to have a good time in Iceland without him. On the other hand, the P.A. was the only important conference of the year and was my one opportunity to present my work to other parapsychologists. Also to complicate everything more, Dick was going.

He had rung a few days before. He was taking a tent and said I could share it with him if I liked. I could imagine us camped in some romantic spot on the island of myths. In some ways I could think of nothing more wonderful, but in another way I did not want to give myself that opportunity. I felt even more guilty. I'd be going off to see Dick too. I said no to Dick's offer, but I still wanted to go to the conference.

Tom was, uncharacteristically, sullen. He told me to go if I really wanted to, but he had plenty of arguments why I shouldn't want to. First and foremost, and true enough, was that I was still quite ill. I thought I was well enough to go, but I was certainly not back to normal—if indeed there is such a thing. I was still overly emotional, weak, and, even to myself, unpredictable.

I went back to my rows of potatoes, hurling up the earth to prove how fit I was and struggling with the arguments. I had to decide. I had to tell Martin my decision. I really wanted to go to Iceland.

Twenty

Is There Psi in the OBE?

I am not very good at making decisions. I tried all the tricks I knew, like writing out a list of pros and cons. That had worked supremely well for really important decisions, like when I had given up the idea of doing medicine and turned to psychology instead. It had made things obvious when I decided not to marry John. Now it didn't work at all. "I want to go," just sat there against, "I'm not better yet, we haven't the money, Tom doesn't want me to go," and so on. I forced myself back to work and hoped the decision would make itself.

I was still working through the evidence on OBEs and finding some of it surprisingly fascinating. There were marvelous experiments done early this century in which mediums were hypnotized and their astral bodies sent off to view distant events, or to sniff bottles of scent, or to taste oranges or bitter aloes (Blackmore 1982a). It was claimed that all sensation left the body and went with the astral double. There were even photographs of the astral forms swaying in the ethereal winds.

The attempt to capture the soul had led to even more bizarre experiments. Patients dying gradually of tuberculosis were placed on special scales to weigh the spirit as it left. And then when cloud chambers were developed to detect small particles in physics, they were adapted to track the paths of the departing soul of the innocent mice, grasshoppers, and frogs that were used for the purpose. Fascinating these were, but not convincing. The experimental controls just weren't good enough (Blackmore 1982a).

More recently there were better-controlled studies looking for evidence of ESP during OBEs. For example, Charles Tart tested several people who claimed to be able to have OBEs at will. They slept in the laboratory and had to try to leave the body and look at a five-digit number on a shelf high above the bed. One subject, a Miss Z, actually succeeded. She got the number exactly right (Tart 1968).

But here again I found myself confronting a familiar problem. It just happened that this successful trial was one in which the number was in the same room as the subject, though on others it had been in a different room. Tart himself argued that Miss Z could not have climbed up to look because of all the wires and electrodes fixed to her head to record her brain waves. However, Adrian Parker, another parapsychologist interested in altered states, pointed out something interesting. If Miss Z had tried to climb up, the brain-wave record would have showed a pattern of interference. And that was exactly what it did show (Parker 1975). As so often in these cases, a repetition under better conditions would have clarified things, but Miss Z was unable to take part in any further experiments. The evidence was tantalizing and worth considering, but the closer I looked, the less compelling it seemed to be.

There were other experiments too (Blackmore 1982a), but no results as outstanding as Tart's. Some were "significant," but they were much like the results of other ESP experiments, just wavering above the magic "significance level." I feared it was a kind of prejudice, but all my experience made me believe it was quite feasible that these marginal results were due to overanalysis or very minor problems in experimental design. Certainly none was repeatable, and certainly none showed any kind of massive psychic effect of having OBEs.

In the attempt to detect the astral body, things looked much the same. Experiments used Geiger counters, infrared and ultraviolet detectors, thermometers and thermistors, detectors of magnetic field strength and flux, as well as cameras and weighing-scales—all to no avail.

Then the idea of using animals as detectors was tried. In a famous study, the experimenter Bob Morris gave his friend, Blue Harary, two kittens. Blue called them Spirit and Soul. The kittens were placed in an open field—a sort of terrifying-to-cats box with a checkerboard floor, bright lights, and smooth walls. Blue went to another room and, after appropriate preparation, "left" his body to come and console and calm them. The behavior of the kittens was monitored and compared for periods in which he was "out" and periods in which he was "in." As predicted, one of the kittens moved around less and cried less when Blue was astrally "there."

However, this only worked with one kitten on one occasion. Later experiments failed. It was argued that this might be because the kittens were getting older or more used to the apparatus. But this seemed reminiscent of all those arguments I had struggled through years before. There was always an excuse. And which ever way you looked at it, there were no repeatable results. As Morris and his coworkers concluded, if anything left the body it was not something that could be consistently detected (Morris et al. 1978).

I sat at my desk, day after day, trying to force all this work into some sort of shape. If I looked out of the window I was only distracted by the sight of so many weeds needing hoeing or rows of seedlings needing thinning, so I looked at the books, alphabetically arranged and overflowing their shelves, instead.

There was a serious problem. The whole issue was clouded by the very existence of the notion of ESP. On the one hand, if people having OBEs could see or affect things at a distance, this might be attributed to the all-powerful psi, and so the evidence would still not prove that something left the body. On the other hand, if they failed, the same old excuses (or reasons) were used to account for the failure. After all, psychic effects were fickle, elusive, and hard to pin down. Either way, no real progress was made in understanding the OBE.

This seemed more and more ridiculous. I tried to imagine what would happen in other sciences if psi were considered as an alternative hypothesis. No research would ever get off the ground. Anything at all can be attributed to psi if you try hard enough. But that is precisely how it is in parapsychology. The idea of psi is constantly getting in the way of testing any other ideas. I realized with a kind of dull anger that the psi hypothesis and all the excuses raised to protect it form a vast barrier to progress in the study of OBEs.

I imagined how it would be without it—forgetting about psi and all the arguments for weak and barely detectable effects. If we just looked dispassionately at the evidence and asked, "Does anything leave the body in an OBE?" then the answer looked clear. It was no.

But I couldn't forget about psi like that. The whole subject was embedded in it. And what about all those spontaneous cases and all that other evidence for psi in OBEs? Didn't they force me to consider it, as they had forced many others before me? Surely I couldn't ignore it all.

I sat there at my desk, trying yet again to clear a way through these arguments. The phone rang. Oh no, not another interruption. I couldn't bear it. And if it was someone calling to tell me about their wonderful psychic experience I would scream!

It was Martin Johnson. I hadn't yet decided whether I should go.

"Is that Sue?"

"Yes. Hello, Martin. I thought you weren't going to ring until Saturday."

"Ah, well, I have some news for you," he said. "I have just been speaking to George Zorab, and he wants to pay half your airfare."

"What? For me?" I asked, "But I've never even met him! Why should he want to pay for me?"

"I don't know exactly," I could almost hear Martin smiling, "but I told him all about you, and I think he wants to help young parapsychologists now while he's still with us. He's very old, you know." I knew that. He was a very well-known psychical researcher who had been publishing for more than fifty years on ESP, poltergeists, and survival after death. Brian Millar had told me how much he liked him.

"That's fantastic," I said. "What can I do to thank him?"

"Oh, he'll be going to Iceland too, so you can thank him yourself."

I ran out into the garden and round and round the lawn. I would go to Iceland. It was wonderful that things had a habit of sorting themselves out. People were wonderful.

I knew Tom wouldn't be as pleased as I was. This present from Zorab just served to show up to both of us the fact that it wasn't entirely the money that was the problem. Tom was worried about me, my wild ways, my illness, Dick, and a whole lot of things. But I decided to go. And I apologized very sincerely to Tom for worrying him so much.

The decision made, I got back to work on all that evidence for psi in spontaneous OBEs. But I didn't have all the books I needed. My own books and journals were mostly on the experimental work. I would have to go to London and use the SPR library.

Also, I was still worrying about Carl. I had written up my report on my visit to his lab back in January and had sent it to the SPR. I didn't like it sitting there, all alone, with no word of corresponding explanation from Carl. He had promised and promised to send in his version, but so far he had not. So, yet again, I rang him. He said he was going to London that week, and we could meet at the SPR at 10:30 on Thursday.

I got to the SPR early. There was Eleanor, ready with a cup of coffee, a great tin of biscuits, and all the latest news on the problems of the SPR. And there was the wonderful library, with every book you could possibly want on the psychic and paranormal. But I wanted to look in the archives first for the actual accounts of experiences that people sent in. I went into the little windowless back room full of rows of bulging files and looked up "astral projection."

"Sue," called Eleanor from the office, "It's Carl on the phone. He says he can't make it for 10:30. He's got tied up and has to have lunch with someone soon. Will 3:00 P.M. do?"

"Yes, that'll be fine," I called back.

There wasn't much under "astral projection." Oddly there wasn't much under "OBEs" either, nor under "traveling clairvoyance."

"Have I missed something, Eleanor?" I went to ask. "I can only find about thirty cases of OBEs in the archives!"

"Ho," laughed Eleanor, "I suppose you think the archives are crammed with interesting material. Everybody thinks that. They think we have so many good cases we don't know what to do with them. But it just isn't true, you know. You should see the stuff we get in the post. Most of it is real drivel. Only the best ones, which have been investigated to some extent, get into the archives, but you'll see what they're like. To tell you the truth," she lowered her voice, as though the spirits of past Council members might be listening, "most of those aren't much good either."

And she was right, as I was not the first to discover. In the SPR files there were a few good cases, but in that one day I went through them all quite carefully. There were no golden nuggets hiding here. The only reasonably documented ones were already in the literature.

Soon, Kevin, my old friend from Oxford, came by. That was a real treat as I hadn't seen him for years. I had yet another cup of tea with him and then suddenly realized it was nearly four o'clock. There was no sign of Carl anywhere. After another hour of rounding up a huge heap of books about OBEs, I had to say goodbye to Eleanor. I would obviously have to wait to hear Carl's version of the events at Cambridge. But I wanted to know very much where those errors had come from. Perhaps, I thought, I would see him in Iceland.

Back home again I was busy. I had to get ready for Iceland. I had to prepare the slides for my papers, and that meant a day in the darkroom at Bristol and getting Tom to help me with my incompetent photography. Then I had to practice what I was going to say and write the final version for inclusion in the conference proceedings. All this had to go hand-in-hand with research for my book. I couldn't let myself get behind. I took scheduled gardening breaks but otherwise just kept at it.

* * *

One Tuesday in mid-August I set off to London to catch the night boat-train. It was a long night: the train to Dover, customs with hordes of people from the train, the ferry to Belgium, and the long wait in Ostend station for the 6:00 A.M. train to Luxembourg—I wondered if I really were there.

I took the opportunity to look around Luxembourg. I loved the aloneness that exploring new cities can induce—at least for a while. I walked miles, diving into interesting-looking bars for cups of coffee and buying buns (always the cheapest way to eat) at a bakery. Finally I arrived at the tiny airport. There, already drinking and very jolly, were George Zorab, Brian Millar, Martin Johnson, and Dick. The conference had already started.

Iceland was fascinating. From the first moment I saw the dark gray volcanic ground with more sheep than blades of grass, I knew that Icelanders would have to be very different from anyone I had met before. With some difficulty we negotiated the journey to Reykjavik University, where we were met by Erlendur Haraldsson, the only Icelandic parapsychologist and most welcoming host of the conference.

They were busy sorting out the usual problems: the people who hadn't come, the ones who had come but hadn't paid. I heard Carl's name mentioned and hoped he was there already. But it seemed he hadn't come. They had all been expecting him earlier that day, but he had not arrived, and no one knew why.

I didn't have a room to stay in, nor did two or three others. Dick announced that he was off to pitch his tent, and Brian kindly offered me his floor, which I was happy to accept. It seemed to be settled, until Erlendur said that if we liked we could all sleep in his lab, a house just a few streets away. That sounded wonderful. And so it was that, after all my good intentions, I found myself rolling out my sleeping bag next to Dick Bierman's.

That first evening nothing much seemed to be happening, so we suggested a party in "our room," and thereafter it became a regular feature of the conference. But if you get the impression that this was just "fun" to be contrasted with the "real business" of the conference, that would be quite wrong. The real business of many a conference takes place in the early hours of the morning and anywhere other than the conference hall. In this case it was over the regular meals of boiled fish and potatoes, varied only by the color of the sauce; in the wonderful open-air swimming pools, where natural hot springs fed pools of every shape, size, and temperature; and at the late-night parties.

The following night, after a long day of paper after paper, dinner was followed by a statistics workshop. At 10:00 P.M., when the conference finally closed, most of us adjourned to go hear Stephen Braude play the piano. He was the pianist and philosopher whose striking arguments intimidated but fascinated me. We had met a few months earlier at a conference in Brighton. There I had presented my ideas on memory, and he had startled me by arguing that the very notion of a memory trace makes no sense (Braude 1979a). I had enjoyed our arguments and was glad to see him again. He was small, with a lithe-looking body, curved to the shape of the long-handled shoulder bag he wore over his faded jeans. His tightly curled, almost frizzy black hair had a hint of gray, and his eyes were deeply bright and alive. I had instantly liked him, and now got the impression that almost every other woman there did too.

The music was difficult, rather formless, but haunting. Stephen played with an intensity that reminded me of John, all those years ago, deeply engrossed in the music of his viola de gamba, in his college room at Oxford.

When he'd finished, Stephen leaned back and looked as though he were shaking something off. He looked tired, stilled, but somehow more relaxed. Evading the hordes of roaming parapsychologists, he grabbed Dick and me, who happened to be nearest.

"I'm angry," stated Stephen quite honestly. "All those people at the back just kept on talking and spoiled it for the people who wanted to listen."

I felt very bad. I had been, at least some of the time, one of the culprits. I muttered something apologetic.

"Oh, it doesn't matter," said Stephen. "Perhaps I should have spoken up at the time. It's just that I felt I was sharing my musical self with people and was treated as if I were sonic wallpaper." I laughed.

"Come on," he added, "Let's get out of here."

We walked down to the sea, only half a mile away, and into another world. The beach near Erlendur's lab was on a widely curving bay with scattered rocks stretching out for miles on either side. The air was still and cold. Even at this time of night, the sun was barely below the horizon, and everything was lit by a pale orange glow, except for the sea, which seemed to be a slick dull gray, and the deep black outlines of masts and rocks. We clambered out over slimy, weed-covered rocks, fewer and fewer among the pools of water, daring each other to go just a little bit farther, until we ran back to safety, with wet feet, gasping in the cold air and falling onto the cool dry sand.

It was much later that I finally got back to "our" room. I have to admit that by then I had mistakenly had far too much of some very excellent grass. Afterward I went walking alone in the twilit midnight streets. I was wonderfully high, wrapped in the familiar closeness of an old friend, buoyed up by the unfamiliar closeness of a new one. I was exhilarated by all that strenuous intellectual effort and the truly beautiful place.

Poised in this pleasure, I wandered the empty streets until eventually I felt like going "home" to sleep. I quietly opened the door and crept in.

Twenty-one

An Experience in Iceland

As I opened the door, the noise hit me. There in our room were a dozen or so parapsychologists sprawled about on the floor and arguing heatedly. Another group was milling around the door putting on their coats and saying goodbye to each other. Only my thwarted expectation of going to bed seemed real. This chaotic social scene, the sort of scene I would normally delight in, seemed uncontrollable and terrifying in my state of mind.

"Hello there, Sue," said Russell Targ, in his slow Californian manner. "We were just talking about the remote-viewing experiments. Did you hear that paper this morning?"

"Yes," I said, my face sticking in the shape of the word. It was all I could manage; and, though it was a sharp contrast to my usual, overly talkative self, I hoped they wouldn't notice. They chatted on, and I smiled and fought with myself to look "normal." Charly Tart was there too, just pulling on his jacket. How I wished I had had the composure to talk to him too. But most of all I wanted to sit down, to get away, and to stop the violent cavorting of my thoughts and fears.

Then Charly leaned gently toward me and spoke quietly. I would have to listen and try to reply sensibly. "Don't worry, Sue. You just have to learn to be on both levels at once."

I froze. He knew. He knew so much. He even knew what to do. I looked up at him, tall above me, and into his eyes. He was smiling kindly and knowingly, almost like the being of my astral plain. I gazed into his eyes with relief and gratitude.

"—or three layers, or more," he went on. I nodded dumbly. I watched as he muttered something noncommittal to the others and casually took off his coat again. I followed him slowly to a vacant patch of floor and he helped me to sit, quietly cross-legged, in front of him.

"Hands and feet," he said.

The effect was just so. I came down. And when he saw that it had worked, he told me other things, about heads and toes and fingers,

183

about balancing the head and navel, about grounding and about flying. And when I had learned those, he taught me about going into the light while staying on the floor.

He knew. I should have realized it before. Of course he knew. And with sudden clarity at last I understood that state-specific sciences were going on here, at the P.A. Convention, at three in the morning. Of course we couldn't write papers about it. It could only be taught and learned in the altered states themselves. It could only be transmitted by people who could achieve those states. For all my doubts about Tart's experimental results and the weakness of his OBE theory, I knew that his idea of state-specific sciences was alive and well.

I was thinking about OBEs too. Different people had the same experiences, but I was quite convinced that wasn't because they could leave their body. There had to be another reason, some cognitive reason. We had to understand the rules governing patterns of thought. Thoughts must be utterly dependent upon lower-level mechanisms, neural mechanisms, but to understand altered states we needed to work on a higher level of representation. I could clearly picture a science of altered states that could cope with what I was learning tonight, could cope with the astral worlds and flights beyond the body, and could relate them all to the way the mechanism of the brain makes some representations possible and others not. Reality is all constructed. That is the basis of cognitive psychology. In altered states, perhaps we just construct different "models of reality." At that higher level a science of altered states would be possible. And it wouldn't have anything paranormal about it either.

But it was all so hard to remember. As I had found so often before, I knew. Something inside me told me that this was right, this was important, but I knew I would forget it. I had also learned many times before, with drugs or in meditation, that there is no easy way to remember. If I struggled to code the ideas into words I destroyed them in the process. If I didn't, then I couldn't grasp them back when I thought about anything else. They were thoughts too far removed from normally structured ideas.

"Do you know about the unobservable event?" asked Charly Tart, breaking into my thoughts but totally in touch with them.

"The unobservable event?" I echoed, a beaming smile stretching my happy face once more.

"I'm sure you've observed it," he said. "It's when you can't remember that you've forgotten something."

My smile broke into a laugh, and my laugh into open-eyed wonder. A vast structure was collapsing into itself and merrily destroying and rebuilding itself. On every level I could think of, this simple sentence meant something quite different: and all of them linked up, from the problems of my memory theory of ESP, to the problems of living, being, choosing, and trying to remember difficult things. I disintegrated in a cascade of impossible ideas.

Charly Tart was gone. He was chatting easily to someone else a few paces away. He could slip from mode to mode with no trouble, being on both levels, or three or more, at once. I couldn't do that. But I could learn. I wanted to thank him for taking the trouble to teach me.

Eventually they were all gone, Stephen too, and I was alone with Dick. Time to clean our teeth and wriggle into our sleeping bags.

I lay there on the hard floor trying to rehearse all that I had learned, sad that I could remember so inadequately and joyful that I had learned so much. I was worried about Dick. I thought perhaps I couldn't cope with wanting him, on top of everything else.

I felt a soft hand run down my side. But it wasn't threatening. It felt like a part of me, caressing myself with familiarity. I lay quite still and smiled. With our sleeping bags between us, we slept our few brief hours tight together.

Then all too soon it was breakfast time, and Dick and I were making toast and talking about each other. It was obvious that we were repressing powerful desires, so what were we going to do about it? Like true parapsychologists, we began to wonder whether this energy couldn't be used to psychic effect. There have long been suggestions that the right motivation is needed for psi. Some theories suggest that psi operates by bringing about unconscious needs and desires. Some people argue that laboratory experiments rarely work because the motivation is lacking—and artificial motivations, like paying your subjects, just aren't a substitute for real-life needs and desires. Well here we had a real-life desire. Could we make it work for psi?

"We could," said Dick. "We take the data from an experiment, printed out of the computer. We choose the right moment to look at the results and then—if the results are significant—no more repressed desires!" He grasped my hand as I laughed. I wasn't sure whether I would like to take on this challenge.

But now we had to get going again. In spite of the lack of sleep, I had to keep alert. That day I was to be chairperson for the whole afternoon session, and for our own Roundtable. The idea of a Roundtable is to get several people together to speak briefly about some topic, less formally than in full papers. I had convened a group to talk about "Reliability and Other Ignored Issues in Parapsychology" (Blackmore, Bierman, and Johnson 1981). Brian sat next to me and was, if anything, even more tired than I was. He paid no attention to my little notes passed surreptitiously across the large table, saying, "Five minutes to go," "One minute left," and even "You MUST stop!" Eventually I kicked him on the ankle. Dick was also there, speaking on negative reliability, and Martin Johnson tackled selective reporting and fraud.

I was nervous. I hadn't had a good night's sleep for days and had been talking, arguing, and thinking nonstop. My mind seemed to be working in fifteen different directions at once. But I wanted to be a good chairperson, and I wanted to give a good paper.

"There are several important issues which seem to have been ignored in parapsychology," I began.

In "normal" psychology, when some measure is taken, like scores on a test, it is usual to check for reliability. For example, you can split the data in half and check that the two halves are correlated, or you can test the same people again some time later and correlate the scores. If there is a close correlation, then the score is reliable. It is a general rule of thumb that the validity of any measure cannot be higher than its reliability. In other words, if your measure is unreliable, you cannot be said to be measuring anything.

I went on to explain how this affects parapsychology. ESP scores are notoriously unreliable. Indeed my own ESP-memory experiments gave correlations close to zero. So if ESP scores were not reliable, could they be valid? Were they measuring anything? Dick Bierman said they were; indeed, his whole argument was that even negative reliability could be seen as a result of psi operating at a different level from the one examined, for example, at the level of the checker, rather than the subject. But, to claim we were measuring anything, we would still have to find reliability somewhere, and so far no one had done so.

"Could we be simply measuring nothing?" I asked, speaking from well-rehearsed memory, in spite of my tiredness. "If we persist in defining parapsychology as the study of psi, define psi negatively, and have no reliable or valid measure of it, what is the future for our subject? We are committing ourselves to an ever-diminishing subject area. Long ago, hypnosis and multiple personality were lost to parapsychology. Today we still study out-of-body experiences, death-bed experiences, apparitions and divination, but if these should turn out to be 'normal,' they too will be lost to parapsychology. I think parapsychology would be much poorer without them."

I sat down, on time, shaking and breathing unevenly, my palms drenched in sweat. As the applause subsided (Had they clapped a lot? Was it all right? Did I sound silly?), I remembered I had to get up again, to invite questions from the floor.

There were lots of questions. I tried to notice everyone and to remember all their names, as well as to answer the questions addressed to me. And all the time my thoughts were hurtling along. I hadn't quite realized how very skeptical was my position. By having to condense my ideas into just ten minutes, I had laid them bare. I was really saying that we might all be measuring nothing at all, and it was time to watch out, or we'd be a subject left with no subject matter.

I also remembered, with a very strange leap of pleasure and anticlimax, that I had always wanted to be a "famous parapsychologist." I may not be very famous, but I was certainly a parapsychologist: up here, chairing the session at the 1980 Parapsychological Association Convention. And what was I doing? I was doubting everything, and criticizing people who had done far more work than I had. Could I really justify it? In the midst of it all I laughed at my own presumption.

I was glad to get out into the clear Icelandic air and to walk the tea break away to calm down. Usually I was keen to talk to as many people as possible, to make as many meaningful points as possible—in short to impress people—but now I was glad to get away, if only briefly. Soon it would be time to change for the celebration dinner.

It wasn't boiled fish! We had the Icelandic specialty of smoked mutton, and it was delicious. We even had some sort of pudding, but there was no coffee to go with Brian Inglis's after-dinner speech.

Brian Inglis, a historian, member of the SPR, and well-known British proponent of the paranormal, held quite contrary views to mine but was persuasive in putting them over. "Power Corrupts: Skepticism Corrodes" was his provocative title (Inglis 1981). He amused us all with some lovely neologisms like the wasting disease of "protocolitis," which causes parapsychologists to become wedded to their protocol and dictated to by the pressures of rampant "skepticaemia." The worst kind of skeptics, he told us, are those who profess an open mind. He would rather have good honest rejection of psi than the pretense of objectivity characteristic of most members of the Committee for the Scientific Investigation of Claims of the Paranormal (CSICOP).

If he expected a good laugh here, this gibe did not achieve it. CSICOP (naturally referred to as the Psi Cops), is a group consisting largely of scientists and stage magicians, who investigate claims of psi as well as such things as astrology, fire-walking, and dowsing. The outcome was generally "debunking," and there were rumors that certain members of the organization were more biased against the evidence for psi than any believers could be for it. However, its journal, the *Skeptical Inquirer,* contains many interesting analyses of psychic claims, and many of its members have produced thoroughly constructive criticisms (Hyman 1985; Kurtz 1985; Marks and Kammann 1980). Inglis may have had the impression that CSICOP and the parapsychologists are sworn enemies, but in fact each is extremely wary of offending the other. After all, each is dependent upon the other. Parapsychology needs to be taken seriously by CSICOP, and CSICOP would not even exist without those claims of the paranormal.

Nevertheless, I was left wondering. Why did it always come down to this: pro or con, for or against, belief or disbelief? Did it have to be a *pretense* of an open mind? Wasn't there such a thing as a really open mind? As we made our way back to the university, I wondered just how open my own mind was.

Before we left Iceland, we had time for a tourist excursion. A dozen parapsychologists in a minibus drove across desolate gray fields of lava to a village full of greenhouses heated by natural hot water. We climbed to a wonderful waterfall and visited the famous geysers. Some of us danced around the water spouts, trying to alter their regular eruptions by the powers of PK, and pushed each other into the tepid muddy waters all around. William Roll apparently got lost, and John Beloff was sent off to find him. Then at the "continental divide" we stood on opposite sides of the chasm and wondered about the trans-Atlantic effect. Would psi work better over on the Western side?

When we stopped for lunch, most of the others went into a little restaurant, but Dick and I had brought sandwiches, and we sat outside on the grass instead, with a view of the bluish volcanic mountains.

It proved to be a fortuitous choice. Suddenly we felt a very strange rumbling in the ground. It got louder and louder and then Dick was shouting and pointing, and we leapt to our feet. A vast column of smoke was pouring up into the sky with a power I had never imagined was possible. While everyone else was eating their boiled fish, Mount Hekla was erupting!

Before I went back to England, I stopped off again in Holland to finish off the work that my illness had so rudely interrupted. There Dick and I could try our special experiment on the powers of motivation. Without looking at them, Dick took the data from an experiment we had been doing and sealed them up in an envelope. We were only to look when we thought the time was right.

That time came one evening at Jerry Solfvin's house in Utrecht. We were very relaxed, very happy, and very excited about the possible outcome. Dick held up the envelope. It almost felt as though we might use retroactive PK to force that computer to produce a significant result. If the p-value was less than .05 then——I took the envelope from him and slowly opened it. Even then I didn't want to look straight away. Finally, I pulled out the paper and stared at it.

"What is it?" they all cried at once. "Is it less than .05?"

I looked nervously at the final significance level.

"Oh no, I can't believe it," I groaned. "It's just over .05!"

We laughed and laughed. It would be, wouldn't it—it just barely missed significance, just teasing us. And then everyone began to wonder, looking for ways to account for the result. Dick reminded me that I had always said that I didn't want to get involved with him, and now I had managed to avoid it. He also reminded me about my illness. Could that also have been a way of avoiding the entanglement? Stupid, I thought! It's just chance—it's just another nonsignificant result. But I suppose, if the truth be known, I was quite relieved!

Twenty-two

From OBEs to Poltergeists

Back at home again I had to tell Tom everything, to relate all these experiences to my ordinary life at home, and to begin on that pile of books about OBEs. I was about to start exploring the last place I thought psi might be hiding, in the spontaneous experience.

I had explored the experimental work quite thoroughly, but I had done very few spontaneous case investigations myself, and I was quite prepared to believe that other people's were more convincing. Several years before, I had received a fascinating letter from Karlis Osis. It was about the time I met Tom, and both of us tackled it together.

I knew of Karlis Osis from his experiments on vision in OBEs (Osis 1978), though I had not then met him. He was research officer at the American Society for Psychical Research, and I was thrilled to hear from him. He enclosed a long, long account of an extraordinary OBE of a Canadian architect. This man had apparently left his body and traveled across the Atlantic to London. He saw a winding cobbled street, busy with people shopping and lined with three-story houses set back behind railings. He had particularly noted the lie of the River Thames and could find on a map the exact place where he had landed, in Fulham in West London.

He wrote that he had asked an English colleague to describe that area to him and said that he had "proceeded to describe the character of the street, the buildings, the style, the building setbacks and entrance yards—all exactly as I had seen them!"

"Come on then," urged Tom. "We can easily go up to Fulham and have a look. I'll take my camera and we can photograph all the details."

We got on a train to London and then on the Underground to Fulham Broadway, clutching a detailed map and hunting down the right street.

We found it easily enough, but what a disappointment! The houses were absolutely nothing like those of the architect's vision. We searched and searched, walked most of the streets of Fulham, and found nothing like it. We pored over maps of London to find any other streets that might lie in similar bends of the river, but when we tried those we met with no more success.

"Didn't he say something about going back in time?" asked Tom. "Perhaps there were once such houses here, but they have been knocked down. We could try the library."

The local librarian was very helpful and provided us with maps and histories. But it was all quite clear. Fulham had only been built with the extension of the railways from central London, and before that there were only green fields there. Whatever the Canadian architect had seen in his OBE, it was not the actual streets of Fulham, either now or in the past. I sent my report and photographs to Karlis Osis, feeling that at least I had done my best.

This case was clearly not veridical, but perhaps others might be. After all, the books were full of them. I recalled from long ago that there were several classic cases of OBEs that appeared in numerous books. One concerned a woman who had apparently carried a toy dog from one room to another while her body was asleep in bed. Another concerned a man who was on a ship crossing the Atlantic when his wife's out-of-body form visited him. Not only did he and a friend see her, but she was able to describe everything about the ship and her husband's cabin. Or so the stories went.

I found both these psychic stories with no trouble. The first was the Landau case, reported in the *SPR Journal* (Landau, 1963). I got the original article and read it with fascination. It was extraordinary really—to see how much fuss could be made of such an unconvincing story. Lucien Landau and his wife (or rather, future wife), tried an experiment in which she was to "leave" her body and carry his diary from her room to his. During the night he awoke to see a shadowy figure in his room. So he got out of bed and followed it, whereupon it led into her room and disappeared. There he saw her body lying asleep in bed. Going back to his room he found her toy dog on the floor. Had her astral form carried it there?

I was certainly not convinced. There was no independent corroboration of any kind. They had left the doors open between their rooms to make it easier, and there was no witness to the fact that the dog had been in her room in the first place, or indeed to any other details of the case. We have only their brief accounts to go on. I don't mean to say that this case is absolutely worthless. If it were one of lots of cases, backed by properly corroborated ones, it might be an interesting (if weak) addition to the literature, but it was cited in book after book as evidence that sometimes people can move things when out of the body. I began to wonder.

The Wilmot case proved much more interesting but not much more evidential. The story was given in Frederic Myers's wonderful book *Human Personality and Its Survival of Bodily Death* (1903). That was taken from an earlier version in the *SPR Proceedings,* and I had fondly imagined that there would be many more details there, but when I checked, I found that the version in Myers's book was the entire story.

We are given the account by Mr. Wilmot, who had been sailing on a ship from Liverpool to New York in 1863 when he saw (and his cabinmate also saw) a female apparition, which he thought was his wife. He says that when he arrived at New York, "Almost her first question when we were alone together was, 'Did you receive a visit from me a week ago Tuesday?' " Apparently she had seemed to go out and seek her husband on the very night of the apparition.

I immediately set about checking details of the ship. I wrote to Lloyds Shipping Register and looked up newspapers from the 1860s. This ship did indeed exist and sailed on that date, but I suddenly realized that there was little point in these time-consuming researches. I don't know why I hadn't noticed the most important fact before—but both sides of the story are told by Mr. Wilmot.

Mrs. Wilmot endorses her husband's version but gives only a short account of her own, in which she briefly mentions what she calls her "dream." There is no description of leaving the body or traveling across the sea to the ship. Even more important, she did not record the "dream" at the time; and, although she says that she might have told her mother about it the next morning, there is no statement from the mother. Thus there is no independent corroboration that the two events occurred on the same night—let alone at the same time. And it wasn't even certain that she had an OBE at all.

Was I missing something? This was a case which had, according to Hornell Hart (1967) been quoted at least five times by 1967. I thought that perhaps this case was so often quoted because it was especially interesting. There might be less dramatic but more evidential cases elsewhere. I wondered which cases were generally considered to be the best evidence. Fortunately Hart had done the useful job of listing cases of ESP projection and giving them all "Evidentiality ratings" (Hart 1954). I searched avidly for the case to which he gave top marks.

It turned out to be the Danvers case, a fascinating little experiment carried out by Frederic Myers, in 1894, with two women, one of whom claimed to be able to visit the other "out of body" (Myers 1903). Myers had a sound idea of experimental design, and in this case he asked Miss Danvers to record her intention to visit her friend beforehand and send it on a postcard to him. He would then know when, and how often, she had tried the experiment, before he received any confirmation that it worked.

In the event, she did write the card, but she sent it on to Myers together with the confirmatory note from her friend. Myers's good intentions had been thwarted, and the simplest experimental control broken, yet this was the case with the highest evidentiality rating!

I hadn't got very far into all this material before a familiar pattern seemed to be leaping out at me. The more carefully I looked, the less evidential the cases seemed to be. My own experience with the Canadian architect's case now seemed to be quite typical, rather than a disappointing exception. Could it be that there simply was no evidence for psi in the OBE?

Perhaps the OBE had nothing whatever to do with the paranormal. I thought again about my own OBE all those years before. It was stunning and important and realistic, but it too fit the pattern. There was nothing paranormal about it. It provided no evidence for psi. Was my book going to be thoroughly skeptical? It certainly looked that way. The more I found out about any topic, the less paranormal it seemed to be.

However, I still wasn't going to conclude that there was no psi anywhere. There were many areas I still had not explored and about which I had to keep an open mind. Perhaps psi was to be found in apparitions, poltergeists, ghosts, or hauntings.

I had never investigated such things before. On the rare occasions when I had been asked to do so, the cases had always disappeared into nothing after the most preliminary investigation. But now the opportunity arose, just when I needed it.

* * *

It began one day at the lab, when I was busy with some tedious data analysis. I got a phone call from someone called Ian, who told me that he ran a local UFO group and that he had been investigating a rather strange case. A family in North Bristol, he told me, had all seen strange lights in the sky above their house. The local UFO group had interviewed them all and kept in touch over a period of weeks, but now they felt they were getting out of their depth. Things in the house had started to move about!

"Would you like to take over from us?" asked Ian.

I wasn't sure I could handle this sort of thing either, but I felt someone ought to help the family, and so, with mixed feelings, I agreed.

The next evening I met Ian, and he took me to visit them. We drove through the boring suburbs of North Bristol, into a perfectly ordinary Council-house estate, and up to the gate of a typical semi-detached house. A woman of about thirty-five opened the door, and Ian introduced me to Helen.*

"Do come in," she said. "Shall I make us all some coffee?"

We sat in their pleasant living room on a large flowery sofa and heard the whole story. Helen had started by seeing the lights through the window at night. At first she was the only one to see them, but later the rest of the family, her husband, Dave, and their three daughters had all seen them too. More recently the lights had stopped and other things had started happening. First the television had mysteriously changed channels on its own. They had no remote switch, I quickly ascertained, and the repairman had assured them several times that there was nothing wrong with the set. Then the clock on the mantelpiece had jumped without anyone touching it. They had heard footsteps upstairs and even the sound of someone pulling paper off the toilet-roll holder, although when they went to check, it was always just as it had been before.

"Do you know what it could be?" Helen and Dave wanted to know. "We really want to understand what is happening. Do you think you could help us?"

I could only tell them that it was typical of a poltergeist and that I

---

*Helen and Dave are not their real names.

would very much like to learn more about it.

"The best thing you could do to help me," I said, "is to keep a diary of all the events that happen. Then we can begin to find out what's going on."

I said this for two reasons. First, I had tried to investigate several previous occurrences but found that when I asked people to do the simplest task, like keeping a record, they failed to do so. If they couldn't do that, then I felt I was unlikely to be able to help them or to get to the bottom of things. Second, I knew that the whole family was worried by the events. I felt that keeping a diary would be a good way to settle things down and alleviate their fears. They would feel that something was being done about it.

I gave Helen a notebook and said I would come back in a few days to talk to the three girls.

"Would you mind if I brought my husband?" I added. I knew that Tom would find this fascinating.

Much to my surprise, when we came back the following week, they had kept the diary beautifully. There, carefully recorded in it, were many misdemeanors by the television, several jumps of the clock, several strange noises upstairs, and two other incidents involving electrical apparatus apparently turning on or off without anyone touching it. Alongside each incident was recorded who had been in the room at the time, and where everyone else was.

"This is wonderful, Helen," I said. "Now we really have something to work on."

"Could I start with the television?" asked Tom. "Would you mind if I had a look at it?"

To their amusement Tom started squeaking and whistling and making all sorts of odd noises until he found out how to change channels. They had no remote switch, but the television was obviously fitted with a receiver. He was soon surrounded by three girls, aged about eight to twelve, all squeaking and whistling too.

"Is the dog around?" asked Tom.

"I'll fetch him," called one of the girls, and a moment later the golden Labrador came wagging his tail into the living room.

"Can I take his collar off?" asked Tom (irrelevantly I thought!). One of the girls took it off and gave it to Tom, who waggled it gaily in front of the television. The channel immediately changed. Was it really that simple?

Apparently it was, but that did not explain the other events, especially the clock that jumped along the mantelpiece. I asked Helen whether I might mark the position of the clock and then we could determine whether it had actually moved or not, that is assuming that no one pushed it. She was quite happy with that, and in fact marked it herself many times. It was quite clear that the clock did actually move. Little streaks of ink could be seen smeared along a few millimeters of the tiles. But why was it moving?

"You'll have to get it looked at by a clock mender," said Tom, very sensibly. So I asked Helen whether I might replace the old blue clock with a different one and see whether that moved too.

"Of course," said Helen, always helpful. "I've got another clock upstairs. We can use that instead."

I took the blue clock home and placed it in pride of place on my desk. There it continued to jump and make strange noises. Meanwhile, Helen replaced the blue clock with a brown one and left it there for a week. And sure enough, they said it had made strange pinging noises, and even moved a little, though not as much as its predecessor. This was getting interesting. Could it possibly be paranormal?

I found a technician at the University who liked mending clocks and watches in his spare time, and I entrusted the blue clock to him. Then I tried to think of other ways of finding out what was going on. My first idea was to use a "minilab." At that time there was a lot of controversy surrounding the use of the minilab (Phillips and McBeath 1983). It is a simple idea. You take an inverted fish tank, fix it firmly onto a solid base, and fill it with items such as pieces of metal, pencil and paper (for ambitious spirits who want to write something), and small objects to be moved. The whole apparatus can then be photographed, and it can easily be determined whether anything has been moved.

I had two purposes in mind. First, I wanted to see whether anything would move; second, I wanted to see whether anyone in the family was hoaxing. I thought that if someone were, he or she would be very tempted to create some artificial "phenomena" in the minilab. I had to build one that was easy to get into but in which I could detect tampering if anyone did so.

"I'd like to bring a small box," I told them all. "It will be like an upside-down fish tank with things in it, and perhaps we can leave it here, near the clock, and see whether anything happens inside it."

"That'll be fine," said Helen.

"Oooh, is it for Mr. Polty?" shouted the youngest of the girls. "We're going to have a Polty Box!"

So off I went to build a polty box.

Twenty-three

More Non-Paranormal Experiences

Now, as always, I had managed to take on too much. Soon after I returned from Iceland, a new term started, and I threw myself into it with far more enthusiasm than strength. I planned a hundred things I wanted to do, and then more, like the poltergeist, always seemed to plan themselves. I vaguely wondered how on earth I would manage if we had children as well, but that, so far, was in the future.

It was now the start of my tenure of the Perrott-Warrick Studentship, and for the first time for years I actually had somewhere to work, apart from my study at home. I was to share Tom's room at the Brain and Perception Lab. Being part of the Medical School, this was a thin long clinical room, with more sinks and taps than I could ever imagine anyone using. It was twice as tall as need be, and Tom, so frustrated at the waste of space, had actually built himself an upstairs half, which you could barely stand in but which could hold plenty of apparatus and books, and even an easy chair. Underneath this idiosyncratic structure, between computers, oscilloscopes, and sinks, I cleared a modest patch of shiny black desk and installed myself.

It was there that I built my Polty Box and began on a series of OBE surveys, which proved far harder work than I had ever imagined. I was still fascinated by that difference between the 8 percent of my students who claimed OBEs, and the 20 percent or more found in other people's surveys. Was it just because my students knew a lot about OBEs?

I decided to repeat the survey with students at Bristol who had not had weeks and weeks of parapsychology lectures. One of the psychology lecturers very kindly "lent" me a large group of his students for half an hour, and I tried it out, giving them all a questionnaire that asked about OBEs, dreams, and various psychic experiences. I was rather encouraged when about 10 percent claimed to have had an OBE (Blackmore 1982b).

This kind of survey is very easy. Indeed all you have to do is to design the questionnaire (which can be tricky, but gets easier with practice, [Blackmore 1985a]) then type it up, duplicate it, and give it to the subjects. I took a short computing course and learned how to use the statistics packages on the big university computer.

However, there are drawbacks. The subjects weren't randomly selected. They were a rather special group of people; they were all the same age and interested in psychology. This group might have quite different experiences from "ordinary" people, and I wanted to know about the OBEs of everyone. Secondly, it still didn't answer my question about my own students. Did knowing more about OBEs make any difference to the answers?

To find these things out I needed to do much more difficult kinds of survey. I started on two.

The first I did with a great deal of help from Dick Bierman. He had told me that every year, at the University of Amsterdam, there is a "test week" in which the students are given hundreds of tests and that anyone can submit things for them to do. This sounded like a wonderful opportunity. I therefore designed a special questionnaire.

There were to be two groups of a hundred students each. One group read a detailed description of several OBEs with definitions and discussion. The other group read about dreams and other more familiar altered states. Then both answered the same questions about OBEs and other states. I wanted to find out whether the extra information would affect the number of students who claimed to have had OBEs.

I sent off the questionnaires to Dick, and he did all the hard work of translating them into Dutch, duplicating them, and giving them to the students.

The results were rather satisfying. Exactly 17 percent of each group claimed to have had an OBE. In other words, it made no difference whether they had read about the OBE or not (Blackmore 1982c).

This was one of the first times since I had started parapsychology that I had actually found something meaningful. I realized the contrast between this and looking for ESP. If you asked people about their experiences, all sorts of consistencies appeared, but if you looked for ESP everything seemed inconsistent and unrepeatable. It was a contrast that became clearer and clearer as my work with OBEs progressed.

The other survey was a mammoth job, something I regretted starting only when it was too late to turn back.

One of the main problems with surveys is getting a random sample of people to question. All my previous surveys had used students; they are readily available and don't complain too much. But if you want to generalize your results to the rest of the population, you need to take a random sample, and that isn't easy.

There are many ways of doing it. The way I chose was to get the Electoral Register, a list of each official resident over eighteen years old, for Bristol and take every five hundredth name on the list (Blackmore 1984a). This would ensure that I had people of all ages, religions, occupational groups, levels of education, and so on. I was very lucky in that the SPR offered me a grant to cover the expenses of this survey, which were not inconsiderable. I knew that making up the lists of names would be hard work, so I paid a student to help with that for a few weeks. Then there was the postage. It is no good sending out a questionnaire just once. Lots of people throw it away or forget about it. So it is usual to send it out three times or even more.

I decided I could afford to send out six hundred questionnaires, allowing for only 40 to 50 percent response on each occasion. I spent ages deciding on the questions. This was my one chance to survey a random sample, so it had to be done right.

First, I wanted to explore the possible differences between the people who claim to have OBEs and those who do not. I surmised that OBEs might be related to certain other experiences. In particular, there is the lucid dream, in which you know *at the time* that it is a dream (Gackenbach and LaBerge 1986). It often feels more "real" than ordinary dreams and also feels somewhat like an OBE. So, this went into the survey. As well, OBEs are often claimed to affect people's beliefs about life after death; so, although I would not be able to infer any causal relationship, I wanted to ask about belief in survival after death.

When I went down to the printing office, they told me it would take two weeks to print the questionnaires, but I had heard that the post office was raising the price of a second-class stamp in a month's time. So I had to get it all finished before then, or it would throw out all my calculations of the total cost. Just as I thought it was ready, a friend, who no doubt had my best interests in mind, told me about the Ethical Committee. Apparently I was supposed to clear the survey through their procedures before I could go ahead.

This was an unexpected nightmare. I rushed along to see the man in charge, and he told me I could have a form (about five pages long and full of idiotic questions about whether I would be giving my experimental subjects any dangerous drugs or not) and that my application could be considered in three weeks time—bang went 20 pounds worth of postage straight away.

Thank goodness for the poltergeist. It was a welcome break from the horrible survey, and now I visited Helen and the children every week. They had kept up the diary, and strange things were happening regularly—never when I was there, of course—but they were all recorded in the notebook: the kettle turning itself on, a lampshade swinging about with no wind or anyone touching it, strange bangings and thumps. And now we also had the "polty box" to look at.

Tom and I, feeling rather silly, had gone out one morning to the local pet shop and bought a fish tank. Tom made a solid wooden base for it. We had to decide how to fix it so that we could tell whether anyone had tried to tamper with it, and Tom suggested that we could do it photographically. So we fixed black cloth to the base and the underside of the tank edges and sandwiched a sheet of photographic paper in between. If anyone opened it, the paper would be exposed.

Fumbling about in the darkroom, we put inside some paper clips, strips of metal, a pencil and paper, some light objects hanging from the "ceiling" on fine thread, and some sand at the bottom. We fitted the whole thing together in the dark; and, very carefully, we drove it over to Helen and Dave's.

"Can we see the polty box?" cried the eight-year-old.

"Here it is," I said. "I'm going to put it on this shelf here, and I hope that the poltergeist might do something with it. But you must be sure not to touch it! If you like you can try to make things move inside it by just looking at it. But don't touch it, whatever you do!"

"I'll make sure she doesn't," offered one of the older girls. Then while they all began peering into it, I set up my camera to take photographs. If anything moved, we would have a definite record of it.

Just then we all heard the key in the front door.

"That'll be Dave home," said Helen. "I expect he's just popped upstairs to wash his hands," she added. But he didn't appear, and we forgot all about it.

It was only when I got back to the lab that Helen rang in a panic.

"Did *you* hear the key in the door and the door opening, Sue?"

she asked anxiously.

"I think so," I said, but now that I thought about it, I couldn't be sure. It was one of those minor events you barely notice. Had I heard it? Or had I only remembered her response to what she thought she had heard? In any case, it hadn't been Dave. He arrived home ten minutes later, and this was yet another event to go in the diary.

A few days later I went back again. I was looking forward to learning whether anything had happened inside the "polty box." It hadn't. Nothing had moved.

"We did try," said the oldest of the three girls. "I sat for hours looking at it, but nothing would move."

"I once thought it had," put in her sister. "When I was watching telly one day after school, I thought I saw that paper clip twizzle round, but when I looked more carefully I don't think it had moved at all. It's most frustrating," she added with a grin.

Most important to me was that obviously no one had touched it. There seemed to be no signs of the "naughty little girl" syndrome here. These three girls were the same age as so many poltergeist children, but unlike many previous ones they didn't seem to be up to any pranks. I had also tried other ways of catching out pranks. I had suggested to them that poltergeists might roll things on the floor. There was no basis for this, but I thought they might pick up on it and start things rolling! But they didn't. This at least reassured me, but I seemed to be getting nowhere. The family appeared to be a lot happier and more relaxed since I had been "investigating." Their father, especially, seemed to accept the events much more calmly than at first. But what had I learned? I had discovered little or nothing about what was going on. I was looking forward to finding out about the clock.

Meanwhile, the survey was getting even worse. The Ethical Committee had at last invited me to meet them, and I walked down the hill to some anonymous office to be given the verdict by the guardians of experimental ethics. There were four of them, mostly of medical background, and their answer was basically "no." They said I couldn't send the questionnaire out more than once; it was an infringement of privacy. I couldn't ask anything about religion; it might upset people. I couldn't ask any questions about death; it might lead to physical and psychological aggression. I was too surprised to argue very coherently. It was only as I walked back up the hill to the Medical School that I began to be angry. They clearly knew nothing whatever of survey techniques—that it was standard to send out repeated questionnaires, that the questions had been carefully designed and based on previous surveys. And anyway, what about all those horrible experiments on rats and cats and pigeons and frogs? I don't suppose those led to physical and psychological aggression! I steamed quietly. I would have to change a few of the questions.

On my way back up the hill I stopped off at the workshops. There was the part-time clock repairer, and he'd got the clock ready waiting for me.

"I don't know why on earth you gave me such a horrible clock," he said. "It's cheap and nasty and obviously hasn't been cleaned for years!"

"But have you found out why it should have been jumping and moving?" I asked impatiently.

"I don't know why you want to know," he grumbled. So I had to explain all about the poltergeist. He was horrified.

"A poltergeist!" he said, straightening himself up to his full height in his dull brown overalls. "We don't admit of such things in our house. A good Christian wouldn't countenance such a thing!"

I was beginning to wish I'd never mentioned it.

"Well, maybe it isn't a poltergeist," I said. "Can't you tell me why the clock should have jumped and moved?"

"Of course I can!" At last he was in his element. "Look at this spring here. There is one like that in your clock, but it was filthy dirty. It can't ever have been cleaned I should think. Now look. When I wind it up, the coils of the spring all stick together, with the dirt and grease. Now watch. As it unwinds slowly, the coils suddenly let go and *pop!* the force of the spring can move the clock along. It's such a cheap, light thing. That's why it jumps. You ought to have had it cleaned years ago. It won't jump again," he added with obvious satisfaction.

I didn't protest that it wasn't my clock. I was just grateful for the information and began to thank him.

"And don't you go meddling with the Devil's work!" he advised me as I left.

I took the clock back to Helen's a few days later. I really didn't know what to say to them all and tried to think of encouraging ways to explain it. At first they didn't ask, so I said nothing. But my enthusiasm was stunted. I pored over the diaries, so carefully written out by Helen and the children. They had really tried to make sense of it all. I was convinced they weren't making it up. But the more closely I looked, the more obvious it was that the moving clock had been the center of it all. I would have to tell them next time I went there. And I wasn't looking forward to that.

Apart from the poltergeist, the book (always nagging at the back of my mind), and the surveys, I had taken on too many other tasks. The SPR was in the throes of acrimonious reorganization; and, while I was glad not to be involved, one outcome was that the Council, or ruling body of the Society, decided that we needed an informal newsletter. They asked me to be the editor. Not really knowing how much work it would be, I agreed.

Then somehow or another I got involved in working for the local hospice. My research on OBEs was naturally related to research on death and dying, and that is why I went to a lecture at the hospice, where a dozen terminally ill patients were gently nursed until they died. But what they needed was not research psychologists but hands to do the cooking and carrying of food and fetching of things for the patients. So I volunteered.

Then that Cambridge business was still worrying me. I had not heard from Carl for ages and seemed no closer to understanding the source of those errors. Yet people kept asking me about what had happened.

More fun were some of the jobs at home. Tom and I had been working on our garage for well over a year, and it still wasn't finished. Some days I would be out there for two hours or more and at the end of it find I had laid only about a dozen concrete blocks. I wasn't cut out to be a builder, and my respect for bricklayers grew stronger. However, we decided that we really had to get the roof on before the worst of winter. We decided on a long weekend to be devoted to the task.

A fellow researcher at the Brain and Perception Lab, John Harris, had once worked as a builder and offered his invaluable help. He taught us how to fix the wall plate, saw the roof timbers, make up the trusses, and fix them to the ridge. In two days we had the entire structure up, and in another had put on felt, battens, and lovely old tiles to match the house. I enjoyed the last bit best, sitting astride the new roof, cementing in the ridge tiles from one end to the other, while Tom mixed the cement and passed the bucket up and down the ladders. It was a great day when we finally drove the old yellow van into its new home.

But this was a temporary break from the dreadful survey. The questionnaire was finally printed, and then I found myself sitting, hour after hour, peeling computer labels off a long roll and sticking them on envelope after envelope. And another week after that I went to our local village post office to buy 50 pounds worth of stamps and stuck them onto envelope after envelope. I was so sick of envelopes that I wished I'd never started. But perhaps the results would justify all that effort. Only a few days after I had sent out the first batch of questionnaires, I began to realize yet more problems. Only about 40 percent replied within the first ten days, and so the second batch had to be a large one, and so did the third. I was back to sticking labels on envelopes again.

Then came the analysis. For each of the 400 or so people who finally replied, I had to type about 40 numbers into the computer, and then I struggled and struggled to master the analyses needed for such large quantities of data.

In the end the results weren't at all exciting. They were good sound stuff; I had done it properly, used a random sample, and could generalize my results reasonably safely to the city of Bristol at large, or even a little further, but I hadn't discovered anything earth-shattering! Thirty-nine people (or 12 percent) claimed to have had OBEs, and most of them answered many more questions about their experiences (Blackmore 1984b).

I suppose the only thing which I still find of interest is the fact that of all these thirty-nine OBErs, only eleven claimed they had seen anything by ESP during their OBEs. And of these, only four bothered to check whether they were correct or not. Obviously I wasn't able to investigate them further, but even if there were a few such claims the implication seemed to be that the typical OBE does not include any paranormal content. Popular books make a great fuss of it, but for most of the OBErs it wasn't important at all.

I now realized that I had long assumed I would have trouble accounting for the paranormal aspect of OBEs. But maybe it wasn't there at all! Not only is the evidence for ESP in OBEs very weak, but the people who have the experiences don't even claim that it is an important feature. There is really no good reason for associating OBEs with the paranormal in the first place—other than that both seem inexplicable.

But there *are* OBEs, and whatever they are they need explaining. There may or may not be ESP.

I thought again of my poltergeist. That too had "existed," in the sense that the family had had some strange experiences and had needed help in sorting them out. But all I had been able to do was to tell them of all the "normal" explanations and help them to work together on it. It seemed that there was nothing paranormal involved at all. They had just created their "Mr. Polty" out of a series of odd events. The television and the clock had started behaving inexplicably, and they had attributed that to Mr. Polty. Then every time they heard an odd noise in the house, or even some perfectly normal sound, they added that to their mental list of what Mr. Polty had done. He had become quite an active fellow without even existing.

Eventually I did tell them all about the clock. They weren't particularly surprised. It was almost as though they had expected it in a way. I got the impression that, in any case, Mr. Polty had outlived his original use—whatever that may have been—and that they were happy to let him "die" in peace. I kept in touch, but it soon became clear that everyone wanted to forget all about Mr. Polty.

Twenty-four

Regression to Past Lives

"Would you like to come to the European Conference on Visual Perception next week?" asked Tom one day.

I hadn't really thought about going, but I felt I could do with a break from my book, and I also wanted to meet "Ding."

Eric Dingwall was (and is) a legend. At my first SPR Annual General Meeting in 1978, I sat quietly in the half-empty hall, while Dingwall, aged and deaf, leapt up and down from his seat in the front row, waving his hearing aid and shouting objections. The chairman, Arthur Ellison, made out that the old man was imbecilic or totally deaf, but it was quite clear that he was neither. His objections were very much to the point and the only interesting part of the meeting. And most impressive of all, he had apparently been causing a similar rumpus at SPR meetings since 1928 or even before.

I also knew of Dingwall from his books on hypnotic phenomena and psychics, his bitterly skeptical writing on psychical research, and—best-known of all—his investigations of Borley Rectory, which was, according to some, the most haunted house in England. But according to Dingwall, it was a perfectly horrible house imbued with a nasty story to suit the inhabitants' greedy ends (Dingwall 1971; Dingwall, Goldney, and Hall 1956).

Since that first impression, I had been corresponding with Dr. Dingwall, and he had invited me to visit any time I could. Here at last was an opportunity, since Tom's conference was very close to where he lived. But it nearly failed altogether. We didn't have time to write and ask if we could visit. We didn't ring him because he couldn't hear the telephone bell; we hadn't yet learned that he sits by the phone from 6:00 to 6:30 every evening in case it rings. So we went there instead.

He lived in St. Leonards-on-Sea, a rather dreary seaside resort with dull blocks of flats along a monotonous beach. We found the great white block where he lived, found the right door, and only then realized that he couldn't hear the doorbell either. He might well be sitting there, all on his own, with us outside totally unable to contact him. I was more sad than annoyed.

However, Tom and I decided to have a quiet half hour on the sunny beach and to drop by again before we went back to the conference. By some stroke of luck, Dingwall, an ancient, decrepit old man with wisps of white hair and a red-veined face, wearing a patched and torn suit, was out in the corridor, disputing with a bewildered neighbor over some detail of the running of the flats.

He was instantly welcoming. He escorted us into his home and immediately regaled us with the most fascinating stories I have ever heard. As he led us through the entrance hall, its walls lined from floor to ceiling with hundreds of books, I longed to ask him about them. I had heard rumors that he had the finest collection of eighteenth-century pornography in the world and that he had written the authoritative text on the chastity belt! His livingroom was also book-filled but seemed strangely not to suit him. I had heard that he and his wife used to own a country mansion, where they had entertained guests in great style, but this was just a modern flat, without any special redeeming features apart from the books.

"She wouldn't have liked it," he said, following my eyes, I suppose, and embarrassing me. "She died, you know. Boxing Day it was. I haven't been able to face Christmas since." I made a mental note to remember this in my next Christmas card to him. "Life's not worth living without her, you know." He looked steadily at Tom. "I expect you know?" Tom nodded his assent, and I couldn't help smiling. This wonderful old man made me feel very young and innocent.

"I hope it doesn't happen to you," he added. "Every night when I go to bed, I hope I won't wake up again. And then every morning I do wake up and I think, 'Oh, no, not another day, spare me another day.'"

I suddenly realized that he hadn't heard a word we had said, not that we had said much. Now the old man sat down carefully in a vast armchair, plugged a hearing aid carefully into his ear, attached it to a microphone on the wide leather arm, and sighed. "That's better, I can hear you now. Sit down, sit down. What do you want to know? I'll tell you what, you can ask me anything you like!"

I took this as a great honor but couldn't for the life of me think of anything I wanted to know. I felt so idiotic, as though I was failing some peculiar test of initiative. But I need not have worried, for he supplied the questions himself, and the answers were wild and strange.

He told us of the books he'd written, starting with one on the deformation of babies' heads, through some unmentionable topic (goodness knows what it could have been, given the ones he did mention), and on to the psychic ones. He began to talk of the people he had known, decades before we were born.

"I knew Crawford, you know," he said. "I suppose you've read his books?" I had indeed. W. J. Crawford had weighed and photographed "psychic structures" emanating from the body of a rather attractive young medium called Kathleen Goligher (Crawford 1921).

"Do you believe in Crawford's results, Dr. Dingwall?" I asked cautiously. "Are there really such things as columns of ectoplasm and psychic rods?" It was extraordinary to be able to ask someone who had actually been involved in psychical research all that time ago.

He gave me a penetrating look. "Before he died—committed suicide, you know," he added, rather conspiratorially, "he said, 'Ding, I have to tell you something. It was all faked, all of it.' " Before I had time to ask him more he was pointing to other books.

"I used to know Aleister Crowley, too."

"You mean *the* Aleister Crowley?" I asked. "The great magician?"

He nodded. "A most remarkable man," he added gravely. "But you must be hungry. Let me just go into the kitchen for a moment and fetch some tea."

"May I help, Dr. Dingwall?"

He turned almost angrily to me, "No, you may not, and please call me Ding." It was an order, not an invitation.

We sat speechless, until he returned with a trolley piled high with bread, rolls, meat, cheese, cakes, and biscuits. Then as we ate, he talked of his exploits during the war when his skills were needed to counter the occultism depended upon by Hitler and of the way he posed as a Finnish mechanic to gain access to the Paris underworld.

"Though I say it myself," he admitted, "the criminal fraternity in England always tell me 'Ding's all right.'"

When our meal was nearly finished he went off to the kitchen again and returned with some ice cream, and as we ate he told us about the case of "Miss B," whose bedroom had walls and ceilings of the finest tooled leather, whose four-poster bed was entirely made of suede, and who wore skin-tight leather from neck to toe.

We could have listened forever, sitting there eating our meal, served with such effort and such kindness by a man whose age (though never divulged) must have been over ninety, who could barely hear and barely see and who seemed far more intelligent than either of us.

It was six years later that he finally died, and during all that time he responded to any letter of mine with intelligent answers and warm advice. When I heard the news, I could only feel glad for him that his last wish was eventually fulfilled, but I couldn't help wondering whether he was happily reunited with his wife or simply existing no more. I had once asked him about his hopes for survival, and he was typically direct. "No one could have tried harder," he said. "If communication with the dead were possible, she would have communicated with me by now—but there's been nothing, not a thing. So I shall just have to wait and see—or not see."

Back in Bristol again, I was starting on yet another task. Months before, I had committed myself to two weekly evening classes on parapsychology. I had expected them to be quite easy, given the years I had taught parapsychology at Surrey. So I now drove the ten miles to the first class, in the beautiful Georgian city of Bath, quite relaxed and confident.

In the appointed schoolroom I found about twenty-five men and women all chattering away as though they had known each other for years. There were only one or two younger than myself and a great preponderance of women. I told them I would spend the first week on a kind of overview of the subject, with some definitions and examples.

"Who would like to define telepathy?" I asked to get them going.

"It's seeing the future," ventured one.

"It's mind-to-mind communication," called another.

"Is it conversing with the spirits?" asked a third.

I wrote down all the answers on the blackboard, and we went through them, discussing what they meant by *mind* and whether they could define *communication.* I thought it went quite well.

At the end I had to collect the money and make a list of the class members.

"I—I—I—I don't want to come any more," said one young man, looking positively terrified; he ran off before I could ask him why.

"I thought we were going to have a proper *group,* not just *classes,* " protested a smart elderly lady who would not have looked out of place in a spiritualist development circle and possibly was hoping this was one.

Then a loud voice struck over the chatter, "I think I speak for us all," it was a portly and serious-looking middle-aged man in the back, "when I say that we don't need all these childish definitions. I have been doing hypnotic regressions for ten years. I know what happens. I've come here for some explanations."

I muttered some sort of reply and left the class feeling hopelessly inadequate, wondering what all the rest of them thought and how much of my planned course I could still use. These classes were obviously going to be harder work than I'd anticipated.

The following week I decided on the topic of "survival." That would be sure to get them interested, even if they already knew all about it.

I began nervously this time, "How many of you expect that something will survive the death of the physical body?" Almost every hand went up. "And how many of you believe that death is the end, and you will just cease being when your body dies?" One timid hand went slowly up, and a few of the others looked surprised and even disdainful at this one outcast.

I went on, "Right. I'd like to ask a simple question and see whether we can get toward an answer this evening. That is, *what* might survive?"

We threw questions back and forth, and eventually I had listed on the blackboard *personality, consciousness, memories, awareness, spirit, soul, astral body, ka,* and *self.*

I launched into familiar arguments against the possibility of the survival of any of these making sense, one by one. I had barely started on personality, discussing its dependence on behavior and bodily actions and its inseparability from a living person, when the "regression" man from last week stood up again.

"I think I speak for us all," he thumped his desk rather startlingly this time, "when I say—forget the rest and get onto spirit!" He smiled self-confidently.

I stood there for a moment, terribly glad I was not a full-time teacher. I looked quickly around, but the blank looks on the faces of the others gave me no aid. "We can consider spirit next if you like," I began tentatively.

Suddenly the others perked up. "No, stick to the list," shouted one young woman.

"Don't listen to him," said another.

"Sit down," said several at once, turning round in their seats to face him.

I must have breathed an audible sigh of gratitude! "Right," I said, confidence at last rushing back, "we'll carry on with the list. We'll get to spirit in a minute."

After the class was over, we all went to the Bunch of Grapes, a lovely old pub in a Georgian square, with heavy brown tables in little alcoves, and mugs of real ale pulled from traditional hand-pumps. It was the first of many such evenings spent discussing the weird and wonderful, and the "regression man," as I always thought of him, turned out to be quite fun.

Those classes also provided all kinds of opportunities I had never expected. The "regression man" even came and did some demonstrations for us, hypnotizing one of his star pupils before our eyes and "taking her back" to a time before she was born.

* * *

This "hypnotic regression to past lives" was something I had a special interest in, and I wanted my students to share in it. There had been many popular books and several television programs about this "new discovery" (Iverson 1977; Wilson 1981). It was claimed that, under hypnosis, many people could be taken back in time to reexperience their birth and even to remember a time before they were born. Remarkable evidence of the veridicality of what they saw was offered time and again. Tom and I had even been lucky enough to get involved in one of these television programs. The producer rang me and asked whether we would like to attend a weekend of experiments on hypnotic regression with the hypnotist Joe Keeton (Moss and Keeton 1979).

We were loathe to give up a weekend's work in the garden, especially in the middle of summer, but eventually we decided to go. And what a weekend it was!

There were about twenty of us in an imposing room at the BBC in Bristol. The large windows were kept firmly shut, and the temperature and stuffiness gradually crept upward as the day went on. Our hypnotist was a short, stout man with a squarish beard, a small straggly moustache, and large square glasses. He slouched horribly in a great armchair and seemed quite used to the stuffy, darkened atmosphere.

He began by hypnotizing everyone, one by one, with a simple procedure—getting us to fix our gaze on the glass chandelier while he convinced us we were falling asleep and going up in an elevator. I found myself happily acquiescing and drifting into a fascinating state in which part of me seemed quite aware of what was happening, while the other responded to all his suggestions about floating, sitting on a beach, or whatever it was.

"When I say, 'It's getting dark outside,' you will go back into this state again," said the soothing voice. "You will only do this if I say the words and if there are other people with you." And he brought me gradually out of it.

As he happily chatted to me again, and the others started talking, he looked toward the windows, "It must be late. It's getting dark outside."

I stopped and thought a minute. Something rang a bell. Oh yes. I laughed out loud, "Oh dear," I exclaimed, "I was supposed to go back into that state, wasn't I?"

He looked despairingly at me. And I was furious with myself. I knew that only those who had "done well" in today's session would have a chance to be regressed on Sunday. All that evening I drilled myself. I walked around telling myself, "It's getting dark outside," and imagining I was going back into that hypnotic state. I did so want to be a good subject.

On Sunday morning, we were all back there again, with the curtains drawn to blot out the cheerful sunshine.

"There are bluebells in the garden, the lake is too full, it's getting dark outside, the clock is running late," said the hypnotist very quickly. And I was gone with the others. I didn't have time to think about it consciously, let alone to pretend. At the sound of those words my head just slumped forward. Before I had time to realize what was happening, I felt utterly relaxed. And so I was regressed after all, but it was Tom, not I, who was the star of the show.

He was hypnotized and told to go back to his childhood, back through his own birth and into a kind of void. Then back still further, until suddenly Tom was struggling to say something.

"Where are you?" asked the hypnotist. "Tell us what you can see."

In a thick, deep, and sexy accent, the prostrate Tom replied, "I am in Vienna." I pricked up my ears. I was so glad that the hypnotist had encouraged us to tape-record everything. This was going to be interesting.

With prompting and encouragement Tom, or whoever he now was, explained that he was the son of a Polish tax collector who had been sent to tour Europe for his education. It was some time during the nineteenth-century, and the coins he used had the head of Franz Joseph upon them.

"You're going back further now," said the hypnotist, in his soft and persuasive voice. "You are going back ten years, ten years back."

Tom wriggled in his chair and sighed. *"Nazywam sie Armin i mam dziesieć lat. Mieszkam w wiosce ze szkola i kościolem. Najchetniej bawie sie w sadzie owocowym."*

"He must be speaking Polish," hissed someone.

"Can anyone understand him?" asked someone else. Apparently no one could.

"But will *he* be able to understand anything now?" whispered another excitedly.

"Do you understand English?" asked the hypnotist, looking somewhat worried. There was no reply. He looked even more worried. "I want you to go forward again, to the time when you learned English." No reply. "You are twenty years old now, twenty years old. Do you understand me?" Still came no reply.

Eventually though, the thickly accented English began again, and Tom was induced to sing Polish songs, which he did in the same deep-throated voice.

Quite a few of the audience, apparently including the hypnotist, seemed to think it was wonderful. His wife even took a photograph with a flash, and when asked why he jumped Tom said he had seen a flash of lightning in the cobbled streets of Vienna. They talked about checking up on the songs and the Polish. This was apparently a very good regression and one to be investigated further. It was only very much later that anyone thought to ask Tom whether he normally speaks Polish and where he learned those songs. The answer, of course, was that he is Polish and learned the songs as a child.

When the curtains were finally opened and the last of the day's sunshine allowed in, we rushed off for a much-needed drink in the bar.

Tom's own account of his experience was fascinating. He said that throughout he had known what was going on, but he was also totally engrossed in the tax-collector's son. When the flash went off, part of him knew it was a camera. Indeed he even identified it, from the sound it made, as a Kodak Instant Picture Camera. Yet he also saw it as a flash of lightning and found himself saying as much. Perhaps most fascinating were the songs. He said it was most frustrating to find that he still couldn't remember that same one line he had always forgotten since he learned the song many many years before. The regression had not only drawn on ordinary memories, but it had even failed to elicit any partly forgotten ones.

Our evening-class regressions were quite tame by comparison, but the general effect was the same; people were able, with very little encouragement, to concoct little stories and live them out under the hypnotist's care. It had a lot to tell us about psychology, but nothing, as far as I could see, about the paranormal.

It was all great fun. We learned a lot and explored a lot of strange things. But underlying the fun was a creeping depression. Something was changing in my whole attitude toward the subject. I thought back over my years of research. Long ago I had concluded that there might be no psi in any of the laboratory experiments, but then I had still assumed it might be hiding elsewhere. I had still been thoroughly hopeful. Then I had explored quite a lot of that "elsewhere" and still found nothing. I had read accounts of spontaneous psychic experiences and found nothing remotely convincing. I had investigated a poltergeist case, ventured into hypnotic regression, tested dowsers, and talked to countless psychics. And in all of this I had found no hint of any evidence for psi. Indeed the deeper I looked into anything, the less paranormal it appeared to be.

I think the most depressing part about it was that I realized all too clearly the problem I faced. People would say, "Oh, but you've only investigated one poltergeist case. That one wasn't a *genuine* poltergeist at all." And I had no answer to that. I couldn't investigate every claim of the paranormal that there ever was. I couldn't prove that psi didn't exist.

It was back to that same old problem again: how to weigh the results of my own failures against everyone else's successes; how to deal with failing to find the possibly nonexistent. If parapsychology had just one repeatable demonstration of psi, I thought, then all would be well. Or even if it had a better definition of psi. But it didn't. It had never had, and it looked as though it might never have in the future. Then we would be stuck forever with this horrible problem.

I also realized something else, and that was even more depressing. Deep down in my heart I knew what I believed. I had had too many negative results, too many hypotheses disconfirmed, too many beliefs knocked down by the lack of evidence. My own arguments told me I ought to come to no firm conclusion, that I should have an open mind, but I didn't. I honestly believed there was no psi! And now, everything new seemed only to confirm that view. I must even admit that I now felt relieved when something turned out to have a perfectly normal explanation. I longed to be able to explain everything away. What a horrible thing to have to admit—I really wasn't open-minded about the possibility of psi any more! For the first time I began to be truly depressed about parapsychology. I just didn't know what to do with my new-found skepticism. I could see why so many people before me had just given up in disgust and left the field.

Twenty-five
_____

The Power of Belief

I wonder how often I have thought of giving up parapsychology and then found myself carrying on? I don't even know what it is that always drives me back to it. I only know that time and time again I have thought of doing something else and then found myself haunted by parapsychology again. This time I could blame necessity rather than desire. I had to finish my book, I had to write up my surveys, and I had to carry on with my classes.

I started the new term with far less enthusiasm than the previous one. Indeed, I drove off to Bath feeling rather despondent and wishing I had not committed myself to yet another ten weeks. There were the familiar faces, all eager to learn about ESP. And what was I going to do? Try a few tricks with them!

I had just read a fascinating book by two psychologists (Marks and Kammann 1980, 4). Its preface immediately gripped me: "ESP is just around the next corner," they wrote. "When you get there, it is just around the next corner. Having now turned over one hundred of these corners, we decided to call it quits and report our findings." They proceeded to explain a few tricks of various magicians, expose some methods used by Uri Geller, and criticize the claims of some parapsychologists. I wasn't convinced they had really turned a hundred corners, but I was fascinated by those very, very simple magic tricks. Could people really be so easily convinced of ESP? I decided to try for myself two tricks reportedly used by an American magician, Kreskin.

At the end of my class I told them all: "I know you think I don't believe in ESP, but the funny thing is that I have quite a knack for *transmitting* messages to other people." (I didn't really expect them to fall for this, but I had to say something.) "I thought we'd try it today before we finish." I went on, "Now I'm going to think of two simple geometrical figures, one inside the other. I'll just think very carefully about them, as clearly as I can, and I want you to see if you can pick them up and draw them yourself. Right, I'm thinking," I paced slowly up and down in front of the class for a few moments, holding my hands to my head.

"Right, I'll draw it on the board." I drew a circle (there were gasps of anticipation) and then inside it a triangle. "Who got it right?"

Everyone was putting up their hands to say they had it, or telling me they had a circle inside a triangle, or that they had thought of that first but changed their minds. Only one or two of them had nothing like it at all.

"Very good," I said. "You see, perhaps you'll convince me there is ESP after all! Now shall we try something a bit different? This time I'll think of a number. Let's see—I'll make it between one and fifty, but I don't want to make it too difficult so I'll give you a few clues." (I paused for a moment.) "Both digits are odd, but not the same—so, for example, it could be fifteen, but not eleven because both are the same. Got it?" They nodded, and I began my thinking and pacing again, concentrating hard on the number 37.

"Right. What numbers have you all thought of?" I wrote their numbers on the blackboard. Nearly half of them had written 37, and those with 35 and 39 thought they were pretty close, and those with 17 thought it wasn't far off. They were all trying to tell me about their "experiences." One told me how clearly the image had popped into her mind, another how it had stood out from the other ideas she had had, another said it just flashed upon him as though it came directly from my mind, and a fourth had felt a strange tingling sensation just as he "got" the number.

It was already nine o'clock and time to go, and they were all packing up their things and chatting. As we walked down to the pub I realized what I had done. I hadn't the heart to call them all back and explain. I hadn't thought I would need to. I hadn't really expected it to work, but then they had all leapt to the conclusion that it was ESP with such speed and such enthusiasm that I hadn't even dared to enlighten them. How pathetic I was! And how easy it was to bow to the social pressure of determined belief!

For those who came to the pub I did explain. Those geometric figures are simply the most commonly chosen ones. Even if I had been thinking about a dodecahedron inside a square, they would mostly have drawn triangles and circles. In fact, I wished I had been thinking about a dodecahedron inside a square, so as to counter their suspicions that it could still have been ESP. And as for the number, well, if you worked it out there were only seven numbers left that fit the conditions and hadn't been given as examples, and people usually tend to avoid the extremes. Thirty-seven is the most common response to that trick.

The funny thing was that even when I had explained all this and we had worked out the probabilities together, many of them were still convinced it was ESP. It was as though, once they had formed that hypothesis, they didn't want to let it go. To many of them, the idea of ESP just made a lot more sense and fit better with their view of the world than did the idea that it was just common patterns of response and tedious probabilities. I was suddenly glad I had to do all these classes. I had lots of ideas I wanted to test.

I had also been reading about the "Barnum effect" (Snyder et al. 1977), the tendency for people to accept certain generalized personality descriptions as true of themselves and not others. Apparently, if they believe the description is supposed to be specific to them, they will rate it even more highly (Snyder 1974). Could people really be so easily duped by generalized personality descriptions?

I knew that many people in the class were interested in divination, the Tarot, and astrology. I was still fascinated with these topics and lectured happily on them. So one week in class, I asked everyone to give me their date, hour, and place of birth. I said that a friend of mine had kindly offered to do an astrological reading for each of them, and I would bring them all the next week.

The next week I brought twenty identical personality readings; each headed with one person's name and birth details, followed by a few questions on how good they thought it was.

"It's most important," I said, "that you don't look at anyone else's. I want you to concentrate on your own reading and answer the questions, uncontaminated by anyone else's." I had to say something to stop them noticing! Even so, one of the brightest of the class, sitting at the back, suddenly put her hand up. I could see her glancing meaningfully at her neighbor's sheet. I rushed over quickly to give her a hint, and, much to my relief, she laughed conspiratorially and didn't let on.

When they had all finished, I asked them how highly they had rated their special astrology reading. It was remarkable. It was just like my Tarot study. On a scale from 1 to 7, most of them had rated their reading as 5 or 6, as accurate and specific to themselves and not other people. Not only that, but they started asking who the astrologer was and if I could ask my friend to do some more readings for their family. Before they got too carried away, I asked whether anyone would volunteer to read theirs to the class. My co-conspirator at the back put up her hand with a smile and slowly and dramatically began reading. There were a few gasps, a few shaking heads, and then everyone was laughing and thumping on their desks and groaning.

"You rotter!" shouted one with a grin.

"You knew we'd fall for it, didn't you?" cried another.

I was glad to be able to explain that everyone had been falling for it for thirty years (it was taken from Forer 1949) and for similar things long before that. They were just like everyone else, and this was a powerful and very human effect. I think they quite enjoyed the temporary deception.

And it certainly made me think about that Tarot study I had done. Not only did I not need the paranormal to account for the success of Tarot readings, but two very simple effects would account for it all. First, people will readily accept a certain kind of reading as true of themselves and not others. And, second, the Tarot reader usually has had plenty of practice. I thought of myself. In all my years of practice with the Tarot had I simply learned to produce readings that were universally applicable, vague, or ambiguous? I even went back and did some further analysis of my own Tarot readings. It did indeed seem that I was good at producing nonspecific and acceptable readings (Blackmore 1983). There didn't seem to be a lot of room left for psi.

So what if there were no psi? I was back to this question and the skeptical hypothesis that ESP does not exist. Like any other hypothesis, it had to be tested. Instead of going on hunting for psi, I would try to find evidence that it does not exist.

This provided an interesting challenge. Clearly, negative results were not much good as evidence. I needed some specific predictions from the skeptical hypothesis. One prediction is obviously that debunking will be successful, but I had had enough of that. It is probably harder work investigating someone else's research than doing new research oneself. All my experience had led me to believe that if I investigated more of other's people's claims, I would find them less and less convincing, but I couldn't be sure of that, and there would always be more claims coming along. No, I had to find some more positive prediction.

The experience with the tricks had given me an idea. I could ask why—if there is no ESP—so many people go on believing in it?

People usually claim that they believe in psi because of their own experience, and surveys showed that things like apparent telepathy and precognitive dreams are cited most often. Interestingly, most such experiences involve some kind of assessment of probability.

As an example, I got a letter one morning from a gentleman in Scotland who recounted a story about his daughter—let us call her Angela. He wrote that Angela and a friend had come to visit him in November 1965 or 1966. They had flown up from London and intended to go back the same way, but he had persuaded them to go by train instead. That night he slept badly and woke very worried about them. The next day he read in the papers that the plane they would have taken had crashed on landing and all on board had been killed.

I get dozens of letters about people's psychic experiences, and most are utterly inconclusive. However, I always feel I should follow up any promising ones, and this one did look promising. He had given the approximate date, and there were other people whom I could ask for their accounts. I decided to follow it up as best I could and wrote to ask him for more details. I didn't realize that this would turn out to be such an interesting case, but the point I want to make is that the "significance" of this story rests on an assessment of probabilities. We think this might be "psychic" because we judge that such a coincidence cannot be due to chance. Surely the man didn't dissuade Angela and her friend from taking the plane, just when it was going to crash, *by chance*. Surely he dissuaded them *because* it was going to crash. We think the coincidence is so unlikely that there has to be a causal connection, and we supply psi to fill the gap.

* * *

People are notoriously bad at judging probabilities (Kahneman and Tversky 1973). We simply cannot assess how likely that coincidence was. We don't know how often he woke feeling uneasy. We don't know how often he had bad dreams, how often his daughter visited him, or how often he tried to talk people out of flying. More important still, we don't know how many other things might have happened that day that he might have considered a *cause* of his uneasy feeling. And even if we did know all these probabilities, we would probably still underestimate the actual chance of that coincidence.

Could this problem underlie everyone's belief in psi? I thought it might, but how could I find out?

"Wouldn't you expect the believers to be worse at probability judgments than the disbelievers?" asked Tom when I told him about my thinking.

What a very good idea! We could set up lots of tests of probability judgments and get sheep (or believers) and goats (or disbelievers) to try them all. Our prediction was that the goats would do better than the sheep; the implication being that it was the erroneous thinking of the sheep that made them opt for a belief in psi.

What we needed were many subjects of varying belief and some simple test that could be made into computer games and be fun to play. This was a good opportunity for me to learn programming, and Tom tried valiantly to teach me. I did actually manage to write part of the programs, but I have to admit that Tom did all of the hard parts.

Soon the programs were all written, our tests were ready, and we had to find subjects to take them. First we got permission from a local girls' school to test fifty of their pupils. We took all the computer gear off to the school and set it up in one of the classrooms. The teachers had organized things wonderfully well, and we found a stream of keen young girls constantly supplied to try the tests.

Fortunately, they seemed to find it fun. They were asked questions about coins falling, about ways of selecting boys and girls for a party, and about taking colored beads from a hat. They had to generate a string of random numbers and, of course, at the very end of the test, they had to answer questions on their beliefs.

We also put up a notice at the Bristol Medical School for volunteers to take the tests there. This provided quite a different crowd, lots of medical students taking a break between classes, some technicians, doctors, researchers, and lecturers. Much to our surprise there was no shortage of volunteers, and we simply stopped when we had tested one hundred.

For the first time in years, the results came out as predicted (Blackmore and Trościanko 1985). Yes, the sheep actually did worse than the goats at almost every task involving probability judgments.

And interestingly, the adults from the Medical School did no better than the schoolgirls. It wasn't just a question of education or intelligence. To take just one example, we asked the following question:

"How many people would you need to have at a party to have a 50:50 chance that two of them will have the same birthday (not counting the year)?"

This is an old, but fascinating, question. It is too hard for most people to work out the right answer, even if they know a bit about probability theory, so most people have to guess. Try it. Given a free choice some people say 365 or 183. Quite a few guess between 40 and 50. In this case we made it easier by giving three choices: 22, 43, and 98. The right answer is, in fact, 22, but I think that most people would be surprised if they went to a party with only 22 guests and found that there were two people there with the same birthday. They might even think it was a "strange coincidence" or even paranormal. The crux is that it need not be someone else with the same birthday as you—it can be any two people.

Not surprisingly, most people got this wrong, but the goats picked the right answer significantly more often than did the sheep. Could this explain why people acquired, and stuck to, their paranormal beliefs?

I was driving back from the school one day, wondering about this. I was in a hurry, and in front of me was a green light. It had been green for some time.

"Stay green, stay green," I thought to myself, as I drove steadily toward it. Just as I had gone too far to brake comfortably, it changed to amber, and I sped on—suddenly realizing what I was doing. I was, unconsciously, imagining that I could influence the lights by wishing it so. Just by whispering "Stay green," I was implying that my thoughts could have a paranormal effect—the effect known as psychokinesis. But it was obviously an *illusion of control* (Langer 1975). I knew I couldn't control the lights by thinking about it, but it was tempting to think I could. This immediately led to a new experiment for Tom and me. We predicted that believers would suffer from a greater illusion of control than nonbelievers. Maybe that was why they believed in psi.

This time Tom designed a coin-tossing game to be played on the computer, in which the subjects were given a button to push to control the coin on the screen and make it land either heads or tails. In fact, some of the time they *could* control it with the button, and some of the time it was purely random. We predicted that the believers would more often suffer from the illusion that they were controlling it when they weren't.

To pull in another hundred subjects on our limited resources, I drew up a large poster that said, "Try our Computer Games. A bottle of Whisky for the Highest Score" and placed it right by the door of the Medical School. In poured the subjects, eager to win, and in poured our results. As before, our predictions were confirmed. The believers thought they had exerted more control over the randomly flipping coins than did the nonbelievers. But as I was testing them and watching them play, I noticed something rather odd. I decided to add a new question. I asked, "Please estimate how many 'hits' (out of 20) you would score if you did the test with your eyes shut."

Now the coin was landing randomly on heads and tails, so with eyes shut, the answer should be 10. Most of the nonbelievers did indeed put 10, but the believers didn't. They put all kinds of answers, from 0 to 20, with an average of 8. This seemed to make sense. Suppose they underestimated the chance probability, then when they scored 10 out of 20, as chance would predict, they would think it was a high score and have to assume some causal explanation of their success. In the absence of anything better, they might assume it was psi. So again, a misjudgment of probability might underlie a belief in psychokinesis (Blackmore and Trościanko 1985).

Could all belief in psi arise this way? It might, but it might not. We had certainly thrown some light on how belief in psi can come about, even when there is no psi. And it was wonderful to have had some predictions confirmed and to have found out something positive at last. However, nothing had really changed. We had not in any way proved that there is no psi. The hypothesis that psi does not exist was still just that—a hypothesis.

Then one evening, I received a phone call. It was the man from Scotland who had written about his daughter and the plane crash.

"Is that Dr. Blackmore?" he asked. "I've just got your letter and you have asked me for more details. So I thought the best thing you could do would be to ring Angela herself. I'll give you her number and you can ring now, before I have a chance to talk to her myself. That way you can hear her side of the story."

I thanked him profusely. He clearly realized how useful it was to have independent accounts. Then I dialed Angela's number, a little nervous about what I would say.

"Parapsychology?" she said. "Oh no, has my father been worrying you with that old story? I suppose he told you that he saved my life, didn't he?"

"Something like that," I agreed with a smile.

"Well, I don't mean to be unkind, and I do appreciate his concern, but it really wasn't half as dramatic as he made out. Did he tell you he persuaded us to take the train? Well, I think that was only to save money, you know. After all, he was paying. And nothing very terrible happened to the plane. I think a stewardess was slightly injured or something. I really am sorry," she added, "but I can't tell you it was all very exciting and psychic."

I thanked her too and, with something approaching exultation, put down the phone. I would make one last check. I went into my study and wrote to ask her if she would mind sending me a written account of her story. Then I wrote a quick letter to the Civil Aviation Authority to ask whether there had been any crashes or other incidents at that time. I imagined it might make rather a nice little story—the father's dramatic "psychic" tale, then her quite different account, and the evidence that there had been no serious crash after all.

"CAA," I read on the envelope of a letter that arrived a few days later. Ah, that must be to tell me about the plane from Scotland.

I wasn't going to be surprised when they said they had no record of a crash. I looked at it casually. "This crash," they wrote, "occurred at 0123 hrs. GMT on 27.10.65 at Heathrow. . . . everybody on board was killed."

I stood there in the kitchen holding the letter. So I was wrong! It had crashed, and presumably Angela would have been killed if she had been on the plane. But what of her story? Had she been making it up or conveniently forgetting the details she didn't like to remember? Of course the story still wasn't good evidence for psi. The father might have invented the story *after* he heard about the crash. Or it might have been a coincidence. Nevertheless, I had been wrong to believe Angela instead of her father. It was just prejudice; my new-found skeptical prejudice. Now I was really confused.

I pulled a chair out from under the kitchen table and sat down, looking at the streaky surface of the old pine table I had spent so many hours sanding and polishing. I had got myself into a right muddle. I had known all along that psi was negatively defined, couldn't be pinned down, and produced only unrepeatability. I had known that the question "Does psi exist?" might be a pointless one to ask. Yet I was still behaving as though it either did or didn't. For years I had assumed it did exist. Now I believed it didn't. But really neither view made sense.

I grabbed the salt shaker: psi does exist. Then the pepper grinder: it doesn't. There were the believers and skeptics, battling away against each other. I crashed the wooden shakers together. But neither side could present a testable hypothesis. My ten years of research seemed to have shown me that, above all else.

I could think of no way of refuting the psi hypothesis. Negative results didn't; debunking positive results didn't; our work on probability judgments didn't. There were always arguments to be found that could bolster the psi hypothesis. Moreover, the non-psi hypothesis was just as irrefutable. People could always argue that any evidence would be debunked in the end. It seemed an impasse. I pushed the salt and pepper roughly across the table and threw the letter into a heap "to be filed."

Twenty-six

The Failure of the Psi Hypothesis

That weekend we had a visitor. I hadn't seen John Dupré for a long time; indeed I had only seen him a few times since we had broken off our engagement five years before. Since then he had studied at Cambridge, married an American woman, and then moved to Oxford, where he had a fellowship. I was glad to find that he got on well with Tom, and now he came to visit us more and more often. This time the three of us set off for a walk to the woods. My old love of arguing with John was instantly rekindled, and we squelched through the winter mud talking about reductionism and supervenience, mental change and physical change, realism, and repeatability. Then as Tom cooked dinner and we sat over drinks in the kitchen, we got onto the problems of parapsychology, the nature of pseudoscience, and the consensus of scientists: Popper, Kuhn, Feyerabend, and Lakatos.

"Now hang on a minute, John. I haven't read Lakatos. Please enlighten me!"

Between swigs of gin and handfuls of crisps, John gave me a potted account. Popper (1959) had talked about the competition between theories; Kuhn about the overthrow of old paradigms by new ones (1962); but Lakatos (1978) looked at scientific progress in terms of rival research programs. Perhaps this would help with my impasse over psi. I would have to get Lakatos's book from the library.

But I already had so much to do, and I wasn't getting on too well with my book on OBEs. There were so many distractions: phone calls, appointments, the house and the garden, lectures, and so much other work I had to do. I wanted to get away from it all. So that is exactly what I did. I took everything I needed for my book and set off down to Salcombe.

It was midwinter and very, very cold. I was alone in the huge house with no heating, and the wet salt wind blew everywhere. I typed wearing a pair of those wonderful gloves with the fingers cut off, and I wrapped myself in sweaters and blankets. The cold was my challenge, and I revelled in enduring it. I used to get up at seven and work all morning without a break. Then in the afternoons I took long walks on the beaches and cliffs before getting back to my work.

That was the time of year I loved: gulls everywhere, driven inshore by rough seas, and hardly another person to be seen braving the biting drizzle. I went out in almost any weather, but one day it was just too wet. I stood on the porch overlooking the estuary and stared out into the grayness. The rain was streaming down the windows and the wind driving it into every little crack. I decided to sit and read instead of braving the weather.

Lying on one of the chairs was a book from the pile I had brought with me. It was the book by Lakatos (1978) that John had recommended to me. I was tempted to go upstairs for something a bit lighter, but laziness won. So I snuggled down into a big wicker armchair, tucked my legs in out of the draught, and began to read.

I was immediately glad that I'd made the effort to go to the library. In trying to characterize scientific progress, Lakatos didn't talk about theories competing with each other but about more progressive research programs ousting those that stagnated. He argued that a research program progresses so long as it keeps predicting novel facts with some success. It stagnates if it gives only post hoc explanations of chance discoveries. He suggested that progress was made by more progressive programs superceding degenerating ones.

The implications for parapsychology seemed clear. I could now look afresh at the two sides of the argument: the believers and the disbelievers. I could ask not which theory was better but which research program was progressing; which showed more "progressive problem-shift," and which was likely to supercede the other.

Looked at in this way, the answer was obvious. I looked through the streaming window to the choppy gray sea of the estuary and the sodden beaches where a few walkers were now braving the day and leaving squelchy footprints among the worm casts at low tide. My favorite view glinted encouragingly back at me.

Neither. The answer was neither. Everything Lakatos said about stagnating research programs seemed to apply to parapsychology—but to both sides. Parapsychology's theoretical growth was negligible. There were theories all right, and very occasionally they predicted some new findings, but generally there had been no discernible theoretical growth in a hundred years. There was always the problem of unrepeatability. Indeed, I began to wonder whether parapsychology's only finding in a hundred years was the unrepeatability of psi (Blackmore 1985b). I chuckled to myself—though it wasn't very funny.

Even more telling was the lack of *problemshift*. One hundred years ago, Myers was asking essentially the same questions parapsychology is tackling now. The methods have changed, but the questions are just the same: Does information travel from one place to another independently of space and time? Can people communicate without using the recognized senses? And after one hundred years we still don't have answers to even these most preliminary questions. We haven't progressed at all. Parapsychology has a stagnant research program.

"So how can it continue?" I asked myself. And here too an answer leapt out of the rain. It continues because there are so many ways that the psi hypothesis can protect itself by retreating into ever weaker and weaker positions. Indeed the whole of my "career" could be seen as illustrating that retreat. As I had faced one "reason" for the non-appearance of psi, there had always been another to take its place, and another and another, until psi seemed as evasive as those little beach worms, always disappearing from sight, leaving only their casts behind to tempt the unwary into thinking they must really be there.

So of course my research lead to skepticism and even disbelief. I could thoroughly sympathize with myself for becoming so aggressively disbelieving! But what of the disbelievers research program? Was that any better? A research program that is based solely on denying claims of the paranormal is just a parasite upon those claims. The best it can hope to achieve is to demolish them. While that may in itself be useful, it cannot replace the claims with something better, because it has nothing but their nonvalidity to argue for. The real contribution of skeptics is in providing viable alternatives to psi, but then, by current definitions, they are no longer doing parapsychology.

So parapsychology itself produces two hopeless research programs, both utterly dependent on the other, both battling over the vanishing remains of a shrinking subject, and both going nowhere.

I threw Lakatos down and looked out the window. The rain was easing up a little. Was the prospect for parapsychology really so dismal? An ever-shrinking subject, tied to definitions that forced people into taking sides and into pointless confrontation, a subject that has led nowhere but to stagnation? I climbed out of my chair, stiff with the cold and damp, and I pulled on my boots. I found some not-too-wet oilskins and headed out into the rain.

* * *

That night, after more work and my lone dinner, I began my OBE practice. Every day I was there, I tried out some technique for inducing "astral projection." As I wrote about the methods in my book (Blackmore 1982a), I tried them out, one by one, getting more and more frustrated at how difficult it seemed to be. I knew what to expect, I had had the experience myself, yet I still couldn't induce it at will.

Now I tried one of the last methods on my list: Robert Monroe's. He was a businessman from Virginia who began having spontaneous OBEs and then developed techniques for teaching others to have them (Monroe 1971). I had not seriously tried this method only because it sounded so complicated and arbitrary. He advised lying in a darkened room, head point magnetic North, repeating certain words five times over, and staring into the blackness at a spot about a foot from the forehead. The idea was to move this spot farther and farther away and to induce a "vibrational state" by reaching mentally for this spot.

It all seemed a bit far-fetched, and I couldn't understand where the vibrations were supposed to come from. Nevertheless, I set to practicing it. To my great surprise I found myself entering a delightful state. I could see nothing, was aware only of the blackness and the spot of concentration, and then everything began to vibrate. On top of that vibration I felt as though I were swinging gently back and forth, almost like being in a hammock, and then my imagery began to flow spontaneously and vividly. Everything I imagined seemed vividly realistic, almost reminiscent of my original OBE.

All the time I was wondering whether the vibration was due to rapid eye movements, such as occur during dreaming sleep, and whether I was falling asleep and experiencing hypnagogic imagery. I had no way of finding out then and there, but whatever the origin of this state I found it easier and easier to induce, and from there to get closer to the OBE. In this way I could test out my own theories about the OBE. So I wrote in the day and practiced each night.

I had also been practicing in a small group. Several of my parapsychology class had joined together for a regular "astral projection" session, and we were trying some of the same techniques. One evening we had an unusual visitor. His name was Vee Van Dam (though whether it was his real name I never discovered). He had written to me about his OBEs several times, and because they sounded so interesting, I invited him to come and talk to us.

I met Vee one afternoon at Bath bus station. It had to be him I saw stepping off the bus. His head was closely shaved, and he wore an old anorak over strangely colored robes. He had said he was Vegan, and I had duly prepared a totally vegetarian meal for him. I drove him home, and we spent the rest of the day deep in discussion on the OBE and the evening together with my group. They were somewhat taken aback by his appearance but fascinated by what he had to tell.

"Can you do it whenever you like?" they wanted to know.

"Could you come and see something here if you wanted to?" they asked.

Vee said that he could usually succeed in leaving his body when he wanted to and that certainly he could see things at a distance. It was even he who suggested the experiment. He said he would like to try to visit my house, out of his body, and see whether he could actually see what was there. I was delighted.

"I could easily put some sort of target out for you," I said. "What sort of thing would you like best? And where should I put it?"

He walked around the house and settled for the kitchen, certainly the warmest and most friendly room in the house. He looked all around and then pointed to a spot on the wall near the back door.

"I think you should put it here," he decided.

It was Vee who suggested I should use a five-digit number, a word, and a small object. He said he thought the numbers would be the hardest, but he wanted to try it. When he had gone, I set it all up. I found twenty small objects and put them in a box, I chose twenty common words and made a neat list, and then I found random-number tables to select the first targets. That evening I pinned up a sheet of paper in my kitchen. In large black writing it said 34802 CAT, and beside it was pinned a matchbox full of matches.

Whenever people come into our kitchen they ask what the numbers are for. I suppose there is always the risk that someone who has seen them will meet Vee or some of the others who subsequently tried the experiment. In the beginning I changed the targets every Sunday night. Then I did it once a month, and finally even less frequently. Several OBErs have now had a go at it, but none has ever succeeded in seeing it. That is, so far. It is still there, and I keep on changing it.

Now none of this was to deny the reality of Vee's experiences. What he experienced was fascinating, and I wanted to learn about it. However, it seemed more and more obvious that the psychic's theories of "something leaving" the body were just inadequate. Not only did they face enormous logical problems, but they just didn't fit with the evidence and with what the experiences are like.

As I worked on the book and worked on myself, an entirely new way of understanding the OBE began to emerge: one based on changing "models of reality."

I kept on coming back to one question: What is altered in an altered state of consciousness? If I could answer that, then surely the OBE would make more sense. Then suddenly, out of all this practice, came an answer. Maybe "we," these conscious-feeling, out-of-body experiencing selves, are no more than models of a self in the world. Maybe being conscious is just what it's like being such a mental model, and when that model changes, then we change. If so, then what is altered in an "altered state of consciousness" is one's model of self in the world or "model of reality."

I went back to the OBE. OBEs very often take place when sensory input is reduced or cut off or just ignored. Under such conditions one's model of reality is bound to be disrupted—but of course we need a model to coordinate behavior and interact with the world. So perhaps the brain, having lost touch with its normal model of reality, tries to construct a new one from memory and imagination. What would this be like? Of course, it might well be a bird's-eye view. That is often how images are represented in memory. Thus the OBE would come about quite naturally.

This provided a new way of understanding the OBE and one that was later to provide several testable predictions (Blackmore 1986a). It treated the OBE as the brain's natural response to a problem. Because it couldn't make sense of its input, it constructed an imaginary world, and that, for the moment, became reality.

I now saw the OBE, not as some psychic, spiritual, or astral phenomenon, but as something much closer to normal realities; a kind of substitute ordinary world. But I could imagine more mystical experiences in which the model of reality would be quite different, perhaps being far simpler or even having no self at all (Blackmore 1986b). Now, far from leaving the occult teachings behind, I wondered whether we couldn't learn from them. Those "astral planes" and "other worlds" might arise for good psychological reasons. With our nervous system being built the way it is, some kinds of imagined worlds might be easy to construct and others might be difficult. So in these altered states, we would all "visit" similar "worlds." Perhaps some kind of rapprochement between psychology and aspects of occultism might be possible. The teachings of adepts and mystics might provide a genuine input into psychological theories if we could accept that they had learned to change their model of reality.

Of course, this theory had nothing whatever to say about the paranormal and no implications either way for the question of whether we survive bodily death. If I had made any progress in understanding the OBE, I had done so without reference to psi.

* * *

One Sunday morning, back home again, I woke early after some vivid and impressive dreams. I had been practicing floating down tunnels the night before and now lay thinking over my ideas on the OBE. I wanted to get some of my thoughts down before they slipped away; and, leaving Tom still asleep in bed, I crept off to my study to write. Somehow I wanted not to type but to write. Out it all poured! I didn't solve all the problems of OBE. And it wasn't until much later that I formalized the ideas a bit better (Blackmore 1984c, 1986b). Indeed, I was later to get exasperated that I hadn't done a better job of it, but I finished the book! By the time Tom had cooked us bacon and eggs and sausages and fried bread, the last chapter was done.

That morning was not the only one that I woke early. I seemed to be having vivid dreams more and more often. Was it my imagination, or was I feeling rather queasy too?

Tom just laughed, "I'll go to the chemist on Monday and buy you something to find out."

When he brought home a parcel from the chemist, I read the instructions carefully. I had to mix a urine sample with the chemicals provided, wait several hours, and then look for a brown ring that might be formed in the bottom of the test tube. I must admit, I couldn't get down to work that morning. I kept thinking about the brown ring. Would it be obvious? Would I know it when I saw it? What if there were only a very faint, not-very-brown ring? Would it count? I think I had been studying parapsychology too long. When the specified time came, I crept cautiously up to the test tube—the instructions said not to jog or disturb it—and looked.

There it was, as clear as anything, a distinct brown ring.

"Tom, Tom, it's worked. I'm—it's—we're—going to have a baby!"

My feelings were a shambles. What would I do? Would I stop my work and give up parapsychology? No, I couldn't do that, could I? But how would a baby fit into our lives, already full of so many complicated things?

I tried to plan things sensibly and wrote to Donald West to ask whether I could have a six-month unpaid break in my studentship. I reckoned that after six months without doing parapsychology I would know whether I wanted to go back to it or not. Perhaps I would find that once I had made the break, it wouldn't hold the same fascination for me. Perhaps I would find I liked being a fulltime housewife and mother, or perhaps I would start doing something completely different after six months, like writing a novel, or painting, or becoming a landscape gardener.

What I didn't realize was that I would never even make it to the end of the six months. Indeed, when little Emily was only three days old, I found myself reading a parapsychology book in the hospital, and within another two weeks I was already worrying about my research again.

Then Tom and I got fascinated by what kinds of sounds babies like to listen to. We invented a system whereby Emily, and later Joly, could control a tape recorder, even as young as two months old. Using that, we were able to determine their musical preferences. But perhaps more important, we discovered how much they loved to play themselves music and stories and how easy it was to give them the chance (Blackmore and Trościanko 1984).

Incidentally, we also learned about how stories can be made. The accounts in the papers of what we had done with the tape recorder for babies seemed to build on each other and, like Chinese Whispers (in

America, gossip or rumor), got more and more unlikely. Then eventually we read in a religious magazine that we had discovered a way to use music to cure juvenile delinquents! I wondered whether the authors realized how fictitious their story was. And I wondered how many "psychic" stories are made this way.

Later still, Dick Bierman told me about his computerized PK experiments using his two babies as subjects. He sent me the programs, and I was then able to test Emily with our computer (Bierman 1985a). To my great surprise, these tests were successful, and it appeared as though Emily might have PK powers. So that led Tom and me to work on possible normal explanations for the results and yet another round of psi versus no-psi arguments (Troscianko and Blackmore 1985; Bierman 1985b). So eventually even the babies became involved in parapsychology!

But for now I had to get used to my new limitations. We were trying to put felt under the tiles on our roof, and it was a terrible job. The roof was not as old as the house, but was probably two-hundred years or so, and under the tiles was an old-fashioned snow-roof, all laths and ancient crumbling plaster that clogged up the lungs and tickled the nose. Then we had to carry the tiles up and down and replace all the rotten wood. After about an hour up there I began to feel frightfully dizzy and weak. Very reluctantly, and with some tears, I concluded that things were never going to be quite the same again. I would just have to give up scrambling about on roofs for a while and have a rest.

Twenty-seven

I Don't Know

The summer found me relaxing in earnest. The book was at the publishers, the piles of things to do "before the baby" were not yet getting urgent, and I set off down to Salcombe for a real holiday. The whole family was there: my mother and father, my younger brother Stephen, and my sister and her latest boyfriend. On the warm sunny days we went windsurfing and walking; on the frequent cold and rainy ones, we sat around in the house playing Scrabble or reading.

One morning we had breakfast together and set about planning the day. It was always hopeless; there were so many people, all of us "organizers" who all wanted to do different things or expected others to want to do different things. Then my father suggested a fishing trip. Tom and I looked at each other.

"We have to go right away, or the boat will be on the mud," said my father.

So Tom and I grabbed our waterproofs and set off with him down to the little boat with its small outboard engine and the lines with spinners to catch mackerel—well, to try to catch mackerel. It was a lovely day, and we pottered out of the harbor, under the shadow of the cliffs, and into open water. As we swept a long circle we kept on putting out the lines and hauling them in again, never catching anything but keeping on hoping, watching the cormorants and seagulls and the sea breaking against the rocks.

Then all of a sudden I began to feel a little queasy. I didn't like this feeling at all. It wasn't like me to feel seasick.

"Would you mind dropping me off on the beach?" I asked my father. "I think I'd rather be on dry land. You carry on fishing."

They dropped me off at South Sands; my favorite beach since I was a child. There, in the shallow water, I climbed gratefully over the side and onto the wet shiny sand, grasping my shoes and socks and jumping as far as I could to keep my jeans clear of the small waves. I ran halfway up the beach and stopped to watch the little boat heading out to sea again.

As I stood and watched, I drew patterns on the wet sand with my toes, squashing the spiraled wormcasts into circles and wiggly lines. "Is it really that bad?" I found myself asking. "Parapsychology, I mean. Is it completely hopeless?"

"No, it's not," answered somebody with more determination than I thought I had. "Because there is still a mystery! There *are* phenomena! There are OBEs, near-death experiences, lucid dreams, apparitions, divination, and mystical experiences. It must be possible to make progress in studying these. They happen—people experience things they cannot explain, that I cannot explain. And of course progress is being made on all of these, isn't it?"

I wriggled my feet into the cold wet sand and tried to think whether it was. Yes, of course it was, but not by parapsychologists! As far as OBEs were concerned there had been no *problemshift* at all. Myers's experiments in 1903 were asking just the same questions as those of the past twenty years (Osis 1978; Rogo 1978; Tart 1968). Only the psychological theories seemed to be getting somewhere—and largely without the hypothesis of psi. Then there was progress being made on lucid dreams and near-death experiences, but outside of parapsychology (Gackenbach and LaBerge 1986; Greyson and Flynn 1984). Perhaps all the real progress was made by people who pursued the phenomena for their own sake and without regard to psi.

So was parapsychology's only finding the unrepeatability of its phenomena?

"No," said that determined half of me again. "That's the whole point. It isn't the phenomena that are unrepeatable. It is psi. Couldn't we have a new parapsychology: one defined, not as the study of psi but as the study of all those interesting phenomena that it has always studied; a new parapsychology uncommitted to psi; a parapsychology with an open mind?"

But even as I thought it, I knew what most parapsychologists would say. Many were genuinely interested only in the paranormal and that was why they were studying it and why parapsychology was defined that way. I didn't expect many supporters for a parapsychology without psi.

I sighed. I had been standing on the beach for a long time, and my back was beginning to ache a little. The boat was nowhere in sight, so I walked slowly up the beach to the road. There I tried to brush the sticky sand off my feet and put on my shoes. I would take a slow and leisurely walk up on the cliffs.

It is half a mile or so along a narrow high-banked lane to the start of the woods. In early spring they are full of primroses competing gamely with the stringent wild garlic. Later on they are dark with bluebells. Now, in July, there were only a few straggling flowers overshadowed by the dense green leaves above. The muddy path is like a leafy tunnel, leading through the trees and on out to the cliffs. There, at last, you come suddenly out onto the rocks and can look back to see the little town sitting on the side of the estuary, looking out to sea. I had always run to that point, as a child, on my early morning walks. Now, with my ungainly shape, I climbed slowly onto the rock. Would my child grow up to run onto these rocks too?

Even then I thought about parapsychology. What would happen? Could parapsychology go on forever, ever shrinking, never progressing? Could it continue, a stagnant field, for another hundred years?

Of course there was always a chance that one day somebody might make that great breakthrough we have always been waiting for. They might find the repeatable demonstration of psi or discover something—anything—about the way psi works, so that it could be positively defined at last. Someone might develop a new theory that suddenly makes sense of all psi's fickleness and elusiveness and explains all those disparate findings. If that happened, then all my arguments would be washed away in a flood of progress.

But on the other hand, it might never happen. Indeed, I would be surprised if it did. It seemed more likely that parapsychology would just go on shrinking and losing all its interesting phenomena, one by one, until nothing was left but its clinging to psi. And psi, as I had learned so painfully, is a useless hypothesis.

So could psi be just a red herring, a very elusive and very alluring red herring, one that had had everyone chasing after it for a hundred years? In the future, when we are closer to understanding man's spiritual nature, will we look back at parapsychology as a pointless detour?

I stood proudly on my rock and remembered my ambitions. I suppose I really had thought that I might be the one to transform parapsychology. Instead, all I had done was to cast doubt and confusion on the whole notion of psi. There was so much that I didn't understand.

I climbed cautiously down off my rock and walked on along the cliffs. Soon the path narrows and turns dry and rocky, meandering as the cliff takes it out to wilder and steeper parts. There, around a jagged headland, the wind blows fiercely, even on a summer's day. I stopped and leaned on the one piece of tilted railing overlooking the small bay. I could see Tom and my father a mile or so out from the shore and far below, pottering slowly, their lines still trailing. They had been at it for hours. As far as I knew, Tom had never caught a fish in his life. It's amazing how long one can go on hoping to find something and never give up, even though you know you may never find it.

I gazed out to sea, at one with the self who had stood there so many times before and gazed out at the same sea. Was I really the same person who had held out so much hope for psi? Would I be able to remember myself now, a year from now, when I had a baby and was a mother? Would I ever understand what it was about memory that fascinated me so? Would I ever know whether there was psi or not? And all those claimed successes I had met with so often, were they really due to psi, or chance, or bad experiments, or what? I didn't know. I hated not knowing, but I really didn't know.

And now I realized, as though I had never realized it before, that sometimes you can't know. And you don't *have* to know. You don't *have* to be able to remember everything, to cling to the past and to knowledge and understanding. You don't *have* to understand everything. I just didn't know: this mental construction of a self didn't know some things.

It was obvious, wasn't it? Even the warring factions inside me seemed to agree. *I didn't know.*

I jumped back from the railing and looked about me. The wild scenery was clear and real, and the wind was harsh and fresh. I threw up my arms to the salty air and yelled into the wind at the top of my voice. "I don't know!"

I ran back up the slope behind me, instantly out of breath, and fell laughing into the damp and prickly bracken. I didn't need to force myself to know all the answers anymore. One answer would do.

"I don't know, I don't know, *I don't know!*"

Twenty-eight

Ten Years On

That is how I left my story, ten years ago; knowing that I did not know. Many of my friends laughed at my temerity for writing it in the first place. "Going to subtitle it *My early years,* are we? So you can write another one soon?" or even, "Don't expect me to tell you anything secret ever again, you might put it in the next book." Perhaps they didn't know that everyone who was quoted in the book was sent a copy to change or delete as they wished. Some people even added bits of their own: "Don't you remember that incident with the beer? You have to put that in." "Don't you remember what he said next? You can't leave that out." And so, by a cooperative venture, the events and conversations were scripted to be as accurate as possible.

But that is all they can be. Memory can never be totally accurate. I know, whatever that means, that I once stood on those cliffs shouting, "I don't know"—but as for the rest . . . was it really a wild and windy day up there? Did I invent the bit about Tom and my dad fishing out at sea? That might have been a different day and I put them together in my memory. Who can tell? My diaries, on which I heavily relied, contain at most a page a day. What is that, from among the myriad events of any single day?

The past is gone. It may be a fiction we cling to, but the truth is that we reconstruct our pasts again and again, and their relation to actual events is tenuous. We may be shocked when people are apparently made to "remember" child abuse that never happened, or "recall" being abducted by aliens who came in through their bedroom ceilings—but we shouldn't be. "False memory syndrome" is only an exaggerated form of the way all memories are: reconstructions of a now-gone past. They may *feel* real, but that doesn't prove they are accurate.

I have to say I *was* shocked when I learned how different were other people's recollections from my own. Hard as I tried to be accurate in what I wrote, other people remembered things a little differ-

243

ently—occasionally a lot differently. At first I tried to find out which was the "true" version, but I soon realized that often there is no true version. Two friends can never find out how they "really" felt the first time they met each other—even if they both wrote diaries or letters at the time. Sometimes I laugh at myself to think of all the great embarrassments of my life, or guilts about my own past actions, which now I suspect others may not even remember at all. Then I speculate about what other awful things I may have done that I have no recollection of but which are important to other people. I can see that all these worries are inventions.

Couldn't I just drop them all?

Is it possible to drop the burden of all that thinking and worrying; to stop constructing a self, with its illusory past and its imagined future? Is it possible to live in the only reality, the present moment? What would it be like? Who would be doing it?

These are real questions, though I admit I am probably more obsessed with them than most people! Looking back, I can see that the questions began in those few hours of what I then called my "out-of-body experience."

Later, in 1975, Raymond Moody wrote his best-selling *Life after Life* and modern research into NDEs began. Only then did I realize that my own experience included all the classic features of the near-death experience (NDE); the dark tunnel with a light at the end, the out-of-body experience, travel to other worlds, meeting wise "beings," and a painful decision to return—and everything seemed so stunningly *real!* The only missing element was the life review but that is, in any case, rather rare in NDEs. So I began to think of my experience as an NDE, even though I had not been near death, and this helped me to understand other people's descriptions when I subsequently spent many years researching NDEs (Blackmore 1993).

Now I tend more often to think of it as a mystical experience. I disappeared into oneness with the universe. I was no longer myself at all, and yet somehow I seemed more alive than ever. You could say that I saw the light during that experience.

This term—the light—is almost a buzzword nowadays, but what does it mean? I don't suppose anyone can really describe it, though poets, mystics, psychologists, and scientists have tried often enough. As for me, I came to a state (or perhaps I should say, there arose a state) in which everything was fine as it was, yet more vibrantly alive and realistic than anything in my life before. I seemed to know, though with a way of knowing quite different from ordinary knowledge, that all was one. I was of no more consequence than that wood louse on the floor, the suffering people in Ethiopia, or the queen of England. Indeed I was all of these things and none of them. There was no separation, no time, and no intention.

If this sounds like coma or death, it is not. Pervading such a state is a kind of aliveness or light. Time and space disappear and everything seems to be one. Breathing is breathing light. And the light seems also to be warm and full of compassion—even if that sounds nonsensical.

I experienced this all those years ago, and have experienced it since. It is this experience that drives the questions; it is this that drives my life as scientist, lover, and mother. Is it possible to return to this state? What is it? What is consciousness anyway? Who am I? These are only the same questions all over again. And I am still looking for answers.

Ten years ago I posed a series of questions (pp. 9–10). It surprises me now, how pertinent they still are and how often I still ask them.

• What does it mean for "me" to recall something which "I" once experienced in the past?

• What is happening when you seem to be in contact with something "larger" than yourself?

• Why is it that some experiences feel "more real" than others?

• How can a physical and physiological brain give rise to consciousness?

These are serious and important questions. The last, in particular, is probably the greatest challenge that contemporary science faces.

So, has parapsychology provided any answers? Ten years ago I described psi as a "red herring." I concluded that it led nowhere and only distracted from the meaningful questions. It is time to take up the threads of my story again and see whether another ten years in parapsychology have changed that conclusion.

It must be obvious that something happened, all those years ago, that dramatically affected my confidence in the ganzfeld. I came home from Cambridge, tearful and exhausted, and unable to talk to anyone, other than Tom, about what had gone on. Now that reports of the incident have been published, I can explain what did happen in that fateful week in Carl Sargent's laboratory.

In this account, I rely on my personal diaries; the notes I made at the time; letters between myself, Carl, and the others involved; and the published and unpublished accounts I wrote in the years that followed (Blackmore 1987).

You may remember that I had gone to the Cambridge Psychology Laboratory after the failure of my own experiments, to try to find out why Carl was getting such exceptionally good results (p. 129). On the day I arrived, I was invited in to observe a typical ganzfeld session. There were Carl and his colleague Trevor Harley, with a student experimenter called Gerry. Trevor was to be the sender, or agent, in this session and he had brought along a friend to be the ganzfeld subject. Everyone was listening to music, drinking coffee, and the atmosphere was very pleasant and relaxed.

I watched as Gerry took the subject into the large and airy experimental room to make him ready for the ganzfeld session. Right in the middle was a mattress on the floor with a red light poised over it. Gerry asked the subject to lie down, taped halved ping-pong balls over his eyes, and placed headphones, playing white noise, on his ears. Having fixed these, he turned on the red light and retired to an observation room next door, from where he could watch the subject and write down everything that he said during the half hour or so of the session. At the end of the session, he and the subject would go through the transcript, compare it with each of four pictures, and decide which one the sender had been looking at.

246

Meanwhile the rest of us, having synchronized our watches, set off down the corridor to Carl's office. I was now going to watch how the randomization was done. This is a critical part of any ESP experiment, since you can only be sure you have ESP if the targets have been randomly chosen, and neither the subject nor the experimenter can find out what they are.

On a shelf to the right of the room was a long row of large brown envelopes, containing all the pictures that would be used as targets, in twenty-eight sets. Each numbered set consisted of four pictures, one of which would be the target that the sender looked at. These possible targets were individually sealed in large brown envelopes labeled A, B, C, and D, and with them was another large envelope containing a complete duplicate set for the experimenter and subject to look at when doing their judging.

The first task was to choose one of the twenty-eight sets. Carl consulted the large book of random numbers and picked one. He gave the four sealed envelopes to Trevor and placed the envelope with the duplicate set in front of him on the desk. This would later be picked up by the experimenter for the judging. Now the critical part began—to choose whether A, B, C, or D would be the target.

In the middle of the desk was a pile of small brown envelopes. Carl again consulted the random number tables, took the pile of small envelopes, cut it according to the random numbers, cut it again, and pulled out one envelope. The pile, he explained, contained twenty envelopes each with a letter inside—five As, five Bs, and so on. He had no idea which letter was inside the one he had picked. He gave it to Trevor and Trevor left. Only when he reached the sender's room, in a distant building, would Trevor open the small envelope, see which letter was to be the target, and open the large envelope containing that target picture. No one else would know, until the subject had made his guess, which picture it was. We sat and waited.

About half an hour later Gerry came in (saying nothing) to fetch the duplicate picture set. Soon afterwards he was back to say that he and the subject had completed the judging. They had studied each picture and given it a score according to how well it corresponded with the notes and recollections of the ganzfeld experiences, and they had ranked the four pictures and chosen the one they thought corresponded best. Gerry had then rung Trevor, across in the next building, to tell him to come over with the answer. We all trooped back to the experimental room where the four pictures were lying on the table. They had chosen a picture of four men carrying trays of food. Trevor arrived, opened his envelope, and showed us. It was the same picture. Another hit!

I was impressed. I knew this one could just be luck, but within a couple of days I watched five sessions. Three produced direct hits; that is the target was ranked at number 1. That meant a hit rate of 60 percent instead of the 25 percent expected by chance. Something was certainly going on. But what?

I can still remember the awkward mixture of feelings this engendered. I was excited but scared, too. Real results were coming in. Either they were psi at last—and I must seriously revise my increasingly skeptical views—or there was some truly devious problem with the design that I had so far overlooked. This second possibility seemed less and less likely as I watched.

However, I couldn't lightly accept the first. I concluded that I would not be doing my job properly if I didn't try to find loopholes and so I applied myself to thinking up every conceivable way round the protocol. I soon realized that I had to keep detailed and accurate notes of everything that went on. I still have these notes and they are available to anyone who wants to consult them.

Right from the start, I could see there was no obvious loophole. All the classic problems had been solved, and very elegantly. There were duplicate target sets so that fingerprints or other clues could not be used. The sender was well away from the receiver and, as far as I could tell, they could not communicate in any normal way. The sender had to bring proof of which envelope he had opened (with the other three still sealed up) so that he could not lie about the randomization when he saw the subject's choice (or when the experimenter rang him). The experimenter might be able to affect the subject's choice during the judging, but this would not matter because he could not know which target had been chosen. It looked watertight.

Feeling as though I was clutching at straws, I decided to check every last possibility.

The thought occurred to me that it would be quite easy to guess which picture a subject would choose, especially if you knew him or her well. People tend to have recurring themes in their ganzfeld experiences, just as they do in their dreams. But how would this help? The protocol made it impossible for anyone artificially to select the target they wanted, didn't it? I wondered whether someone could mark the little brown envelopes with letters in, and so fix which picture was to be the target. I checked the envelopes and could see no signs of marking, nor any easy way of identifying them. I held them up to the light. Inside, the letters were well wrapped up and could not be seen at all. I wondered whether the whole pile might be switched for a different one that looked the same but contained all Cs, for example. I checked and was sure it was not.

I wasn't entirely happy about making these covert observations. I felt it was necessary, to be sure the experiment was working properly, and Carl had generously given me the run of his room and invited me to watch every aspect of the procedures. But I felt like a spy. I was already looking forward to the day—soon I hoped—when I would run out of ideas and have to conclude that the results were real. I could then turn my energies to facing up to psi!

Another idea came to me. Could a determined experimenter "push" a subject to pick a given picture during the judging? After all, this was a lengthy process in which the experimenter and subject together discussed the experiences and compared them with the pictures. The experimenter could certainly have some influence here. But he couldn't possibly know what the target was, could he, so how could this matter?

I suddenly realized something terribly obvious. I did not yet fully understand the implications of this complicated randomization procedure. The twenty little envelopes contained five As, five Bs, and so on. But after one had been selected, there would only be nineteen left in the pile. It would now be biased against the letter that had been selected. So what happened next? Carl explained that the replacement took place after each trial, or at least before the next one began. Obviously the missing envelope had to be replaced with one that was the same letter, to bring the pile back into balance. That meant, I realized with foreboding, that somewhere there had to be little envelopes with known letters.

There were. These were kept in four small drawers to the left of the desk. After each trial the experimenter could look up which letter had been the target in that trial, take a corresponding envelope from the drawers to the left, and put the pile back into balance. The next trial could then proceed.

The faint sickness I had been feeling over the past couple of days began to get worse. I hated feeling like a spy and had to struggle with myself to work out what was right. If there was really psi going on here it was very important and we needed to know. Equally, if there was not, we had to know what was wrong. If nothing was wrong, my trivial observations would not matter. They could all laugh at me if they liked, but I would be glad I had checked everything and would be able to say that—as far as I was concerned—the experiments were perfectly well carried out and the results genuine. So I carried on.

With drawers containing known envelopes, all sorts of new ideas were possible. Some one might make a mistake. They might replace the wrong envelope and no one would realize this had happened. The pile would then be biased, for example, containing an extra A or too few Ds. But this would not really matter. At least, it could hardly be blamed for the tremendous excess of hits I had seen. Such an accidental bias might conceivably produce a change of a few percent, but not the string of hits we seemed to be getting. What was more worrying was the possibility of manipulation.

This was getting really devious, I thought, but then I must see this through. What if the person who did the randomization just took a known envelope from the drawer instead of one from the pile? If he knew the subject well he might be able to guess which picture would be picked and so create a hit. This would be far more effective than a simple accidental bias in the pile, but surely no one would. . . .

I could check. Throughout the history of parapsychology people have suspected other experimenters. I thought of Hansel snooping about in Rhine's lab (Hansel 1966), of Price's speculations in the 1950s, and of the many people who argued over Soal's results (pp. 116–17). Here I could at least check up on my suspicions. If the randomizer deliberately took a known envelope from the drawer, the pile would still have twenty envelopes and someone might notice. So the sensible thing for him to do would be to remove another envelope from the pile and hide it, or destroy it. In this case two envelopes, not one, would be used up in one trial. Also the drawer would be opened and a known envelope removed *before,* not *after,* the trial.

I could easily see whether this happened.

In addition, the pile of twenty would become biased. This I could not check without opening the envelopes, and I did not want to do this.

I wished only to make observations that did not interfere with the running of the experiment. I decided this would be the very last check I would make. I carefully counted the number of envelopes in each of the four drawers and wrote a list in my notes.

It was now Saturday evening. Carl and his group worked ever so hard. We finished about 7 P.M. and were due to start again after lunch on Sunday. I went gratefully to bed, totally oblivious to what the next day would bring.

On Sunday afternoon I watched yet another hit, the fourth so far, and then a near miss (the target was ranked second). The third session of the day was about to begin and I was writing up my notes. "I am really seeing it working," I wrote. I checked the list of envelopes. After the previous session, the main pile should contain nineteen envelopes, which it did. The drawers, from A to D, contained 11, 19, 9, 17.

With Carl's encouragement I had been watching, and then taking part in, every aspect of the experiments. For this session I was to help set up the subject and then watch from the observation room. A student called Keith was running this session and, officially, Carl was to have no role in it at all. Carl rushed in and out again. "Carl flitting about, seemed anxious and distracted," I wrote in my notes. The notes seemed to be getting a bit out-of-hand but I really did not know what was important and what was not, so I simply recorded as much as I could.

It was an odd session. For this experiment the subject had to have only fifteen minutes in ganzfeld, and he said very little during this time. So when it came to judging the four pictures, he and Keith seemed to be having a lot of trouble. In the midst of this Carl unexpectedly appeared and took over. He checked the notes and began pointing out similarities to the pictures, especially to one of them. In no time it seemed that B was the best correspondence, but the marks were very close. Keith was trying to keep up with Carl. He rapidly added up the scores for each picture (in fact wrongly, as we later discovered) and asked the subject for his final guess. "B," he said. Back came Trevor, with the familiar big envelope—and a B. Yet another direct hit!

I added a few lines to my notes: "Carl came in for judging, pushed to B—anyway B chosen—was B—hit!!" I looked back over my previous notes. Five direct hits out of eight. It really was impressive. I had a lot to think about.

That night there was to be a meeting of the Cambridge SPR and I was looking forward to having something to take my mind off the experiments, but first I had to check the drawers and finish my notes.

I walked back to Carl's office. The door was open, as usual, and I could see the pile of envelopes on the desk. Nineteen—correct. I opened the four drawers and counted, writing down the numbers one by one: 11, 18, 9, 16. I counted again, and again. Oh no. There it was. The thing that deep down inside I had never really expected. One of my crazy predictions had come true. Two envelopes were gone, not one.

I counted again, with shaking hands. Which was gone? Which should have gone? The target for the previous trial had been D, so for the normal replacement a D should have been used. That was right— a D had gone. But what else was missing? It was a B.

Could that missing B have been used for the trial we had just completed? Could someone have taken that B from the drawer instead of from the pile? I began to feel sick. I was in danger of panicking. Only then did I realize that right up to that point my speculations had been purely academic. I hadn't really believed in them. Now it was serious. I had made a prediction about a method of cheating and it had come true. I had to think.

I tried to calm down. I had thought that Carl had pushed the subject toward B but this could have been a coincidence and, most importantly, Carl had had nothing to do with the randomization. Trevor had been the sender and would have done the randomization himself just before the trial began. There could have been no way in which Carl could have known the target was B, and so there was no point in his trying to influence the subject. I breathed more easily. I completed my notes and gratefully set off for a distracting evening with the CUSPR.

On Monday things seemed far better. We had two more sessions, a hit with Carl present and a miss with him absent, and the replacements all went correctly. I spoke to no one about my fears, though I kept thinking of ways to disprove them. If I was right, an extra envelope should be somewhere, possibly hidden. I would surely have no chance of finding that. But more importantly, the main pile should now be biased and would probably contain an extra B. Of course I couldn't check that without asking Carl. I decided to pluck up the courage and speak to him at the next opportunity.

It was on Tuesday morning that we learned Carl had the flu. And so I ended up sharing some of my fears and suspicions with Trevor, though I did not tell him about Sunday's events. Trevor was straight and helpful. He clearly believed completely in the results and was sick of my endless doubts. If I wanted to find out the truth, he said, then we should open all the envelopes and find out. And that is just what we did.

I checked my notes. There were nineteen envelopes. The last target had been A and not yet replaced. So the pile should be 4, 5, 5, 5. I opened them all and laid them out carefully—5, 6, 4, 4. So there it was. The pile was biased. There was an extra A and an extra B.

Now it was obvious that this could have happened purely by accident. Someone might have been careless in replacing the envelopes, but Trevor didn't think so. He explained that Carl always did the replacement himself and would not make such mistakes. I wondered whether there might be errors in the drawers, too. We opened the envelopes there and found two Ds under the As.

Trevor was not as worried as I was. He began doing some calculations. From this he concluded that any bias in the main pile would have only a negligible effect on the results. It could not produce anything like the 60 percent hit rate we had been seeing. I agreed; I had thought this through many times. But why, he wanted to know, had I expected an extra B? Now I had to tell him about Sunday afternoon.

He remembered Sunday afternoon all too well. And this is what he told me. The session was to be a short one, only fifteen minutes, so there would be little time for the randomization, and Trevor knew that he would be able to get there only just before it started. He had therefore asked Carl to make sure everything was ready for him, so that he could do the randomizing quickly. Apparently Carl had mistakenly thought that Trevor meant that he (Carl) was to do the randomization. Trevor arrived to find the picture set and the little brown envelope already selected. Not thinking this mattered, Trevor took the pictures and went off to be the sender.

This wouldn't matter, Trevor insisted, because Carl was not the experimenter and would not be there at the judging. But of course he had been. Officially Carl had had nothing to do with this trial. His name would not be in the record book at all. However, I now knew that he had done the randomization, been at the judging, and apparently encouraged the subject to choose B. B was the target and a B had gone missing from the drawer.

We decided to put everything back, not as it had been, but as it should have been. We got new envelopes of the same sort and put all the little letters back inside. Then Trevor began thinking about how he could prove that the problem was not serious. He needed the record book but couldn't find it. It was in searching the office, looking for it, that we found more envelopes, hidden under books and papers: a C, a D, three As, but no Bs. Trevor could think of no reason why they should have been there, and explained that, for the start of this series of experiments, he and Carl had made up equal numbers of envelopes for each letter, in a kind of envelope they had never used before. We put everything back and decided to do nothing for the moment.

The next day Carl was still ill. We did two more sessions with the students but both were misses. It was not until the following day that we were able to speak to Carl.

I had hoped to do this myself, but in the end it was Trevor, not I, who told him what had been going on. By the time I spoke to Carl he knew what had happened. He spoke very calmly and coldly. He said that the B had gone missing from the drawer because he had found a bent envelope in the main pile and had had to destroy it. He claimed to have told Trevor this at the time and Trevor now seemed to re-member the event, although two days before he had been unable to think of any reason why a B should disappear.

Carl said that the errors in the pile and drawers were just that, er-rors. They could easily have come about by accident and, in any case, would have little effect on the results. He said the envelopes found around the room must have been left over from a previous experiment.

Feeling leaden and confused, I apologized and Carl accepted. He said he had been more upset on Trevor's behalf than his own, and be-cause of all the other people I had troubled with my doubts and sus-picions.

It was my last day in Cambridge. We discussed what checks could be made now and agreed that we could discuss them all when I re-turned for a further three weeks in January.

That night I sat alone in confusion. I had not found the answer. I had apparently upset lots of people. Nothing was clear or simple. I wrote in my diary, "I don't think I've ever felt so very alone, so very responsible and quite so lost in all my life." And that was how I re-turned to Pear Tree Cottage for Christmas.

*   *   *

I never did go back. I wrote to Carl to suggest dates and plans for our work together, but he did not reply. Finally I rang him and that was when he told me that he never wanted to see me in his lab again. I can't say I blamed him but it destroyed my last hopes for getting to the bottom of what had happened without having to tell anyone else about it.

By then only Tom, and a very few people in Cambridge, knew what had gone on. I had told no one else, but I could not keep it that way forever. I felt I had to find out the truth behind Carl's results and this kept me going. I thought it important. If psi exists then science needs to know about it, for the world cannot be the kind of place most scientists assume. Proof of psi's existence would change our views of human communication, and even of space and time. This was far more important than the details of any one person's life, or their feelings or difficulties. I believed it was right for me to persevere. That, as far as I can tell, is why I went on trying to understand whether Carl's results were genuine or not.

I had to write a report for the SPR, who had funded my visit. I decided I would send this to Carl and invite him to write his own version. Both versions would then be available, and I hoped that people who read them would make up their own minds and some kind of consensus would arise. Perhaps other people would decide where the truth lay. I only hoped that journalists, or others who wanted to make a nasty story out of it, wouldn't get hold of the report and make things even harder for Carl. So I marked my report "confidential," meaning that only SPR members could read it.

As it turned out, nothing went as I had naively hoped. I didn't realize that almost no one would bother to read the report and that even people who did read it would fail to understand it, nor that Carl would never write up his version. I didn't reckon on the rumors, which would increasingly proliferate for years to come. I never imagined I would later be accused both of trying to "cover up" the truth by failing to publish my findings (how unfair that seemed!) and of starting the rumors myself (when I had tried so hard to avoid doing so). I did not foresee what would happen when other parapsychologists asked to look at Carl's data.

The reason others wanted the data was simple. If fraud had taken place there would be tell-tale signs to look for. Adrian Parker and Nils Wiklund, parapsychologists from Sweden, made one proposal of this kind and asked for the data.

I was thrilled about this. The worst thing was not knowing. If someone else, quite independently, made checks on the data, we might find out—or at least get closer to the truth. I felt so responsible. I did not know if I was in the process of wrongly destroying the work and career of the best psi experimenter there was.

Carl refused to make his data available. After informal requests for the data failed, an official request was made through the Parapsychological Association (PA). This also failed and in 1984 the PA established a committee to investigate. I gladly supplied all the information I had and once again (naively) hoped that this would settle the matter.

It did not. Carl was reprimanded for failing to respond to their request for information within a reasonable time, but still no one could be sure what had really gone on in his experiments.

Finally, in 1987, the whole affair was published in three articles in the SPR journal. I wrote a report. Trevor Harley and Gerry Matthews responded and said that I was guilty of "extreme prejudice in her reporting of the events and in their interpretation" (Harley and Matthews 1987, p. 199) and that the best interpretation of the events was minor experimental error. Carl entitled his response "Skeptical Fairytales from Bristol" and accused me of suppressing evidence and of having nothing but my own testimony to recount. He gave alternative explanations of everything I had observed and said that he was not prepared to supply his data either to me, because I had had plenty of time to see it in Cambridge, nor to Parker, whom he accused of being incompetent and "an accomplished libeller" (Sargent 1987, p. 217). He concluded: "If I learned one thing in parapsychology, it is that results and statistics and data never changed anyone's mind about anything: experience is the only arbiter" (Sargent 1987, p. 217).

* * *

Does it matter what happened in Cambridge all those years ago? Sadly I think it does, although we still do not know the truth. There are so few strong pieces of evidence for psi that each one is important in the overall quest. Yet this one is clearly marred, at the very least by a series of accidental errors. Carl has now left the field of parapsychology, but the data he gathered then in Cambridge carry on today as part of the evidence presented for psi.

The data are there in the 1985 Ganzfeld Debate. In this famous dispute, critic and psychologist Ray Hyman analyzed the forty-two experiments then published using what is called meta-analysis. This allows one to compare the results of many experiments, to find an overall effect size, to detect common patterns, and of most relevance here to test whether the overall effect can be attributed to flaws in the experiments. He argued that many of the studies were flawed, and that the better the quality of the study, the smaller the psi effect. Nine of the studies were Sargent's.

Chuck Honorton, originator of the Ganzfeld-psi experiments, then carried out his own analysis, using twenty-eight of the forty-two studies (those that reported the number of direct hits). He concluded that there was a reliable effect that did not depend on any one experimenter and was not related to the quality of the study. This seemed to be good evidence for the reality of psi in the ganzfeld.

What worried me was that Honorton had classified Sargent's nine studies as *adequate* for randomization (one of the several possible flaws he considered). But seven of these had used the method I observed in Cambridge. So I repeated Honorton's calculation counting these as flawed for randomization and found a significant correlation (r = -.32, t = 1.73, p<.05, 1-tailed) between randomization and z-score, therefore agreeing with Hyman. I submitted a brief paper on this to the *Journal of Parapsychology* in January 1987. In February the editor wrote to inform me that it would be published, but in fact it never was. I never found out why.

Meanwhile, the Ganzfeld Debate led to a healthy exchange between parapsychologists and skeptics, and to everyone agreeing on what would constitute a good experiment. On this basis, Chuck Honorton designed his now-famous *autoganzfeld* experiments (Honorton et al. 1991). These use a completely automated procedure in which all stages of the experiment, from target selection to judging and recording the results, are controlled by a computer. The methods appeared to be extremely rigorous; the results were highly significant and the findings in line with those of the meta-analysis. Moreover, the effect did not appear to depend on any one experimenter or lab.

All this assumed greater significance when Honorton teamed up with Cornell University psychologist Daryl Bem to provide a review of the ganzfeld literature for a mainstream journal. It was published in what is probably the world's most prestigious psychology journal, *Psychological Bulletin,* to be read widely by psychologists who mostly know nothing of the past history of the subject.

They presented the same meta-analysis and the same *autoganzfeld* data, and concluded that "the psi ganzfeld effect is large enough to be of both theoretical interest and potential practical importance" (Bem and Honorton 1994, p. 8).

Readers will learn that "one laboratory contributed 9 of the studies. Honorton's own laboratory contributed 5. . . . Thus, half of the studies were conducted by only 2 laboratories" (p. 6). What they will not know is *which* laboratory this was. There is no mention of either Cambridge or Sargent, no references given to these studies, and certainly no hint that any doubt has been cast on them.

It makes me wonder about the point of all that painful investigation, when the findings are so quickly forgotten—or deliberately glossed over. Perhaps this does not matter, since further analyses show that the effect does not depend on these two laboratories. But as far as I am concerned, I cannot help wondering about all those other labs and what I would find if I spent a week in any of them. But I doubt I ever shall. I can only say that the whole episode has dented my confidence in psi. It seems that every time I really delve into some aspect of the evidence, it simply slips away.

Ernesto Spinelli never published his results in full. I had hoped that he would present a proper, detailed account of all his methods and results, for others to evaluate. As it is, only sketchy accounts have appeared. So, although Spinelli completed the mammoth task of testing over a thousand children, we still cannot confidently accept his conclusions.

I have not pursued the question of psi in children, though I did design some experiments to test twins. These showed that pairs of twins did better than other pairs when the sender was given the choice of a target (as in Spinelli's experiments)—in other words, when *thinking alike* could help them. In a true telepathy condition they did no better than other pairs and no better than chance (Blackmore and Chamberlain 1993).

Despairing of finding psi myself, I spent many years trying to understand why people might believe in the paranormal even if it doesn't exist (Blackmore 1992). I found that sheep (believers) were more prone to making probability misjudgments, which might lead them to think that perfectly ordinary coincidences need a psychic explanation. I also found that sheep are more willing to "see" things in confusing pictures, and to "hear" things in noise—suggesting that they may live in a more richly meaningful world, but at the cost of seeing some things that are simply not there. This work is interesting (at least to me) but it can never resolve the debate over psi. All these correlates of belief could equally be there whether psi exists, or whether it does not.

So does it? The ganzfeld work is making the biggest impact at the moment. Sadly, Honorton died in 1993, at the age of forty-six. His death was a blow to the field, and makes it harder to evaluate the evidence. However, others are carrying on with the *autoganzfeld*. Among them is the laboratory of the Koestler Chair at Edinburgh University, where Professor Robert Morris now leads a small team of parapsychological researchers. Perhaps we will one day find out whether the effect is real or not.

There are several other lines of research that appear promising. These include remote viewing, PK on living systems (Braud and Schlitz 1994), and remote staring, that is, the ability to detect when someone is looking at you (Braud, Shafer, and Andrews 1993). Probably the most important, however, is PK with random number generators. Vast numbers of trials, conducted in many laboratories, apparently show small but reliable effects of intention on physical systems (Radin and Nelson 1989). In addition there are other meta-analyses which show apparently reliable effects; for example, in precognition (Honorton and Ferrari 1989) and PK with dice (Radin and Ferrari 1991).

Perhaps I should be convinced by all, or some of these. The trouble is that my experience teaches me not to be. Everywhere I have looked psi has seemed to slip away from me. And I cannot look everywhere.

I can only hope that if psi is real, it will jump up and down in front of me and shout "change your mind." And, since I have changed my mind more than once in the past and survived, I know I can do so again.

I also know that the very idea of psi has got me nowhere. Parapsychology is often held up as the science of the future, the science that will tackle all those human questions about the nature of mind or the farther reaches of human experience, the science that will force a new paradigm to topple the old and even serve as a route to spirituality. But it does not deliver.

The reason, I suggest, is not that there is no psi, for with its negative definition and all its other problems, we can never be sure of that. The real reason is that putative paranormal powers have absolutely nothing to do with the real mystery. The real mystery is there all right —in our questions about mind, consciousness, and mystical experience. I made the stupid mistake of looking to psi for those answers. I shall not do so again, for parapsychology cannot provide them.

This is a strong statement, but one I stand by. I once described psi as a "red herring" and I say the same now. If you want to understand the basis of mind, the nature of consciousness, or who you are—psi will not help you.

Let me then pick up the threads of a few things that have helped; things that have touched at the heart of that mystical experience all those years ago.

Thirty

Feeling Real

In 1986 we went to live in Tübingen, a beautiful town on the banks of the river Neckar in the south of Germany. Tom had a scholarship there for a year and we had rented a huge old apartment barely furnished or heated, but with the park on one side and the river on the other. I was writing *The Adventures of a Parapsychologist* in between looking after the children. Emily was then four and Jolyon was two—hard work.

Things were not altogether happy, although I know I did well at persuading myself they were. Fun as it was to be in a new country, I felt trapped. Superficially, theoretically, we had a happy and equal relationship. We were both academics, of a sort; Tom did much of the shopping, and some of the cooking and child care. But in fact I was in the situation that so many women find themselves in. We were there for Tom's job, not mine. He had a career and I did not. I had to remember which day was playgroup, organize the baby-sitter, constantly be aware of where each child was. I was the one who was with the children all day long, sometimes wanting to scream and scream—for all that I loved them. This is the reality of having young children.

I was glad to be with them, not to have to work full-time, to bring them up myself in their most formative years. But it is hard.

How much this had to do with my inner state, I cannot say. However, I remember one particular morning, though it probably happened many times, looking out over our little balcony, while Jolyon clattered about on the bare wooden floor in the playroom behind me. I gazed out across the vast plane trees below. They didn't seem real. I pinched myself and it didn't help. I blinked and tried to look this way and that, as though to catch them out. In some horrible way I didn't feel as though I were really there at all.

Later I took the children to the park with their friends. "Ente, Ente," they all shouted, and ran down to the duck pond. "Sind sie

261

Schwannen?" I asked tentatively. Howls of laughter. "Nein, Schwäne," the older girl corrected my attempts at the plural of "swan," while the little ones chanted, "Swannen, Swannen." I prodded the trees and touched their bark. Sometimes they did feel real. "Mummy, Mummy." What was that I had said to our neighbors last night? They seemed upset. Was it my fault? What could I do about it now? "Mummy, Joly's throwing mud." "Coming." Where was the other boy? Would I get any time to work today? Perhaps if they slept after lunch. "Mummy, Mummy!" Was anything real?

That summer I was helping to organize a conference, though since it was to be in Wales, I was too far away to be much help. It was on "Eastern Approaches to Mind and Self "—not a good title perhaps, but a fascinating theme.

My involvement had begun when I met John Crook a few years before. John was a lecturer in ethology, the science of animal behavior, at Bristol University. He had once been well known for his studies of birds and primates, but was now becoming more interested in consciousness. Indeed, when I asked some of the students about his course on cognitive ethology, they said it was really about Buddhism!

John runs Buddhist retreats in a remote farmhouse in mid-Wales and in January 1982 I had plucked up the courage to go on my first retreat.

Nineteen eighty-two was the coldest winter for many years, and I drove the hundred or so miles, in our ancient drafty car, through increasingly desolate countryside. Everything was covered with snow, and as the road meandered up into the Welsh mountains, the snow got deeper and deeper. Darkness falls by four o'clock at that time of the year, and it was already evening.

When I reached the little village of Pant-y-Dwr, I carefully followed the instructions: "Turn left at the post box, along the lane, left again into the farmyard." The lane was a narrow cutting made by the snowplow and its walls were ten feet high. There was no going back if it was the wrong lane. John had told me to park at the farm below because the half mile of rough track up to his house was impassable and I would have to walk. There was no phone up at the house and I would just have to find it alone. I was eight months pregnant.

To my intense relief, John and the others had seen the lights of my car and set off down the hill with a spare walking stick. They were there to meet me at the farm and show me the way through the white fields to the Maenllwyd.

The Maenllwyd is a tiny Welsh hill farm, of dark gray stone, nestling in the valley of a small stream. Below lie the road and villages; above is the bare sheep-scattered hillside of bracken and heather. Once occupied by poor sheep farmers, it must have been a hard way to make a living.

We pushed open the front door and a flurry of snow rushed in with us to the living room, where a small group was sitting cozily round a roaring log fire. The rest of the room, as far as I could see by lamplight reflecting on stone walls, contained a few ancient armchairs and a long table for meals. They showed me around. At the back was a tiny kitchen, with a stone floor and a range for cooking. There was no gas, no electricity, and, for this retreat, no running water. The cold had burst all the pipes. I should say that I was let off the daily task of breaking ice and fetching water from the stream, on account of my huge size and cumbersome shape.

Everything seemed to be ice. We were awakened at 5 A.M., to run up and down the hill before the first meditation session, in which we sat, on stools or cushions, facing the blank white wall. The whole retreat was held in silence, and each day was a round of half-hour meditation sessions, interspersed with exercises and work periods. Washing up, cleaning, or cutting up the vegetables for meals were a pleasure compared to the hours of sitting. Cold and longing for sleep, we could finally crawl into stiff, icy sleeping bags at 10 P.M. Every day seemed like a week, but I began to learn, for the first time, what it means to look into one's own mind.

There I sat, hour after hour, cold and uncomfortable, moaning and complaining to myself, peaceful or joyful, exasperated or frightened, just staring at a blank white wall. Every crack became a vision of torture or sex. Every bump a landscape of hills or a pit of fears. Every faint blotch a reminder of something I had done wrong, was proud of, hated myself for, or. . . . As John once said, "The thing about meditation is that there is only you and the wall, and you can't blame the wall."

I came to know the Maenllwyd well. The barn is now a meditation hall, but there is still no electricity or telephone to remind you of the ordinary world. I have since been there for many retreats, and to meetings of a small group of psychologists interested in Buddhism and

The Adventures of a Parapsychologist

meditation. Apart from our enjoyable meetings, this group led to one of the first books linking Eastern thought to Western psychology (edited by Claxton 1986), and we organized the conference in Wales (Crook and Fontana 1990).

The idea was to bring Western psychologists together with Eastern scholars, Hindus, Buddhists, and practitioners of different traditions and doctrines. In the end it was the psychologists and the Buddhists who found common ground and great inspiration. I remember talking to a lively young Englishman called Chogyal, resplendent in his robes, about dying in each moment and springing up anew (or ever-dissolving-and-reforming mental models?) and suddenly he said that one can jump off the cycle of death and rebirth. "Wow," I wrote in my diary that night. "So that apparently crazy idea has a very simple foundation in experience."

My own lecture was on mental models and mystical experience (Blackmore 1990), but I felt very much out of my depth. All around me people seemed to be talking about mindfulness—and I didn't know what it was.

It got to me. What *was* mindfulness?

As far as I could understand, being mindful meant being in the present moment, paying attention only to what is happening *now*, not thinking of past or future. This didn't sound very complicated, and seemed an odd thing to be so concerned about. Could that be all there was to it? Could I be mindful? Didn't just thinking about it make you mindful? How could I know if I wasn't?

I would have to try it. Now.

Don't think, just pay attention.

I did. And now. Oh dear, this is a bit weird. If I think about what to do next I am no longer mindful. If I decide to be mindful for an hour I am not being mindful now. If I think about what I am doing, I am thinking, not being mindful. I just have to do it.

I did.

When the conference ended I had to catch the bus back to Heathrow. There was little time to spare and I had to wait ages for a lift to the bus station. I didn't fret, being mindful of the street sounds and sights. Eventually I found myself running flat out across the tarmac to catch the bus just as it was leaving; not thinking, being in the present, running. When thoughts arose, as they did all the time, I met them with something John Crook had taught us as a technique for meditation. When a thought comes along (or anything else for that matter) just meet it with "Let it through. Let it be. Let it go." In other words: Don't block it. Don't do anything with it. Don't hang onto it. "Let it go. Let . . ." I sat on the bus, and at the airport. "Let . . ." The plane was called.

Back in Germany, a few days later I wrote in my diary: "I am pursuing my policy of living in the moment—of reminding myself of 'mindfulness.' It is hard to write about because writing makes it hard to do. However, I shall try. I find it sometimes very hard. It is a strain and I imagine it shouldn't be. On the other hand I am finding I forget less and less often. The state is perhaps less obviously 'different' than it was at first, but I am getting more used to maintaining it through talking, acting and deciding. I am amazed at some of the effects . . . I enjoyed everything as it was happening and didn't keep wishing we were doing something else (as I might easily have), and somehow the whole day seemed to be pervaded by a kind of peacefulness which took me by surprise. Is it really that easy to find peace? Perhaps it is, but of course it is at the cost of giving up a lot of things."

Maybe this is what makes mindfulness so hard. Among the things that have to be given up are fretting about what to do next; trying to make sense of past events; going over conversations to decide whether you said the right thing or not; speculating on future events and looking forward to them; carrying on imaginary conversations; rehearsing anger at other people for their stupidity, forgetfulness, or unkindness. These, I soon discovered, were the ordinary contents of my ever-restless mind. Is this such a loss? They are indeed hard to give up. At first you think you won't be able to do anything if you don't think all the time. But it isn't true. And once the burden has gone—what relief!

For me, one of the hardest was bedtime and giving up idle fantasies as I fell asleep. Maintaining awareness instead seemed comfortless at first, but it no longer seems so.

To this day I don't know how it happened, but I kept this up for seven weeks. At the end of that time the proofs of my book defeated me. I could not remain "present" during hours of checking text for errors. The ability, or determination, never came back in the same form, though I have practiced mindfulness more or less assiduously ever since.

For many years I wondered whether being mindful would ever get any easier. It did not seem to. Yet I think in the end it begins to spring up of its own accord, out of the blue. Being here; everything just as it is, fresh and undistorted by associations, needs, or intentions.

At that same time I finally established a regular practice of meditation, after many abortive attempts. I have never done a lot, just a few minutes a day, but every day. During that period of intensive practice it was almost a relief to sit down and be mindful of a blank wall or the carpet, rather than all that action and color. This regular habit seems, very slowly, to effect great changes. At last it all began to seem real; there was no more need to pinch myself.

*   *   *

I now suspect that those plane trees seemed unreal because my mind was such a mass of fears, plans, hopes, horrors, worries, and responsibilities. There was no space left over for the immediate world of trees and sky and birds, or the needs of people around me. If things begin to seem unreal I no longer blink, pinch, or try to grasp them; experience tells me to let go and let them be.

Of course I still have plans, hopes, and fears, and letting go is not easy. Somehow we just do seem to want to hang onto things—especially to ourselves.

The most crucial lessons for me have been of losing things I thought I needed the most. My memory theory of ESP was one. The reality and importance of the paranormal was another. Yet I let these go, and the world did not disintegrate. Indeed, only by letting go of my own theories have I been able to progress to new ones. I no longer fear being proved wrong, or working out for myself that I am wrong. There are plenty more theories where they came from, and a great freshness in clearing away the rubbish.

The worst was losing Tom.

Tom fell in love with someone else, and I could hardly complain, for I had done the same thing many years before. However, this time was different. He wanted to leave us and live with her. I fought like mad. Both of us fought like mad and we were horrible to each other for a while. Our marriage, our family, and our happy home in Pear Tree Cottage were everything to me and I could not imagine life without them. I felt a failure as a lover, a wife, a mother, and a human being. I would be—horror of horrors—a single parent. Emily and Jolyon would be part of a broken family. I clung desperately to the myth of what I thought we had been. I can even remember the moment when I felt it all crashing down around me. Oddly enough, though, when I finally stopped fighting, I found a new life beginning.

Tom now lives on a narrow-boat, a traditional English canal barge, in Bristol docks. Emily, Jolyon, and I finally left Pear Tree Cottage and came to live in the city, too. The children now live half the time with me and half with Tom on the boat, seeming to thrive on this new life, cycling to school from one place or the other, carrying piles of books (that is Emily), or half-constructed planes and a pet rat called Shniffles (that would be Jolyon). My garden is more modest but the vegetables no worse. And we live with Adam Hart-Davis, with whom I write books, make television programs, and love.

In 1992 I was offered my first ever real job as senior lecturer in psychology at the University of the West of England in Bristol. Although it seemed an honor at the time, I soon reduced the job to part-time. I now teach courses in parapsychology and the psychology of consciousness, supervise research students, and still carry on with my own thinking and writing.

My life now is a complicated juggling act between students and lectures, television and radio studios, garden, home and the kids, research, and writing. I sometimes wonder who this person is; Susan Blackmore—rent-a-skeptic for the chat show, producer of sound bites, and provider of an alternative argument for every claim. Who is she? "She" is something concocted by all the people out there who have views about her.

That "her" has little to do with the moment-to-moment arising of experience here, in working, traveling, digging the garden, cooking meals, setting off with Adam and the kids for a holiday in Salcombe, or visiting Tom on the boat. Consciousness is something quite different from all those concocted selves.

Then there is "Mummy." I sometimes think that having children is all about letting go—from the moment they leave your own body and become separate creatures. They stop drinking your milk and eat solid food; they go off on their own to school and make friends you have never even met. I suppose my greatest fears are still for them, that they will be knocked off their bikes and killed, will fall into the canal and drown, or be attacked by a sex-crazed murderer. But these are all fantasies and not here in the present. All I can really do is love them when they are here, teach them what I can, and let them go. Letting go in every moment is good practice for these grander kinds of letting go.

So who is doing all this?

When the incessant commentary slows down, it becomes less and less clear who is doing anything. Indeed, sometimes there does not seem to be anyone in there doing anything at all. Meditation and mindfulness both seem to wear away at the sense of a little self inside who does things.

At first I found this disconcerting. I had read and heard plenty about the Buddhist idea of no-self and this fitted perfectly with the obvious scientific point that if you look inside the brain, there is no little person in there pulling the strings. There are only millions and millions of neurons and synapses. But in terms of *experience* the idea is distinctly creepy. If there is no one in there, who is actually making the decisions?

I tried to find out. If the idea that "I" was acting and doing and deciding was an illusion, then it should be abandoned. So, could I *not* act, do, or decide?

I was driving home from Bristol one day, back to Pear Tree Cottage. There are two possible routes; either you turn left at the Chelwood traffic lights and go through the lanes, or you go straight on along the main road. The main road is longer and rather boring, but the single track lanes can be slow; meeting a tractor, or even another car, means reversing and waiting. Which way should I go today?

I sat waiting for the lights to change and wondered what would happen if I simply did not decide. A flash of fear gripped me. Surely I would crash through the fence and into the hedge between the two.

The lights changed. A hand grasped the gear lever, a foot pressed the pedal, the steering wheel moved to the left, and we set off down the lanes. The decision was made without "me." "I" wasn't needed.

I gradually extended that new attitude to other, more tricky decisions, and I now practice this way of living. Ten years ago I wrote: "I am not very good at making decisions" (p. 175). I wouldn't say that now. Decisions seem much easier without the false idea of a "self" who makes them, or to whom the outcome matters one way or the other.

I sometimes think I am just a beginner when it comes to these practices, when countless people throughout the ages have discovered all sorts of things about the nature of mind, self, and awareness through years of practice and diligent application. The training must be at least as long and arduous and intricate as training to become a nuclear physicist, a concert pianist, or even a parapsychologist. But at least I have begun. And I am grateful to all the people who kicked me in that direction, and guided me on the way, because you cannot take a university degree in self-observation or the development of awareness.

*   *   *

Many people associate meditation with religion and New Age ideas; with mysterious energies or psychic forces; with going to higher planes or better worlds; with an inner soul or spirit that is separate from the body and can be born again. Yet meditation itself, as direct experience, has nothing to do with any of these. Indeed, meditation and mindfulness seem not to take one away to another world, but to reveal the immediate and glorious presence of this one.

Meditation and mindfulness can be seen simply as disciplines of the mind. Being in the present requires no God and no psychic forces; implies no life after death or personal reincarnation. Indeed, being in the present can give rise to a sense of eternity in every moment, which obliterates the desire for any other kind of immortality.

I once referred to "The First Mistake" that I made: that is, in thinking that parapsychology would help me to understand consciousness, altered states, and the nature of my own mind. I was looking for a spiritual path and I turned to the paranormal. I now realize I am not the only one to make that mistake. All around us people assume that psi is the way to the light; that spirituality, mystical experience, and the exploration of consciousness have something to do with the paranormal. I don't think it is true.

The spiritual path may be very simple. The gradual weakening of self-related desires leads to a different way of living. Simply doing these practices could be called a spiritual path. If so, there is no need for religion, doctrine, God, or the paranormal.

It is a scary way. You cannot be the detached observer of classical science because "you" are inevitably changed in the process of learning. However, you can be disciplined, structured, and critical. There is no real conflict with science.

My hope is that what feels like clarity of vision really is so; that the many different paths people take all lead to similar insights and understanding; that they all reveal the light that is here and now—not somewhere else. If so, we may discover a new way of studying consciousness that begins from self-discipline and personal insight, but crosses into objective understanding. This would be a new science of consciousness indeed. It seems to me that this is the way to learn about mind, self, and consciousness. This, not parapsychology, is the way to tackle all those questions that set me off in the first place.

In this way I have come to what many people find a very odd position. I see it as perfectly logical, but I know others find it confusing. I practice and encourage meditation, though I do not believe in raising energies, chakras, or reincarnation. I investigate claims of the paranormal, even though I doubt any of them is valid. I advise people how to have or control their OBEs, though I don't think anything leaves the body. I study how NDEs transform people's lives, though I argue that this has more to do with the dissolution of an illusory self than with life after death. I talk about spiritual experience, though I do not believe in spirits. I try to live here and now.

As for the paranormal, I still don't know.

Alcock, J.E. *Parapsychology: Science or Magic?* (Oxford: Pergamon Press, 1981).

Ashton, H.T., Dear, P.R., Harley, T.A., and Sargent, C.L. "A Four-subject Study of Psi in the Ganzfeld," *Journal of the Society for Psychical Research* **51** (1981):12–21.

Avant, L.L. "Vision in the Ganzfeld," *Psychological Bulletin* **64** (1965): 245–58.

Beloff, J. "Belief and Doubt." In *Research in Parapsychology 1972*, ed. W.G. Roll et al. (Metuchen: Scarecrow Press, 1973), pp. 189–200.

——, ed. *New Directions in Parapsychology* (London: Elek Science Books, 1974).

Bem, D.J., and Honorton, C. "Does Psi Exist?: Replicable Evidence for an Anomalous Process of Information Transfer," *Psychological Bulletin* **115** (1994):4–18.

Bierman, D.J. "A Retro and Direct PK Test for Babies with the Manipulation of Feedback: A First Trial of Independent Replication Using Software Exchange," *European Journal of Parapsychology* **5** (1985a):373–90.

——. "An Impossible Artifact," *European Journal of Parapsychology* **6** (1985b):99–103.

Blackmore, S. J. *Parapsychology and Out-of-the-body Experiences* (London: Society for Psychical Research, 1978).

——. Correspondence, *Bulletin of the British Psychological Society* **32** (1979):225.

——. "Correlations Between ESP and Memory," *European Journal of Parapsychology* **3** (1980a):127–47.

——. "A Study of Memory and ESP in Young Children," *Journal of the Society for Psychical Research* **50** (1980b):501–20.

——. *Extrasensory Perception as a Cognitive Process.* Unpublished Ph.D. thesis (Guildford: University of Surrey, 1980c).

——. "Report of a Visit to Carl Sargent's Laboratory in Cambridge." Unpublished paper, Archives of the Society for Psychical Research, 1980d.

271

Blackmore, S. J. "The Extent of Selective Reporting of ESP Ganzfeld Studies," *European Journal of Parapsychology* **3** (1980e):213–20.
———. "Errors and Confusions in ESP," *European Journal of Parapsychology* **4** (1981a):49–70.
———. "The Effect of Variations in Target Material on ESP and Memory," *Re-
search Letter* **11** (Utrecht: Parapsychology Laboratory, 1981b):1–26.
———. *Beyond the Body* (London: Heinemann, 1982a).
———. "Out-of-body Experiences, Lucid Dreams and Imagery: Two Surveys," *Journal of the American Society for Psychical Research* **76**
(1982b):301–17.
———. "Have You Ever Had an OBE?: The Wording of the Question," *Jour-
nal of the Society for Psychical Research* **51** (1982c):292–302. See also
Correspondence, *JSPR* **52** (1983):152.
———. "Divination with Tarot Cards: An Empirical Study," *Journal of the So-
ciety for Psychical Research* **52** (1983):97–101.
———. "ESP in Young Children," *Journal of the Society for Psychical Re-
search* **52** (1984a):311–15.
———. "A Postal Survey of OBEs and Other Experiences," *Journal of the So-
ciety for Psychical Research* **52** (1984b):225–44.
———. "A Psychological Theory of the Out-of-Body Experience," *Journal of
Parapsychology* **48** (1984c):201–18.
———. "Some Advice on Questionnaire Research," *Parapsychology Review*
16, no. 5 (1985a):5–8.
———. "Unrepeatability: Parapsychology's Only Finding." In *The Repeata-
bility Problem in Parapsychology*, ed. B. Shapin and L. Coly (New York:
Parapsychology Foundation, 1985b), pp. 183–206.
———. "Where Am I? Viewpoints in Imagery and the Out-of-body Experi-
ence," *Journal of Mental Imagery* **11** (1986a):53–66.
———. "Who Am I?: Changing Models of Reality in Meditation." In *Beyond
Therapy*, ed. G. Claxton (London: Wisdom, 1986b), pp. 71–85.
———. "A Report of a Visit to Carl Sargent's Laboratory," *Journal of the So-
ciety for Psychical Research* **54** (1987):186–98.
———. "Mental Models and Mystical Experience." In *Space in Mind,* ed. J.
Crook and D. Fontana (Shaftesbury, Dorset: Element, 1990), pp. 66–75.
———. "Psychic Experiences: Psychic Illusions," *Skeptical Inquirer* **16**
(1992):367–76.
———. *Dying to Live: Science and the Near-death Experience* (London:
Grafton; and Amherst, N.Y.: Prometheus Books, 1993).
Blackmore, S.J., Bierman, D.J., and Johnson, M. "Reliability and Other Ig-
nored Issues in Parapsychology. Roundtable." In *Research in Parapsy-
chology, 1980,* ed. W.G. Roll and J. Beloff (Metuchen: Scarecrow Press,
1981), pp. 14–15.

Blackmore, S.J., and Chamberlain, F. "ESP and Thought Concordance in Twins: A Method of Comparison," *Journal of the Society for Psychical Research* **59** (1993): 89–96.

Blackmore, S.J., and Trościanko, T.S. "A Baby-Operated Tape Player," *Bulletin of the British Psychological Society* **37** (1984):A53.

———. "Belief in the Paranormal: Probability Judgements, Illusory Control and the 'Chance Baseline Shift,'" *British Journal of Psychology* **76** (1985):459–68.

Blavatsky, H.P. *Isis Unveiled* (London: Rider, n.d.).

Boring, E.G. Introduction to C.E.M. Hansel, *ESP: A Scientific Evaluation* (New York: Scribner's, 1966).

Brandon, R. *The Spiritualists* (London: Weidenfeld and Nicolson, 1983).

Braud, W., and Schlitz, M. "A Methodology for the Objective Study of Transpersonal Imagery," *Journal of Scientific Exploration* **3** (1989): 43–63.

Braud, W., Shafer, D., and Andrews, S. "Reactions to an Unseen Gaze," *Journal of Parapsychology* **57** (1993): 373–90.

Braude, S.E. *ESP and Psychokinesis: A Philosophical Examination.* Philosophical Monographs (Philadelphia: Temple University Press, 1979a).

———. "The Observational Theories in Parapsychology: A Critique," *Journal of the American Society for Psychical Research* **73** (1979b):349–66.

Broad, W., and Wade, N. *Betrayers of the Truth* (New York: Simon and Schuster, 1982).

Bursen, H.A. *Dismantling the Memory Machine* (Dordrecht: D. Reidel, 1978).

Carington, W. *Telepathy: An Outline of Its Facts, Theory and Implications* (London: Methuen, 1945).

Castaneda, C. *The Teachings of Don Juan: A Yaqui Way of Knowledge* (Berkeley: University of California Press, 1968).

Claxton, G., ed. *Beyond Therapy: The Impact of Eastern Religions on Psychological Theory and Practice* (London: Wisdom, 1986).

Cox, E. In *The Philosophy of Parapsychology,* ed. B. Shapin and L. Coly (New York: Parapsychology Foundation, 1977), pp. 169–70.

Crawford, W.J. *Psychic Structures* (London: Watkins, 1921).

Crook, J., and Fontana, D., eds. *Space in Mind: East-West Psychology and Contemporary Buddhism* (Shaftesbury, Dorset: Element, 1990).

Dingwall, E.J. "The Need for Responsibility in Parapsychology: My Sixty Years in Psychical Research." In *A Century of Psychical Research,* ed. A. Angoff and J.B. Shapin (New York: Parapsychology Foundation, 1971).

Dingwall, E.J., Goldney, K.M., and Hall, T.H. *The Haunting of Borley Rectory* (London: Duckworth, 1956).

The Adventures of a Parapsychologist

Drucker, S.A., Drewes, A.A., and Rubin, L. "ESP in Relation to Cognitive Development and I.Q. in Young Children," *Journal of the American Society for Psychical Research* **71** (1977):289–98.

Eccles, J. "The Human Person in Its Two-way Relationship to the Brain." In *Research in Parapsychology 1976*, ed. J.D. Morris et al. (Metuchen: Scarecrow Press, 1977), pp. 251–62.

Forer, B.R. "The Fallacy of Personal Validation: A Classroom Demonstration of Gullibility," *Journal of Abnormal and Social Psychology* **44** (1949):118–23.

Gackenbach, J., and LaBerge, S., eds. *Lucid Dreaming: New Research on Consciousness During Sleep* (New York: Plenum, 1986).

Gauld, A. *The Founders of Psychical Research* (London: Routledge and Kegan Paul, 1968).

Gibson, H.B. "The 'Royal Nonesuch' of Parapsychology," *Bulletin of the British Psychological Society* **32** (1979):65–67.

Gregory, R.L. *Eye and Brain* (London: Weidenfeld and Nicolson, 1966).

Green, C.E. *Out-of-the-body Experiences* (London: Hamish Hamilton, 1968).

Greville, T.N.E. "On Multiple Matching with One Variable Deck," *Annals of Mathematical Statistics* **15** (1944):432–34.

Greyson, B., and Flynn, C.P., eds. *The Near-death Experience: Problems, Prospects, Perspectives* (Springfield, Ill.: C.C. Thomas, 1984).

Hansel, C.E.M. "A Critical Review of Experiments with Mr. Basil Shackleton and Mrs. Gloria Stewart as Sensitives," *Proceedings of the Society for Psychical Research* **53** (1960):1–42.

———. *E.S.P.: A Scientific Evaluation* (New York: Scribner's, 1966).

———. *ESP and Parapsychology: A Critical Re-evaluation* (Amherst, N.Y.: Prometheus Books, 1980).

Haraldsson, E. "Representative National Surveys of Psychic Phenomena: Iceland, Great Britain, Sweden, USA and Gallup's Multinational Survey," *Journal of the Society for Psychical Research* **53** (1985):145–58.

Harley, T., and Matthews, G. "Cheating, Psi, and the Appliance of Science: A Reply to Blackmore," *Journal of the Society for Psychical Research* **54** (1987):199–207.

Hart, H. "ESP Projection: Spontaneous Cases and the Experimental Method," *Journal of the American Society for Psychical Research* **48** (1954): 121–46.

———. Book Review, *Journal of the Society for Psychical Research* **61** (1967):173–78.

Heywood, R. *The Sixth Sense* (London: Chatto and Windus, 1959).

Honorton, C. "Meta-analysis of Psi Ganzfeld Research: A Response to Hyman," *Journal of Parapsychology* **49** (1985):51–86.

Honorton, C., Berger, R.E., Varvoglis, M.P., Quant, M., Derr, P., Schechter, E.I., and Ferrari, D.C. "Psi Communication in the Ganzfeld," *Journal of Parapsychology* **54** (1990):99–139.

Honorton, C., and Ferrari, D.C. "Future Telling: A Meta-analysis of Forced Choice Precognition Experiments, 1935–1987," *Journal of Parapsychology* **53** (1989):281–308.

Honorton, C., and Harper, S. "Psi-Mediated Imagery and Ideation in an Experimental Procedure for Regulating Perceptual Input," *Journal of the American Society for Psychical Research* **68** (1974):56–68.

Hyman, R. "The Ganzfeld Psi Experiment: A Critical Appraisal," *Journal of Parapsychology* **49** (1985):3–49.

Inglis, B. "Power Corrupts: Skepticism Corrodes." In *Research in Parapsychology 1980,* ed. W.G. Roll and J. Beloff (Metuchen: Scarecrow Press, 1981), pp. 143–51.

Irwin, H.J. "Out of the Body Down Under: Some Cognitive Characteristics of Australian Students Reporting OOBEs," *Journal of the Society for Psychical Research* **50** (1980):448–59.

———. "Fear of Psi and Attitude to Parapsychological Research," *Parasychology Review* **16**, no. 6 (1985):1–4.

Iverson, J. *More Lives Than One* (London: Pan, 1977).

Johnson, M. "Problems, Challenges and Promises." In *Research in Parapsychology 1976,* ed. J.D. Morris et al. (Metuchen: Scarecrow Press, 1977), pp. 231–49.

Jung, C.G. *Synchronicity: An Acausal Connecting Principle* (London: Routledge and Kegan Paul, 1955).

Kahneman, D., and Tversky, A. "On the Psychology of Prediction," *Psychological Review* **80** (1973):237–51.

Kuhn, T.S. *The Structure of Scientific Revolutions* (Chicago: University of Chicago Press, 1962).

Kurtz, P., ed. *A Skeptic's Handbook of Parapsychology* (Amherst, N.Y.: Prometheus Books, 1985).

Lakatos, I. *The Methodology of Scientific Research Programmes.* Philosophical Papers, vol. 1 (Cambridge: Cambridge University Press, 1978).

Landau, L. "An Unusual Out-of-the-Body Experience," *Journal of the Society for Psychical Research* **42** (1963):126–28.

Langer, E.J. "The Illusion of Control," *Journal of Personality and Social Psychology* **32** (1975):311–28.

Marks, D., and Kammann, R. *The Psychology of the Psychic* (Amherst, N.Y.: Prometheus Books, 1980).

Markwick, B. "The Establishment of Data Manipulation in the Soal-Shackleton Experiments." In *A Skeptic's Handbook of Parapsychology,* ed. P. Kurtz (Amherst, N.Y.: Prometheus Books, 1985), pp. 287–312.

Markwick, B. "The Soal-Goldney Experiments with Basil Shackleton: New Evidence of Data Manipulation," *Proceedings of the Society for Psychical Research* **56** (1978):250–81.

Maslow, A. *The Farther Reaches of Human Nature* (New York: Viking, 1971).

Medhurst, R.G. "The Origin of the 'Prepared Random Numbers' Used in the Shackleton Experiments," *Journal of the Society for Psychical Research* **46** (1971):39–55. Corrections **46**:203.

Millar, B. "The Observational Theories: A Primer," *European Journal of Parapsychology* **2** (1978):304–32.

Monroe, R.A. *Journeys Out of the Body* (New York: Doubleday, 1971).

Moody, R.A. *Life after Life* (Atlanta, Ga.: Mockingbird, 1975).

Morris, R.L., Harary, S.B., Janis, J., Hartwell, J., and Roll, W.G. "Studies of Communication During Out-of-Body Experiences," *Journal of the American Society for Psychical Research* **72** (1978):1–22.

Moss, P., with Keeton, J. *Encounters with the Past* (London: Sidgwick and Jackson, 1979).

Muldoon, S., and Carrington, H. *The Projection of the Astral Body* (London: Rider, 1929).

———. *The Phenomena of Astral Projection* (London: Rider, 1951).

Myers, F.W.H. *Human Personality and Its Survival of Bodily Death* (London: Longmans, Green, 1903).

Osis, K. "Out-of-Body Research at the ASPR." In *Mind Beyond the Body,* ed. D.S. Rogo (New York: Penguin, 1978), pp. 162–69.

Owen, I.M., and Sparrow, M. *Conjuring up Phillip* (Ontario, Canada: Fitzhenry and Whiteside, 1976).

Palmer, J. "Scoring in ESP Tests as a Function of Belief in ESP. Part I. The Sheep-Goat Effect," *Journal of the American Society for Psychical Research* **65** (1971):373–408.

———. "Scoring in ESP Tests as a Function of Belief in ESP. Part II. Beyond the Sheep-Goat Effect," *Journal of the American Society for Psychical Research* **66** (1972):1–26.

———. "The Out-of-Body Experience: A Psychological Theory," *Parapsychology Review* **9** (1978):19–22.

———. "A Community Mail Survey of Psychic Experiences," *Journal of the American Society for Psychical Research* **73** (1979):221–52.

Parker, A. *States of Mind: ESP and Altered States of Consciousness* (London: Malaby Press, 1975).

Phillips, P.R., and McBeath, M.K. "An Attempted Replication of the Cox Films of PK." In *Research in Parapsychology 1982,* ed. W.G. Roll et al. (Metuchen: Scarecrow Press, 1983), pp. 113–15.

Popper, K. *The Logic of Scientific Discovery* (London: Hutchinson, 1959).

Price, G.R. "Science and the Supernatural," *Science* **122** (1955):359–67.

Price, H.H. "Haunting and the 'Psychic Ether' Hypotheses," *Proceedings of the Society for Psychical Research* **45** (1939):307–43.

Radin, D.I., and Ferrari, D.C. "Effects of Consciousness on the Fall of Dice: A Meta-analysis," *Journal of Scientific Exploration* **5** (1991):61–83.

Radin, D.I., and Nelson, R.D. "Evidence for Consciousness Related Anomalies in Random Physical Systems," *Foundations of Physics* **19** (1989): 1499–1514.

Randi, J. *The Magic of Uri Geller* (New York: Random House, Ballantine Books, 1975).

———. *Flim-Flam!* (Amherst, N.Y.: Prometheus Books, 1982).

Raudive, K. *Breakthrough* (New York: Taplinger, 1971).

Rhine, J.B. *Extrasensory Perception* (Boston: Boston Society for Psychical Research, 1934).

———. "A New Case of Experimenter Unreliability," *Journal of Parapsychology* **38** (1974):218–25.

Rogo, D.S. *Leaving the Body* (Englewood Cliffs, N.J.: Prentice-Hall, 1983).

———. ed. *Mind Beyond the Body* (New York: Penguin, 1978).

Roll, W.G. "ESP and Memory," *International Journal of Neuropsychiatry* **2** (1966):505–12.

Roney-Dougal, S.M. "A Comparison of Subliminal and Extrasensory Perception Using the Ganzfeld Technique." In *Research in Parapsychology 1978,* ed. W.G. Roll (Metuchen: Scarecrow Press, 1979), pp. 98–100.

Rushton, W.A.H. "Letter to the Editor," *Journal of the Society for Psychical Research* **48** (1976):412–13.

Sargent, C. "Skeptical Fairytales from Bristol," *Journal of the Society for Psychical Research* **54** (1987):208–18.

Sargent, C.L. "Exploring Psi in the Ganzfeld," *Parapsychological Monographs,* no. 17 (New York: Parapsychology Foundation, 1980).

Sargent, C.L., Harley, T.A., Lane, J., and Radcliffe, K. "Ganzfeld Psi-optimization in Relation to Session Duration." In *Research in Parapsychology 1980,* ed. W.G. Roll et al. (Metuchen: Scarecrow Press, 1981), pp. 82–84.

Schmidt, H. "Towards a Mathematical Theory of Psi," *Journal of the American Society for Psychical Research* **69** (1975):301–19.

Scott, C., Haskell, P., et al. "The Soal-Goldney Experiments with Basil Shackleton: A Discussion," *Proceedings of the Society for Psychical Research* **56** (1974):41–131.

Sidgwick, H. "Presidential Address," *Proceedings of the Society for Psychical Research* **1** (1882):7–12.

Sinclair, U. *Mental Radio* (New York: Albert and Charles Boni, 1930).

Snyder, C.R. "Why Horoscopes Are True: The Effects of Specificity on Acceptance of Astrological Interpretation," *Journal of Clinical Psychology* **30** (1974):577–80.

Snyder, C.R., Shenkel, R.J., and Lowery, C.R. "Acceptance of Personality Interpretations: The 'Barnum Effect' and Beyond," *Journal of Consulting and Clinical Psychology* **45** (1977):104–14.

Soal, S.G. "A Reply to Mr. Hansel," *Proceedings of the Society for Psychical Research* **53** (1960):43–82.

Soal, S.G., and Bateman, F. *Modern Experiments in Telepathy* (London: Faber and Faber, 1954).

Soal, S.G., and Goldney, K.M. "Experiments in Precognitive Telepathy," *Proceedings of the Society for Psychical Research* **47** (1943):21–150.

——. "Letter," *Journal of the Society for Psychical Research* **40** (1960): 378–81.

Solfvin, G.F., Kelly, E.F., and Burdick, D.S. "Some New Methods of Analysis for Preferential-Ranking Data," *Journal of the Society for Psychical Research* **72** (1978):93–110.

Spinelli, E. "The Effects of Chronological Age on GESP Ability." In *Research in Parapsychology 1976,* ed. J.D. Morris, W.G. Roll, and R.L. Morris (Metuchen: Scarecrow Press, 1977), pp. 122–24.

——. *Human Development and Paranormal Cognition.* Unpublished Ph.D. thesis (Guilford: University of Surrey, 1978).

——. "Paranormal Cognition: Its Summary and Implications," *Parapsychology Review* **14**, no. 5 (1983):5–8.

——. "ESP in Young Children: Spinelli Replies," *Journal of the Society for Psychical Research* **52** (1984):371–77.

Tart, C.T. "A Psychophysiological Study of Out-of-the-Body Experiences in a Selected Subject," *Journal of the American Society for Psychical Research* **62** (1968):3–27.

——. "States of Consciousness and State-Specific Sciences," *Science* **176** (1972):1203–10.

——. *States of Consciousness* (New York: Dutton, 1975).

——. "Acknowledging and Dealing with the Fear of Psi," *Journal of the American Society for Psychical Research* **78** (1984):133–43.

Thouless, R.H. *From Anecdote to Experiment in Psychical Research* (London: Routledge and Kegan Paul, 1972).

Trościanko, T.S., and Blackmore, S.J. "A Possible Artifact in a PK Test for Babies," *European Journal of Parapsychology* **6** (1985):95–97.

Ullman, M., Krippner, S., and Vaughan, A. *Dream Telepathy* (New York: Macmillan, 1973).

Walker, E.H. "Foundations of Paraphysical and Parapsychological Phenomena." In *Quantum Physics and Parapsychology*, ed. L. Oteri (New York: Parapsychology Foundation, 1975).

Weiner, D., and Bierman, D.J. "An Observer Effect in Data Analysis?" In *Research in Parapsychology 1978*, ed. W.G. Roll (Metuchen: Scarecrow Press, 1979), pp. 57–58.

White, R.A. "The Influence of Experimenter Motivation, Attitudes, and Methods of Handling Subjects on Psi Test Results." In *Handbook of Parapsychology*, ed. B.B. Wolman (New York: Van Nostrand Reinhold, 1977), pp. 273–301.

Wilson, I. *Mind Out of Time* (London: Gollancz, 1981).

Wittgenstein, L. *Zettel*, ed. G.E.M. Anscombe and G.H. von Wright (Oxford: Blackwell, 1967).

Wolman, B.B., ed. *Handbook of Parapsychology* (New York: Van Nostrand Reinhold, 1977).

randomization, 130, 247–53, 257
Raudive, K., 115
real, 67, 92–95, 97, 102, 103
Raudive voices, 115
reincarnation, 264, 269, 270
relaxation, 112
reliability, 186–87
remote staring, 259
remote viewing, 183, 259
repeatable experiment, 66, 69, 72, 96
replication, 82
Rhine, J.B., 83, 94–97, 116, 141, 250
Rhine, L., 94–97, 141, 153
Robinson, J., 162
Rogo, D.S., 240
Roll, W., 30, 33, 188
Roney-Dougal, S.M., 65–66, 69, 93, 99, 124–25, 126
Rushton, W.A.H., 172

samadhi, 15
Sargent, C.L., 28, 47, 66–67, 69, 93, 99–102, 106, 120–22, 124–26, 129, 131, 132, 140–41, 143–44, 148, 178–80, 205, 246–58
Schmidt, H., 137
Schouten, S., 136, 139, 142
Scott, C., 117
selective reporting, 142–44, 148–49, 186
self, 7, 123, 154–55, 161, 213, 234–35, 242, 244, 268–70
self-image, 172
Shackleton, B., 96, 116
sheep (believer in psi), 58, 224–26, 259
sheep-goat effect, 58
Sidgwick, H., 82
Sinclair, U., 33
skeptical hypothesis, 222–23
skeptics, 30, 58, 82, 113, 117, 138, 148, 231, 257

Soal, S.G., 83, 96, 116–17, 142, 153, 250
Society for Psychical Research (SPR), London, 9, 22, 43, 51, 82, 115, 117, 131, 134, 153, 178, 187, 205, 209. *See also* American Society for Psychical Research
grant, 125–26, 129, 131, 132, 201
lecture, 130–31
Cambridge University SPR, 66, 100, 130, 252
conference, 120
Oxford University SPR, 8, 13
report in journal, 255, 256
Surrey University SPR, 33, 37, 40, 41
Solfvin, G.F., 30, 64, 67, 136, 189
soul, 154, 175, 213, 269
Spinelli, E., 22, 24, 27–28, 31, 45, 56, 71–82, 84–89, 91, 116, 120–21, 258
spirits, 14, 38, 41, 154, 175, 212, 213, 269, 270
spiritualism, 13, 15, 38, 83, 212
spirituality, 260, 269
Spurling, B.M., 151, 153
stacking effect, 47
Stanford, R., 30
state-specific memory, 159–60
state-specific sciences, 92, 159–60, 184
states of consciousness, 97, 159
subliminal perception, 99
survival, 7, 178, 213, 235
synchronicity, 33

Targ, R., 183
tarot, 31, 39–41, 54, 97, 113, 134
experiments, 61–70, 93–94, 105, 122, 167, 221–22